Frederic William Farrar

Chapters of Language

Frederic William Farrar

Chapters of Language

ISBN/EAN: 9783337085070

Printed in Europe, USA, Canada, Australia, Japan

Cover: Foto ©Paul-Georg Meister /pixelio.de

More available books at **www.hansebooks.com**

CHAPTERS

ON

LANGUAGE.

BY THE

REV. FREDERIC W. FARRAR, M.A.

LATE FELLOW OF TRINITY COLLEGE, CAMBRIDGE;
HON. FELLOW OF KING'S COLLEGE, LONDON;
AUTHOR OF 'THE ORIGIN OF
LANGUAGE' ETC.

Non excogitandum neque fingendum, sed inveniendum quid Natura faciat aut ferat. — BACON.

'Ἐγὼ μὲν οὖν περὶ τούτων ὡς εὗρον καὶ ἀνέγνων οὕτως ἔγραψα· εἰ δέ τις ἄλλως βουλήσεται δοξάζειν περὶ αὐτῶν, ἀνέγκλητον ἐχέτω τὴν ἑτερογνωμοσύνην. — JOSEPHUS, *Antt.* x. 11, 7.

LONDON:
LONGMANS, GREEN, AND CO.
· 1865.

LONDON
PRINTED BY SPOTTISWOODE AND CO.
NEW-STREET SQUARE

TO

R. B. LITCHFIELD, ESQ.

IN MEMORY OF

MANY YEARS OF FRIENDSHIP,

THESE PAGES

ARE AFFECTIONATELY DEDICATED.

PREFACE.

WHEN, more than four years ago, I published my book on the 'Origin of Language,' it was, I believe, the only book distinctly devoted to that subject which had appeared in England since the end of the last century. Since that time Philology has been daily gaining ground as a study of infinite importance, and I believe that the stimulus it has received has been mainly due to the eloquence and genius of Professor Max Müller, whose first series of Lectures was published in 1861. The views however which it was the object of my Essay to explain and illustrate, although they were propounded by philologists of the most unquestioned eminence, have found in Professor Müller a strong opponent, and therefore have met in England with but few converts and fewer supporters.

Nevertheless after constant study, and the most candid consideration of the objections urged against them, I believe that those views, in spite of the vehement assaults directed against them, remain absolutely unshaken. Now, if they are true, they furnish to Etymologists so simple and luminous a principle whereby to guide their researches, and they throw so strong a light on one of the most interesting problems that can be presented for our solution, that it is most desirable that they should not be dismissed unexamined and with a sneer. I have therefore devoted some portion of this book to a careful, detailed, and respectful review of all that has been urged against them, and I have thought it due to the high authority deservedly attributed to Professor Müller's opinion, to state those objections in his own language. The answer may not be convincing to every one, but at least it will be admitted that the objections have been fairly met. I hope that I have never used a single expression inconsistent with the high respect which is due to the courtesy, learning, and ability of so eminent an opponent.

The controversial part of the book however only occupies a few chapters, and even in these I have steadily kept in view the object of bringing the theory into clearer and fuller relief,—of placing it as far as possible on a scientific basis,—of removing the misrepresentations which have clustered round it,—and of supplying linguistic facts and illustrations which might be valuable to the student without any reference to his particular views. And, besides this, there are whole chapters of the book which have no controversial aspect whatever, and which may, I hope, contain suggestions not wholly unworthy of consideration by scholars of every shade of opinion.

I should not for a moment venture to speak of my work in these terms if it contained nothing beyond the results of my own thought. But besides my own reasonings and speculations it sets forth the views of those who are incomparably more entitled to a hearing. A glance at almost any page will show that the authorities quoted are neither few nor unimportant; and, as I have carefully avoided an idle parade of learned names, I can assure the reader that there are very few references in the book — certainly none of any importance — which have not been derived immediately from my own reading. And, more than this, I have often fortified my position by the authority of others in cases where the thought was my own, and was expressed in my own language. In one or two places, which are always carefully pointed out, I closely follow the reasonings of the late Professor Heyse, whose book (*System der Sprachwissenschaft*) is one of the wisest and most beautiful treatises on this subject which have ever fallen into my hands. The reader too will find constant allusions to other profound philological writings, which I have always studied with great profit. I have placed at the end of the book a list of the works from which I have derived most advantage, and which have been most constantly in my hands.

In conclusion I have only to thank those critics who bestowed such indulgent consideration on my previous labours. Their approval, and the still more valuable notice of my work by some very eminent scholars, both English and continental, have encouraged me to proceed. My present book is solely addressed to serious students. I am indifferent to the view taken of it by the prejudiced and the ignorant; yet as I am solely actuated by a desire for truth, I have tried to eliminate every expression which was likely to cause needless offence. If any such have escaped my notice I trust that they will be attributed to a lively interest in my subject, and that no one will consider them to have been dictated by a presumptuous or unkindly tone of mind. I shall be the first to regret it, if I have ever been misled by the zeal of controversy into any want of amenity or moderation.

I cannot hope to have escaped errors, and for these I venture to ask an indulgent consideration. These pages have been written, and the proof-sheets corrected, under a pressure of other avocations which has often made me hesitate whether I ought not wholly to abandon this subject to those who can study it under greater advantages. Any mistakes into which I have fallen are due to this cause, and not either to wilfulness or carelessness. Whether they are pointed out by friendly or by unfriendly critics, I shall always be ready to acknowledge and to correct them with cheerfulness and candour.

HARROW: *August*, 1865.

SYNOPSIS.

CHAPTER I.
LANGUAGE A HUMAN DISCOVERY.

	PAGE
Nothing humanly discoverable has been made a subject of revelation	1
Language was humanly discoverable	3
Certainty of its non-revelation	5
Scripture asserts its discovery by man	7–8
'God said'	8
Adam, the Name-giver	10
Nature's teaching	11
Slavery to the letter	12

CHAPTER II.
THE EXPERIMENT OF PSAMMETICHUS.

The story probably true	14
It confirms inferences from other data	14
(i.) Deserted children would probably evolve a language	15
(ii.) Animal-names among the earliest words	16
(iii.) Animal-names naturally Imitative	17
Their value as suggesting the Idea of Language	19
Wild-children. Their Onomatopœias	20

CHAPTER III.
THE NAMING OF ANIMALS.

Primitive *necessity* for Onomatopœia	22
Classification of animal-names	23

xii   SYNOPSIS.

	PAGE
The class under which they must have originally fallen	24
Australian names for animals	24
Chinese Onomatopœias	25
Animal-names in Sanskrit	26
In Hebrew	28
In Ancient Egyptian	29
Names adopted by Colonists	30
They are either (1) Borrowed native names	30
Or (2) Expressive of attributes	30
Or (3) Misapplications suggested by analogy	31
Or (4) When invented are *invariably* Imitative	34
Imitative words invented in modern Argots	35
Why *new words* must be Imitative	37
Inferences	37

CHAPTER IV.

THE INFANCY OF HUMANITY.

Primitive inferiority of Man	39
Man created with only the capacity of Speech	41
Even if Language were revealed	41
A priori objections are valueless	41
And presumptuous	41
And contradictory of existing facts	42
Existing degradation of human races	43–6
The 'state of nature' not necessarily miserable	46
Fancies *versus* Facts, respecting the first men	47
The Darwinian hypothesis	49
Language furnishes fresh proofs of our position	52–3
Bizarre complexity and cumbrousness of savage dialects	53
Opinion of Mr. Garnett	54
And of Mr. A. Gallatin	55
Inference	55

CHAPTER V.

PSYCHOLOGICAL DEVELOPMENT OF THOUGHT.

'Invenisse non instituisse'	57
Admitted fewness of roots	58
Very few words *necessary* for the wants of life	59
Germs of Speech developed by the Intellect	59–62
Realisation of the Ego	62

SYNOPSIS. xiii

	PAGE
Gradual distinctness of Sensuous Impressions	63
Sensations become Perceptions	64
Intuitions	65
Representations	65
Concepts	66
Words correspond to Representations	67
Illustration of the Process	67
Recapitulation	69

CHAPTER VI.

POSSIBLE MODES OF EXPRESSING THOUGHT.

Tactile Language	71
Art, a Language addressed to the Eye	72
Language of Gesture	73–6
Its advantages and imperfections	77
Superiority of Audible Language	79

CHAPTER VII.

SOUND AS A VEHICLE OF THOUGHT.

Analogies of Light and Sound	81
The Voice	82
Its penetrative power	83
Machinery by which it is produced	84–5
Elementary Sounds	86
Material of Speech	87

CHAPTER VIII.

INTERJECTIONS.

Ultimate identity of Interjection and Onomatopœia	88
Two classes of Interjections	89
Interjections in different languages	90–1
Horne Tooke's denunciation of them	92
Interjections are parts of Speech	93
The source of many words	94
Their value in Etymology	96
'Roots'	96
Dignity of Interjections	98
The part they play in Literature	98–100

	PAGE
Their high linguistic importance	100
Originally more numerous	101
Impressions provoke expressions. Ancient stories	101-2
The Idea of Speech	103

CHAPTER IX.

LAUTGEBERDEN, OR VOCAL GESTURES.

The term due to Heyse	104
Expressions of the will	105
Recapitulation	106
What is Prof. Max Müller's view?	107

CHAPTER X.

VOCAL IMITATIONS.

Epicurus	109
Instinct of Imitation	109
Onomatopœias imitate the *subjective* impression	110
Story of Phædrus	111
Diversity of Imitations for the same Sound	112
Not mere passive echoes	114
But ideally modified	114
Names for Thunder	115
Instinctive evolution of Language	116-7
Myths, indicative of Onomatopœia	117

CHAPTER XI.

FROM IMITATIVE SOUNDS TO INTELLIGENT SPEECH.

Sounds developed into words	121
Connection between Sound and Sense	121
Sounds, to become signs, must have been self-explaining	122
The only theory of Language	123

CHAPTER XII.

ONOMATOPŒIA.

Matter-words and Form-words	124
Sounds as the signs of other sounds	126
Vocal imitation only a stepping-stone for Language	127
Sounds became Words	128
Imitation the starting-point	128

CHAPTER XIII.

OBJECTIONS TO THE THEORY; HOW REFUTED.

	PAGE
First objection. '*Onomatopœias few in number*'	130
Dictionaries of them	132
They become greatly *modified* in form	132
Just as alphabetic letters lose their pictorial significance	134
The Hebrew Alphabet	136
Closeness of the Analogy	137–8
New words, not self-explicative, never succeed	138
Second objection. '*Animal-names not Imitative*'	140
A few such instances would prove nothing	141
But nearly all of those adduced *are* Imitative	141
As may be seen by their cognate forms:	
The word 'Goose'	143
The word 'Hen'	144
The word 'Dove'	145
The word 'Hog'	164
The word 'Cat'	146
The word 'Dog'	147–9

CHAPTER XIV.

FERTILITY OF ONOMATOPOETIC ROOTS.

Third objection. '*Onomatopœias are sterile*'	152
The root 'cuckoo'	152
The root 'cru'	153
General predicative 'roots' inconceivable	154
Onomatopœia a luminous principle of Etymology	155
Immense fertility of Imitative roots	156
Fertility of the primitive sounds ma, ta, da, &c.	157–61
Onomatopœias even among the numerals	162

CHAPTER XV.

DIGNITY OF ONOMATOPŒIA.

Language an echo of Nature	165
Fourth objection. '*Onomatopœias are modern*'	166
If true, an argument in their favour	167
Their function in Poetry	168
Harmonies of Language	169

CHAPTER XVI.

SUPPOSED ILLUSORINESS OF THE SEARCH.

	PAGE
The search not 'lawless' but the reverse	171
Errors of 'scientific' Etymologists	174
Prof. Müller's instances all fail	174
The interjections Fie! &c.	174–6
'Squirrel'	176
'Katze'	176
'Thunder' Onomatopoetic in all languages	177
Examination, and probable history of the word	178–82

CHAPTER XVII.

REFLEX IMITATIVE TENDENCY OF LANGUAGE.

The charge of 'fancifulness'	183
Falls to the ground	184
Views of St. Augustine	185
Contain a residuum of truth	186
Instances	187

CHAPTER XVIII.

THE PART PLAYED BY THE IMAGINATION.

'How are ideas not expressive of sound to be accounted for by Onomatopœia?'	190
Illustration of the subject from the Chinese Ideography	192
Fancy indispensable	193
Close analogy to the Progress of Language	194
Verbal roots *could not* have been the earliest	196
Feebleness of abstraction among uncivilised races	199
'Ideas of going'	201
'Ideas of standing'	202
'Ideas of tasting'	202

CHAPTER XIX.

METAPHOR.

Sound, the exponent of things soundless	205
All impressions subjective	206
The Sensorium Commune	207
Instinctively observed analogies of different senses	208
Light and Sound	209
Other senses	211

SYNOPSIS.   xvii

	PAGE
Genders	. 212
Catachresis	. 212
'The Pathetic Fallacy'	. 214
Personification	. 214
Human relationships attributed to things inanimate	. 215
The Unseen described by analogy	. 216
Analogies to describe the Soul, &c.	219–21
Localisation of the passions	. 221
Hieroglyphics	. 222
Colours in metaphor	. 223
Metaphor among the Numerals	223–26

CHAPTER XX.

METAPHOR IN VARIOUS LANGUAGES.

Metaphor most abundant at earliest stages	. 227
Hebrew vagueness of terms	. 229
Hebrew Metaphors	. 230
Metaphors in Greek Tragedy	. 231
Metaphor and National Character	. 231
Kafir Metaphors	. 233
Malay Metaphors	. 233
Chinese Homonyms	. 234
Metaphors in the Argot	236–7
Evanescence of conscious Metaphor	. 237
Universal consequent confusion of Metaphors	. 239
Especially in Shakspeare	. 240
Metaphor, happily indispensable to Language	. 241
Their illustrative Power	. 242
Languages without Metaphor	242–4
What the results would be	. 245

CHAPTER XXI.

OTHER LINGUISTIC PROCESSES.

Recapitulation	. 247
Struggle for existence among words	. 250
Different possible characteristics. 'Left'	. 251
Contradictory roots	. 251
Their explanation	. 252
Antiphrasis	. 253
Errors about it	. 254
Proclus's fifteen methods	. 255
Reducible to three or four	. 256

CHAPTER XXII.
THE NATURE OF WORDS.

	PAGE
Analogists and Anomalists	258
Confusions of the subject	258
Heraclitus	260
Democritus	261
Weak arguments on both sides	262
Universality of Analogist views	263
The Jews Analogists	264
Paronomasia	265
Mystic import of words	266
And names. Biblical Etymologies	267
'Adam'	268
Insulting name-changes	271
Myths about Adam	272
Import of names among the Greeks	272–5
Among the Romans	275
Among the Moderns	276
Alterations of names	277
Euphemism	278
Its source	278–80
The primitive granite of Language	280
Dangerous hypocorisms of Vice	281
The 'fatal force' of words	283

CHAPTER XXIII.
THE NATURE OF WORDS—*continued.*

Sound and sense	286
The Senses, and the Understanding	287
The three factors of a word	287
Words express nothing of the nature of things	288
They teach us nothing about things	289
Which is a knowledge impossible to us	290
And they teach us nothing about our abstract nature	291
A knowledge no less impossible to us	291
They merely express *relations*	292
And even as the signs of our conceptions they are essentially imperfect	293
Instances	294
They are the starting-point of the full-grown Intelligence	295
But the goal of its earlier development	295
Their immense historical, intellectual, and moral importance	296–7
Conclusion	298

ERRATA AND ADDENDA.

Page 42, line 11, *for* which *read* whom.

,, 43. See some examination of the question about races with a deficient language in Mr. E. Burnet Tylor, *Researches into the Early History of Mankind* (p. 77 sq.), who also has some admirable chapters on gesture language, picture writing, &c. Unfortunately Mr. Tylor's work appeared after my own was in print. I am glad to find in his two chapters on myths abundant confirmations of the arguments which I have used in a paper on 'Traditions real and fictitious' in the *Trans. of the Ethnol. Soc.* 1865.

,, 156. The Essay of Buschmann's here referred to will be found translated in the sixth volume of the *Philological Society's Transactions* (1852-1853). Buschmann shows that even as far back as the Etymol. Magnum these sounds had been noticed, thus: πάππος δὲ ἀπὸ τῆς τῶν παίδων τῶν μικρῶν προσφωνήσεως, ὥς φησιν Ὅμηρος, ποτὶ γούνατα παππάζουσιν (*Il.* v. 406). ὀνοματοπεποίηται οὖν ἡ λέξις.

,, 197, line 5. Similarly 'parts of speech' have little or no existence in the gesture-language of deaf mutes.

,, 212. Mr. Mayhew has collected some amusing anomalies to which the German genders are liable: thus, Der Löffel, the spoon; *die* Gabel, the fork; *das* Messer, the knife: Der Anfang, the beginning; *die* Mitte, the middle; *das* Ende, the end; *die* Tinte, the ink; *das* Papier, the paper, &c. Obviously there is no universal principle at work here, but only the play of a bizarre and arbitrary fancy.

,, 233. For some specimens of Australian metaphors, see the *Transactions of the Ethn. Soc.* 1865, p. 292.

,, 281. In the passage of M. Vámbéry's travels here alluded to, he says that the value of a dress is in Turkestan mainly estimated by the stiffness of the *sound* which it makes. 'The Oriental,' he observes, ' is fond of the *Tchak-tchuck* or rustling tone of the dress.' (*Travels*, p. 173.)

ON LANGUAGE.

CHAPTER I.

LANGUAGE, A HUMAN DISCOVERY.

Πάντα θεῖα καὶ ἀνθρώπινα πάντα.—Hippokrates.

GOD, who, in the words of Lactantius,[1] was 'the artificer alike of the intelligence, of the voice, and of the tongue,' gave to man, with those three gifts, the power of constructing a language for himself. Now we are entitled to conclude from the widest possible observation of God's dealings with the human race, that He never bestows *directly* what man can obtain for himself by the patient and faithful use of intrusted powers. Science, for instance, by which we mean the sum total of all that has been discovered respecting the laws of nature, has furnished the human race with blessings of inestimable value; and yet its secrets were never[2] revealed by a voice from heaven, and, although within the reach of human industry, were absolutely unknown

---

[1] 'Deus et mentis, et vocis, et linguæ artifex.'—Lactant. *Instt.* vi. 21.
[2] 'The Scriptures have *never yet revealed a single scientific truth.*'— Hugh Miller, *Testimony of the Rocks*, p. 265.

to the ancient Hebrews. The living oracles intrusted to *their* charge spoke much of the nature of God, and revealed to the world that which, of himself, man could but dimly and most partially discover or understand— his relation to his Creator, the scheme of the divine government, and the means appointed for the purification and deliverance of the soul. The high majesty and grandeur of this revelation, its sacred origin and unspeakable importance, must not blind us to the fact that there are *other*[1] revelations also, which unveil to us in all their marvellous magnificence the works of God, and which yet were never accorded to Psalmist, or Priest, or Prophet, but to those great benefactors of their race who from time to time have been inspired to devote lives of ardent and devout study to the observation of the laws which God has imposed on His created Universe. It is hardly possible to exaggerate the blessings which science, by thus deciphering the divine records of Creation, has conferred upon mankind; yet her lessons have never been whispered by angel or lawgiver, but, if we may borrow a poet's simile, they have been unclenched by sheer labour from the granite hand of nature; they have ever been not immediate but mediate; not revealed to the idle, but discovered by the patient; not direct from God, but granted indirectly through the use of appointed means. Men have attained to them, not by gliding down the lazy stream of dogmatic inference, but by

Springing from crystal step to crystal step

---

[1] 'Deus naturâ cognoscendus, dein doctrinâ recognoscendus.'—Tertullian. '*Duo* sunt quæ in cognitionem Dei ducant, *Creatio et Scriptura.*' Aug.

of that bright ascent which leads to the serene heights of knowledge. 'And because all those scattered rays of beauty and loveliness which we behold spread up and down all the world over, are only the emanations of that inexhaustible light which is above, they have climbed up always by those sunbeams to the Eternal Father of Light.' God *never* lavishes gratuitously that which man can earn by faithful industry: this is an axiom which may be confidently claimed, a truth which may be broadly asserted, of every discovery which was *possible* to the intelligence of man.

That language *is* such a discovery—that it *is* possible for man to have arrived at speech from a condition originally mute, merely by using the faculties which God had implanted—has been proved repeatedly, and will, we hope, be further illustrated in the following pages. Even those who cling with tenacity to a belief in the revelation of language are compelled to admit the[1] *possibility* of its invention. How, indeed, can this be denied when it has been a matter of constant observation that deaf and dumb children, *before they have been taught*, can and do elaborate for themselves an intelligible language of natural and conventional signs? If, then, the invention of a *voiceless* language, addressed to the eye instead of the ear,—a language so much more cumbrous and difficult than articulate speech, and one in which the learner can receive little or no assistance from the multitudinous echoes of external nature,—be thus easily within the range of human capabilities so unusually limited, we must conclude that a *spoken* language of which man

---

[1] Chastel, *De la Raison*, pp. 283, 295. Dug. Stewart, *Phil. of the Mind*, iii. 1. Comp. Horne Tooke, *Divers. of Purley*, i. 2.

must at once have perceived the analogon among the living creatures with which he was surrounded, and which required for its ample commencement *no achievement more difficult than the acceptance of sounds as the signs either of sounds or of the things which the sounds naturally recall*, was one which man, by the aid of the divine instincts within him, would spontaneously and easily invent, with nature as his beneficent instructress, and all the world before him as the school wherein to learn. We may therefore conclude, as Dante[1] did five centuries ago,

> That man speaks
> Is Nature's prompting, whether thus or thus
> She leaves to you as ye do most affect it;

'Entia non sunt multiplicanda præter necessitatem,' said William of Occam; 'frustra fit per plura quod fieri potest per pauciora.' It is astonishing how much spurious philosophy and spurious theology is cut away by this razor of the Nominalists. Those theologians who, by the liberal intrusion of unrecorded and purely imaginary miracles into every lacuna of their air-built theories, do their best to render science impossible, have earned thereby the merited suspicion of scientific men. Nevertheless, all *but* the most obstinate and the most prejudiced even of theologians ought to admit that if man *could* have invented language, we may safely conclude that he[2] *did;* for the wasteful prodigality of direct interposition and miraculous power which plays the chief part in the idle and anti-scriptural exegesis of many churchmen finds no place in the divine economy of God's dealings displayed to us either in nature, in

---

[1] Carey's Dante, *Parad.* xxvi. 128.
[2] Zobel, *Urspr. d. Sprache*, ad f.

history, or in the inspired Word itself. This single consideration ought to be sufficient for any mind philosophically trained; but as too many engines cannot be employed against the invincible bastions of prejudice, let us proceed to further and yet more conclusive arguments. I have stated elsewhere [1] the *positive* reasons which are adequate to disprove the revelation of language. The whole character of human speech, its indirect and imperfect methods, its distant metaphoric approximations, its traceable growth and decay, the recorded stages of historic development and decadence through which it passes, and the psychological and phonetic laws which rule these organic changes, furnish us at once with a decisive criterion of its human origin. An invention which, in spite of all its power and beauty, is essentially imperfect, could not have come direct from God. The single fact that the spiritual and abstract signification of roots is *never* the original one, but always arises from some incomplete and often wholly erroneous application or metaphor, is of itself adequate to confirm an *à priori* probability. The vast multitude [2] of human languages—certainly not fewer than 750 in number—differing from each other in words, in structure, and in sound, points inevitably, as we shall see hereafter to the same conclusion.

Speech, moreover, is the correlative of the understanding.[3] It can express nothing which has not been

---

[1] *Origin of Lang.*, pp. 23–29.

[2] The number is very uncertain. Pott reckons about a thousand, *Die Ungleichheit d. Menschl. Rassen.* 230-244. Adrian Balbi reckons 860, *Atlas Ethnogr. Dissert. Prélim.* lxxv. sqq. Crawfurd, *Ethnol. Trans.* i. 335, 1863.

[3] Heyse, *Syst. d. Sprachwissenschaft*, p. 51. We do not deny to language a certain *maieutic* power which enables us to bring our con-

developed by intelligence and thought. It can have no existence independent of, or separate from our conception of things. It may be *unable to keep pace with* the advancing power of abstraction, but it never can by any possibility anticipate or outstrip it. A language without corresponding conceptions would be a babble of unintelligible sounds; 'for words,' says [1] Bacon, 'are but the image of matter; and, except they have life of reason and invention, to fall in love with them is all one as to fall in love with a picture.' If then a language were dictated, or in any other manner directly revealed to the earliest men, the comprehension [2] of ideas must necessarily have been inspired with the signs which expressed them; in other words, the full-grown understanding must have been created together with the language, since the only difference between the imitative vocal faculty of children and some animals consists in the fact that with animals the sound in most instances remains a sound, while the understanding of man teaches him the conceptions *pari passu* with the sounds, so that *the sounds* become *signs*. But to assert in this sense the *creation* of the human understanding, is, after the manner of certain ignorant divines, to force upon us as an article of faith, that which is nothing more than

ceptions into clearer light, by reducing them into shape, and by enabling us to reason respecting them; but when Hamann calls speech the '*Deipara* unserer Vernunft,' it is easy to see that the expression can with at least equal truth be *reversed*.

[1] *Advancement of Learning*, p. 100; compare the dictum of the Buddhist philosopher: 'Le nom et la forme ont pour cause l'intelligence; et l'intelligence a pour cause le nom et la forme.'—Burnouf, *Le Lotus de la bonne Foi*, p. 550. 'Wie der Mensch eine Einheit von Geist und Leib, so ist das Wort die Einheit von Begriff und Laut.'—Becker, *Organism d. Sprache*, § 1, 2, 4. Hermann, *Das Problem d. Sprache*, p. 1.

[2] Maine de Biran, *Orig. de Lang.* Œuvres inéd. iii. 239.

an arbitrary[1] and anti-philosophic hypothesis. For to suppose the creation of a full-grown understanding contradicts the very nature of the understanding as 'the[2] faculty of relations or comparisons.' An understanding can no more exist without having passed through the very processes which constitute its activity, than a tree can show its thousand layers of wood without having passed through as many seasons of growth and change. The impulse to self-development, and the capacity for it, are indeed innate in the higher races of man; but to assert that the *results*[3] of this impulse were revealed, is to contradict both History and the order of nature. For nothing is more certain, even as an historical fact, than that man did not come into the world with his abstract ideas ready made; nothing is more certain than that the *growth* of abstract ideas can be distinctly traced, and that, to be primitive, a word[4] *must* express some material image.

For all reasoners, except that portion of the clergy who in all ages have been found among the bitterest enemies[5] of scientific discovery, these considerations have been conclusive. But, strange to say, here, as in so many other instances, this self-styled orthodoxy, more orthodox than the Bible itself, *directly contradicts the very Scriptures which it professes to explain*, and, by sheer

---

[1] Maine de Biran, *ubi supr.* p. 233.
[2] Sir W. Hamilton, *Discussions*, p. 4, note.
[3] Heyse, *l. c.*
[4] Benloew, *Sur l' Origine des Noms de Nombre*, pp. ix. 7.
[5] Witness the lives of Vigilius, of Giordano Bruno, of Vanini, of Galileo, of Kepler, of Descartes, of La Peyrère, of Dr. Morton, of the early geologists, and of hundreds more. There is hardly a single nascent science against which theological dogmatism has not injuriously paraded its menacing array of misinterpreted or inapplicable texts.

misinterpretation, succeeds in producing a needless and deplorable collision between the statements of Scripture and those other mighty and certain truths which have been revealed to Science and to Humanity as their glory and reward. *On the human origin of language, the voice of the Bible coincides perfectly with the voice of reason and of science.* In the passage which deals directly with the origin of language, the Bible implies, as distinctly as it is possible to imply, that language [1] resulted from the working of human faculties, and was *not* a direct gift from God to man.

We shall consider the chief passage in Genesis immediately: but before doing so it is necessary to clear away a preliminary misconception. We find repeatedly, in the earlier chapters of the Bible, the expression 'God said;' and as this is used before the mention of Adam's gift of speech, it is at once inferred that language was revealed. Surely, such a method of interpretation, stupidly and slavishly literal, and wholly incapable of rising above the simplest anthropomorphism, shows that that vail which was upon the hearts of men when Moses was read in their synagogues some 1800 years ago, is by no means as yet removed! Luther, far more advanced, and far more liberal than many modern theologians, could enforce the explanation that 'God said' had nothing to do with the voice or articulations of human language; Bishop Patrick could write 'wherever in the history of the creation these

[1] Any one who wishes to support by authorities the Revelation of language has on his side Mohammed and some of the Rabbis! See Kircher, *Tur. Bab.* iii. 4, p. 147. Michaeler, *De Orig. Ling.* Vien. 1738. Everything that *can* be said on the question is to be found in M. de Bonald, Ladevi-Roche, and Süssmilch, *Versuch eines Beweises dass die erste Sprache ihren Ursprung vom Schöpfer erhalten habe.*—Berl. 1766.

words are used, *God said*, it must be understood to mean 'He[1] willed;' nay, more, St. Gregory of Nyssa could vigorously and eloquently denounce the hypothesis of a revealed language as [2] 'Jewish nonsense and folly' (φλυαρία καὶ ματαιότης 'Ιουδαϊκη), and St. Augustine could unhesitatingly write " *Vidit (ratio)* imponenda esse rebus vocabula, id est significantes quosdam sonos:' yet some modern writers, essentially aggressive and essentially retrogressive,—doctors of that school which learns nothing, and forgets nothing, and whom eighteen centuries have only pushed back behind the earliest Fathers in tolerance and liberality,—can only see in the certainty of a language discovered by mankind 'a materialist,[3] and deistic hypothesis!' Before being guilty of an inference so groundless as the supposed revelation of language from the obiter dictum of an 'auctoris aliud agentis'—an inference which contradicts the express assertion of the Jehovist when he is treating *directly* of the subject—might they not have observed that the same expression is used by the Elohist of God's laws *respecting animals?* 'And God blessed them (*i.e.* great whales, and every winged fowl, &c.),

---

[1] As indeed it is rendered in the Arabic version.

[2] *Contra Eunomium Or.* xii., Aug. *de Ordine*, ii. 12. Cf. St. Basil, *Orat.* ii., and Severianus, *De Mundi Creat.* (Bibl. Patr. xii. 119).

[3] M. Ladevi-Roche, who in his treatise, *De l' Origine du Langage* (p. 7, 1860, Bordeaux), undertakes to resuscitate the moribund reasonings of M. de Bonald. Such arguments in this day are an anachronism, and they are not worth the trouble of refuting. There is nothing of the slightest value in his little treatise, and Science can afford to despise the declamatory anathemas hurled by the most ignorant of men at all her votaries, from Thales and Anaxagoras down to Darwin and Lyell. 'Cette opinion semblait abandonnée, quand elle a été relevée de nos jours par une école d'un zèle fougueux et plus orthodoxe que la Bible, et qui semble avoir pris à tâche de réaliser le fameux *Credo quia absurdum.*'—Baudry, *De la Science du Langage*, p. 32.

saying, Be fruitful, and multiply, and fill the waters in the seas, and let fowl multiply in the earth' (Gen. i. 22). Are we then to infer from this that God also revealed a language to animals,[1] and invented a dialect for birds and whales, or rather are we to open our purblind eyes to the fact that *the letter killeth,* and the spirit giveth life?

But, as I have said already, the assertors of revealed language distinctly contradict the very book to which, in their desire to usurp the keys of all knowledge, they groundlessly appeal as a scientific authority. For what does the Jehovist say? 'And out of the ground the Lord God formed every beast of the field, and every fowl of the air; and brought them unto Adam *to see*[2] *what he would call them: and whatsoever Adam called every living creature, that was the name thereof.* And

---

[1] Cf. Steinthal *Gesch. de Sprachwissenchaft,* § 15. Charma, *Ess. sur le Langage,* p. 247.

[2] לִרְאוֹת = to try. In the Arabic version it is wrongly rendered 'to teach,' 'ut ostenderet ei quod vocaret.'—Walton's *Polyglot.* On the other hand the Chaldee version renders 'man became a living animal,' (לְנֶפֶשׁ חַיָּא) by 'a speaking spirit' (לרוח ממללא). If these versions were correct, it is obvious that the texts would contradict each other as much as they do in M. Ladevi-Roche's inference from Gen. ii. 19. 'Ce que signifie que l'homme avait été créé pensant et parlant' (p. 9). One of the rabbis explains 'that was the name thereof,' to mean its name in the thought of God before Adam uttered it. Hamann, Herder's friend, approves this explanation, and illustrates it by 'the Word was God.'— John i. 1. For a mass of idle learning (?) on the subject of Adam's ὀνομοθεσία, see Clem. Alex. *Strom.* i. 335; Jos. *Antt.* 1, 2; Fabricius, *Cod. Pseudep.* v. 6; Buddæus, *Hist. V. T.* i. 93; Heidegger, *Hist. Patr.* i. 148; Witsius, § 3, 162; Carpzov. *Apparat. Crit.* p. 113; Otho, *Lex. Rab.* s. v. Adam; Hottinger, *Hist. Or.* 22, &c. After diligent examination of these passages, and many more on the same topic, I may safely say that more really valuable exegesis may be found in a sentence or two of Steinthal, *Urspr. d. Sprache.* p. 23; *Gesch. d. Sprachwissensch.* p. 12, 15.

Adam gave names to all cattle, and to the fowl of the air, and to every *beast of the field*' (Gen. ii. 19, 20). When we remember the invariable tendency of the Semitic intellect to overlook in every instance all secondary causes, and to attribute every result *directly* to the agency of superior beings, it is clear that by no possibility could the writer have given more unmistakeable expression to his view that language was the product of the human intelligence, and had no origin more divine than that which is divine in man.

Nature with its infinity of sweet and varied sounds was ringing in the ears of primal man. 'Heavens!' exclaims Herder, 'what a schoolroom of ideas and of speech! Bring no Mercury or Apollo as a *Deus ex machina* from the clouds to earth. The whole many-sounding godlike nature is man's language-teacher and Muse. She leads all her creatures before him; each carries its name upon its tongue, and declares itself vassal and servant to this veiled yet visible god! It delivers to him its markword into the book of his sovereignty, like a tribute, in order that he may by this name remember it, and in the future use and call it. I ask whether this truth, viz., that the understanding, whereby man is lord of nature, was the source of a living speech which he drew for himself from the sounds of creatures, as tokens whereby to distinguish them,— I ask whether this dry truth could in Oriental fashion be more nobly or beautifully expressed than by saying that God led the animals to him to see what he would name them, and the name that he would give them, that should be the name thereof? How, in Oriental poetic fashion, can it be more distinctly stated that man discovered speech for himself out of the tones of living

Nature, as a sign of his ruling intelligence? and that is the point which I am proving.'[1]

There are other meanings of the passage in Genesis, full of profundity and moral value. This is not the place to dwell upon them, although they have almost universally been overlooked; but what we *may* at once conclude from the passage is this—that in this case, as in so many others, those who oppose science and try to sweep back with their petty human schemes of interpretation its mighty advancing tide, are usually as much at variance with the true meaning of Scripture, as they are in direct antagonism to reason and truth. 'The expressions of Moses,' says one [2] whose orthodoxy none will call in question—the late Archbishop Sumner in his 'Records of Creation'—'are evidently adapted to the first and familiar notions derived from the sensible appearances of the earth and heavens; and *the absurdity of supposing that the literal interpretation of terms in Scripture ought to interfere with the advancement of philosophical inquiry* would have been as generally forgotten as renounced, if the oppressors of Galileo had not found a place in history.'

---

[1] *Abhandlung über den Urspr. d. Sprache.* p. 77. This is one of the most eloquent and delightful essays ever written. That Herder should have lived to retract it, and retrograde into the orthodox mysticism of Hamann is truly astonishing. He gave up his own invincible arguments to acquiesce in an opinion which had been contemptuously rejected by Plato two thousand years before him, and which had even been refuted by a Father of the Church—Gregory of Nyssa—when it had been supported by Eunomius, the Arian Bishop of Cyzicus.

[2] Abp. Sumner, *Records of Creation,* i. 270.

CHAPTER II.

THE EXPERIMENT OF PSAMMETICHUS.

Καὶ ἐσίοντι τὰ παιδία ἀμφότερα προσπίπτοντα ΒΕΚΟΣ ἐφώνεον.
Herod. ii. 2.

LET us try for a moment to pass back in imagination to the dawn of humanity. Let us try to conceive—not as an idle exercise of the fancy, but in accordance with inductive observations and psychological facts—the processes by which the earliest human beings were led to invent designations for the immense and varied *non-ego* of the universe around them.

The analogy between the childhood of our race and the childhood of every human being has been instinctively observed, and has been used for the purpose of linguistic experiments. Whether Frederic II. (of Germany) or James IV. (of Scotland)[1] ever shut up children in an island or elsewhere, with no attendants, or only such as were dumb, may not be certain; but after due deliberation, I strongly incline to accept as a fact the famous story which Herodotus received from the Egyptian priests, that a similar attempt to discover the original language was made by Psammetichus, king

---

[1] See *Origin of Lang.* p. 9 and p. 14, where I have given some reasons for not rejecting the story about Psammetichus, as is done by Sir G. Wilkinson (Rawlinson's *Herod.* i. 251) on very insufficient grounds.

of Egypt. I am not aware that a single valid argument has been adduced against its authenticity. Not only does the story carry with it, in its delicious *naïveté*, the air of truth, but also it is quite certain that a nation, so intoxicated with vanity on the subject of their transcendent age as the Egyptians were, would never have *invented* a story which unjustly conceded to the Phrygians a precedence in antiquity. Accepting the story, therefore, we disagree from Professor Max Müller[1] in despising all such experiments, and, on the contrary, regard this fragment of practical philology as one of extreme value, and all the more valuable because, as he justly observes, all such experiments would now be 'impossible, illegal, and unnatural.' For the story, if it be true, establishes three most important conclusions, which are in themselves highly probable—viz., 1. That children *would* learn for themselves to exercise the faculty of speech; 2. That the first things which the young Egyptian children named were animals; and 3. That they named the goats, the only animals with which they were familiar, *by an onomatopœia*; for that Bekos, the word uttered by the children, is simply an imitation of the bleating of goats[2] is evident. It is

---

[1] *Lectures, First Series*, p. 333. He is so far right that the experiment would be inconclusive; but why? because to make it valuable we should require *an indefinite number of children and an indefinite length of time*. But our assertion of the human origin and gradual discovery of language rests on quite other grounds.

[2] 'Bekos' is (if we regard *os* as a mere Greek termination added by Herodotus) the exact and natural onomatopœia for the bleat of a goat, as has been noticed by English children; and it is in fact so used in the chorus of more than one popular song, and in the French *becqueter*. The fact that *no suspicion of such an explanation of the sound* occurred to Psammetichus, or any of those who heard the story, is an additional confirmation of its truth. It is strange that no Greek was ingenious enough

to us a strong internal evidence of the truthfulness of the story that it furnishes us with conclusions so exactly in accordance with those at which we arrive from a number of quite different data. The radii of inference from many other sources all converge to the common centre of a similar hypothesis. And be it observed that the facts, so far from being invented in confirmation of any such hypothesis, were interpreted by the Egyptian philosophers in a totally different, and indeed in a most ludicrous manner. The confirmation ought to remain unsuspected, because it is wholly unintentional.

(i.) As regards the first of these conclusions—that children left to themselves would evolve the rudiments of a language—Max Müller says that it 'shows a want of appreciation of the bearings of the problem, if philosophers appeal to the fact that children are born without language, and gradually emerge from mutism to a full command of articulate speech. We want no explanation how birds learn to fly, created as they are with organs adapted to that purpose.' The illustration appears to be unfortunate in many respects, and wholly beside the mark. Every bird flies at once and instinctively when its organs are full-grown—the action is as instinctive to them as sucking is to every infant mammalian; but the exercise of speech is an action infinitely complex, and innumerable accidents have proved that a *single* child growing up in savage loneliness would have *no* articulate language. But is it by any means certain that this would be the case with a *colony* of infants, isolated and kept alive by some casualty which prevented them from

to hit on this explanation, although they had the onomatopœias βῆξ, βήσσω, βηχία, &c. Compare the French name for a goat *bouc*, Germ. *boc*, Ital. *becco*, &c.

learning any existing dialect? The question cannot be answered with *certainty,* though it seems probable that as our knowledge advances we may be able to affirm that such must and would be the case. It is a well-known fact that the neglected children in some of the Canadian and Indian villages,[1] who are often left alone for days, can and do invent for themselves a sort of *lingua franca,* partially or wholly unintelligible to all except themselves. And if it be objected to this illustration that these children have already heard articulate speech, which, on the theory of a human invention of language, would not have been the case with the earliest men, we again appeal to the acknowledged fact that deaf-mutes have an instinctive power to develope for themselves a language of signs—a power which continues in them *until* they have been taught some artificial system, and which then only ceases because it is useful no longer;—just as in the animal kingdom an organ decays, and becomes rudimentary when its exercise ceases to be of any importance to the possessor.

(ii.) Our second observation from the story of Herodotus was that the first things which the children named were animals; and this too is precisely in accordance with every-day facts. Even a young infant learns very soon to distinguish practically between the animate and the inanimate creation; and few things excite its astonishment and pleasure more than the various animals around it. Careful observation of the progress of children in the power of using speech will soon convince any one that they learn to name the dog, the cow, the sheep, and the horse among their earliest words, and indeed

[1] Mr. R. Moffat testifies to a similar phenomenon in the villages of S. Africa, *Mission. Travels.*

soon after they have learnt to attach significance to those natural sounds by which all nations express the relationships of father[1] and mother. Thus, in representing the *animals* as the first existing things which received their names from the earliest man, the Jehovist of the Book of Genesis wrote with a profound insight into the nature of language and the germs out of which it is instinctively developed.

(iii.) But, thirdly, from the fact that the only sound used by the Egyptian children was an imitation of the sounds made by the only living things with which they were familiar, we saw another indication of the fact that onomatopœia (which is only a form of the many imitative[2] tendencies which characterize the highest animals) is the most natural and fruitful source out of which the faculty of speech was instinctively evolved;— the first stepping-stone in the stream which separates sound from sense, matter from intelligence, thought from speech;—the keystone of that mighty bridge which divides the δύναμις from the ἔργον, the faculty from the fact. In this point also our inference is curiously confirmed by a variety of observed phenomena.

What, for instance, *are* the names by which, in the present day, children first learn to distinguish animals? *Are they not invariably onomatopoetic?*[3] Is any one acquainted with any child, ordinarily trained, which first learned to call a dog, a cow, or a sheep by their names, without having learnt, by means of the nursery

---

[1] See Buschman, *Ueber d. Naturlaut.*

[2] The cause of this particular development of the imitative instinct will be explained hereafter.

[3] A horse does not *frequently* neigh; and this is probably the reason that in so many dialects the childish onomatopœia for it is derived, not

onomatopœias, that a sound may stand for a thing? *This* is the most difficult lesson of all language; and when, by the use of a few words, the child has once learnt it,—when it has once succeeded in catching this elementary conception,—the rest follows with astonishing rapidity. Hence, *very few* onomatopœias, and these borrowed from the commonest and simplest objects, are sufficient for the purpose. What the child has to learn is, that a modification of the ambient medium by a motion of the tongue can be accepted as a representation of the objects which are mirrored upon his retina—in other words, that the objects of sight may be recalled and identified by articulated sounds. But how is he to learn this marvellous lesson? Only by observing instinctively that since certain things give forth certain sounds, the repetition of the sound, by an inevitable working of the law of association, recalls the object which emits it. Nor is it the slightest objection to this to say that the child does not learn the onomatopœia for itself, but learns it from its nurse. Supposing that

---

from the sound it makes, but from the sounds (Lautgeberden) addressed to it, e. g. in English *gee-gee*; in parts of Germany, on the other hand, *hotte-pärd;* in Finland *humma*, &c. See Wedgwood, *Etym. Dict.* s. v. Hobby, ii. 246. (That *horse* is itself an onomatopœia seems probable from the cognate form *hross*, Germ. *Ross*.) The fact, then, that a young child names a horse from the sounds used in urging horses on, only shows how *widely various are the points which may suggest the onomatopoetic designation.* Similarly in Spain a mule-driver is called *arriero* from his cry *arri*, and in the French argot an omnibus is *aie aie*. The whole observation illustrates the active, living power of speech, which is no mere dead matter that can be handed over from father to son. See Heyse, *Syst. d. Sprachwissenschaft*, § 47. Even a watch is to a child invariably a *tick-tick*, and the very same onomatopœia is used in the Lingua Franca of Vancouver's island, and in which we also find 'hehe,' 'liplip,' 'tam-water,' &c. for 'laugh,' 'boil,' 'cataract,' &c.

we grant this, what does it prove? Simply the fact that every nurse and every mother is guided by the swift, beautiful, and unerring beneficence of instinct to follow the very same process which the great mother, Nature, adopted when man was her infant child;—or let us say, in language more reverent, and not less true, that such a process is in instinctive unconscious accorddance with the great method of the Creator. For the whole *idea of language,*—the conception that those impressions which the brain mainly receives through the sense of sight may be combined and expressed by means of the sense of hearing, influenced through the organs of sound,—the discovery, in fact, of a common principle, by virtue of which unity and coherence may be given to every external impression,—all lies in the discovery, by a child, that a rude ideal imitation of the bark of a dog may serve as a sign or mark for the dog itself. Hence, although Professor Max Müller's designation of the onomatopoetic theory of language as the 'bow-wow theory,'[1] was accepted by all flippant minds as a piece of crushing and convincing wit, it is really nothing but an undignified way of expressing that which is, as we shall see *by his own admission,* a great linguistic probability, and which at any rate deserves respectful consideration because it has been deliberately accepted by some of the greatest thinkers and the greatest philologists of the century.

Plutarch tells us the commonly-accepted Egyptian legend that Thoth was the first inventor of language;

[1] We are glad to find an expression of half-regret for this unfortunate term in later editions of Prof. Müller's lectures; to abandon it finally would be but a graceful concession to the many eminent men who have held the view.

and he adds the curious tradition that, previous to his time, men *had no other mode of expression than the cries of animals*. That such may well have been the case is illustrated by the fact that it has been found to be so among wild children lost in the woods and there caught long afterwards. Thus we are told of Clemens, one of the wild boys received in the asylum at Overdyke (an asylum rendered necessary by the number of children left destitute and uncared for in Germany after Napoleon's desolating wars), that 'his knowledge of birds and their habits was extraordinary,' and that 'to every bird he had given a distinctive and often very appropriate name of his own, which they appeared to recognise as he whistled after them;'[1] a sentence which can only mean that his onomatopœias were of the most objective or simply-imitative kind. Here, then, in historical times, is a surprising, unquestionable, and most unexpected confirmation of the inferences which we felt ourselves entitled to draw from the story of Psammetichus. Without dwelling on the arguments adduced in a previous[2] work, or attaching too much importance to the fact that the aborigines of Malacca 'lisp their words, the sound of which is like the noise of birds,' or that the vocabulary of the Yamparicos is 'like the growling of a dog, eked out by a copious vocabulary of signs,' we may find a very strong indication of the reasonableness of

---

[1] See an interesting paper on *Wild Men and Beast Children*, by Mr. E. Burnet Tylor, *Anthropol. Rev.* i. p. 22; and Ladevi-Roche, *De l' Orig. du Lang.* p. 55. H—t. *Hist. d'une jeune Fille sauvage*, Paris, 1775. Tulpius, *Obs. Med.* p. 298. Camerarius, *Hor. Subsec.* Cent. 1. Francf. 1602. *Dict. des Merveilles de la Nature*, § v. *Sauvage*. Virey, *Hist. du Genre Hum.* i. 88 and ad f. &c.

[2] *Origin of Lang.* p. 75 seqq.

our belief in the certainty that the more savage (*i.e.* the more natural and primitive) any language is, the more invariably does it abound in onomatopœias, and the more certain we are to find that the large majority of animals has an onomatopoetic designation.

CHAPTER III.

THE NAMING OF ANIMALS.

'Fingere ... Græcis magis concessum est, qui sonis etiam quibusdam et affectibus non dubitaverunt nomina aptare; *non aliâ libertate, quam quâ illi primi homines* rebus appellationes dederunt.'
QUINCTILIAN, *Instt. Or.* viii. 3.

EVERY fact which as yet we have passed in review would lead us to the conclusion that the first men, in *first* exercising the faculty of speech, gave names to the animals around them, and that those names were onomatopoetic.[1] It is hardly too much to say that *they could not have been otherwise.* For unless we agree with the ancient Analogists, and see a divine and mysterious connection, a natural and inexplicable harmony between words and things, by virtue of which each word necessarily expresses the inmost nature of the thing which it designates; or unless we are Anomalists, and attribute the connection of words with things to the purest accident, and the most haphazard and arbitrary conventions;—unless we declare ourselves unreservedly

---

[1] The word 'onomatopœia' is now universally understood to mean a word invented on the basis of a sound-imitation. It may be worth a passing notice that Campbell's use of it in his Rhetoric (ii. 194), to signify the transformation of a *name* into a word, as when we call a rich man a Crœsus, or as in the line 'Sternhold himself shall be *out-Sternholded*'—is, so far as we are aware, wholly unauthorised.

the champions of one or other of these equally exploded views, or accept in their place some mystical or inexplicable theory of 'roots,' we must be prepared with some other explanation which shall exclude from language alike the miraculous and the accidental. What this explanation is will appear hereafter; but at present we may say that, having disproved the *revelation* of language, we cannot suppose its development possible without *some* connection between sounds and objects. Now, as we have seen already, no connection is so easy and obvious, so self-suggesting and so absolutely satisfactory, as the acceptation of a sound to represent a sound, which in its turn at once recalls the creature by which the sound is uttered. If we consider the natural instinct[1] which leads to the reproduction of sounds, the brute imitations of wild-men and savage children, the onomatopoetic stepping-stones to speech adopted by *all* children, and the *à priori* presumption just explained, little or no doubt upon this point can remain in any candid mind.

But we can go yet further by examining the *actual* nomenclature of animals in existing languages.

If we consider any number of names for animals in any modern language, we shall find that they fall into various classes, viz.: 1. Those for which no certain derivation can be suggested; 2. Those derived from

---

[1] This *imitativeness* (in which lies the tendency to onomatopœia) is found even in animals. I once possessed a young canary which never sang until it had heard a child's squeaking doll. It immediately caught up and imitated this sound, *which it never afterwards lost*. It is well-known that nest-birds, if hatched by a bird of another species, will reproduce, or attempt to reproduce, its notes. There are good reasons for believing (since wild dogs do not bark) that the bark of the domestic dog is the result of hearing the human voice. See *Rev. des deux Mondes*, Feb. 1861.

some analogy, or characteristic, or combination of characteristics which the animal presents; 3. Those which are distinctly onomatopoetic in origin or in form.

The first class of words cannot of course furnish us with any linguistic inferences, and may here be left out of the question;[1] under the second and third classes fall *all names of recent origin; and if, as the Bible asserts, and as has been shown to be independently probable, animals were the first objects to receive names, they* MUST *have received names belonging to the third class* (*viz.*: *onomatopœius*), *because no previous words would have existed wherewith to designate or combine their observed qualities.*

But the imitative origin of animal names is not only à *priori* most probable, but reasoning à *posteriori* we see it to be generally the fact. If we would discover any analogies for the speech of primitive man, we must look for them in the languages of those savage nations who approach most nearly to the condition in which man must have appeared upon the earth. Yet if we examine the vocabulary of almost any savage nation for this purpose, what are we certain to discover? *That almost every name for an animal is a striking and obvious onomatopœia.*

Take, for instance, the following names of some of the few birds and animals found in Australia:—

    Ke-a-ra-pai. The white cockatoo.
    Waì-la. The black cockatoo.
    Ka-rong-ka-rong. A pelican.

---

[1] We assume, however, that every word *has* a reasonable derivation if we only knew what it was; just as we know that no *place* in the world ever received a name which could not be accounted for, though there are hundreds of such names of which we can *now* give no explanation.

Ki-ra-ki-ra. The cock king-parrot.
Kun-ne-ta. The hen king-parrot.
Mo-a-ne. The kangaroo.
Nga-ü-wo. The seagull.

These are chosen almost at random from 'Threlkeld's Australian Grammar,' and in other cases the author himself calls marked attention to the similar origin of others, as follows:—

"*Kong-ko-rong.* The emu, *from the noise it makes.*" p. 87.

"*Pip-pi-ta.*[1] A small hawk, *so called from its cry.*" p. 91.

"*Kong-kung.* Frogs, *so called from the noise they make.*" p. 87.

"*Kun-bul.* The black swan, *from its note.*" p. 87.

Or again, let us take some specimens from a North American[2] dialect—the Algonquin. *Shi-sheeb*, duck; *Chee-chish-koo-wan, kos-kos-koo-oo*, owl; *oo-oo-me-see*, screech-owl; *mai-mai*, redcrested woodpecker; *pau-pau-say*, common woodpecker; *shi-shi-gwa*, rattlesnake; *pah-pah-ah-qwau*, cock.[3]

In Chinese, too, a language which is generally believed to retain more of the characteristics of primitive speech than any other, 'the number of imitative sounds is very considerable.' A few may be seen quoted by Professor

[1] Compare the English name *Pippit*; the Latin *Pipilare*, &c.

[2] The highly euphonic character of the *New Zealand* language renders it unsuitable for illustrating the point before us; otherwise one can hardly avoid seeing onomatopœias in *Ti-oi-oi, Aki-aki, Akoa-akoa*, the names of different birds, *Pipipi*, the *turkey*, &c. See the *Ch. Miss. Soc.'s New Zealand Gram.* Lond. 1820.

[3] I have borrowed these Algonquin words from a suggestive chapter in Dr. Daniel Wilson's *Prehistoric Man*, i. 74.

Müller in the first series of his Lectures (p. 252); but in point of fact they constitute a whole class. The sixth class of Chinese characters is called Hyai-Shing 'meaning and sound.' "These," says Marshman,[1] in his Chinese Grammar, "are formed by adding to a character which denotes the genus, *another which denotes the imagined sound of the species*, or the individual signified. They adduce by way of example *kyang*, which, by adding to *shooi* water, the character *kong*, forms a character which denotes a rapid stream, from an allusion to the sound of its water when rushing down with violence. And also *ho*, the generic name of rivers, which is formed by adding to *shooi*, water, *ho* the supposed sound of a river in its course." These, with the signs Chwán-chyn, are about 3,000 in number.

Savage languages are, as we have already observed, the best to show us what *must* have been the primitive procedure; but we can trace the same necessary elements of words in languages far more advanced. In Sanskrit, for instance, is not gô, the original of our cow[2] (Germ. *kuh*; comp. the words *bos*, βοῦς, βοάω, γοάω), a direct imitation of the sound which the English child imitates by *moo* (comp. *mugire*)? Is not *bukka* a goat (comp. *bukkana* barking, bukhâra the lion's roar, βύσσω, βύκτης, bucca, buccina, buck, butt) a very obvious onomatopœia? Is not *çukara*[3] a pig (cf. σῦς, sus, Irish *suig*, Welsh *hwch*, Russian *cushka*) as transparently onomatopoetic as *krakara* a partridge, *hiṅkâra* a

---

[1] Marshman, *Chinese Gram.* p. 24. It must be admitted that his explanation is not particularly lucid.

[2] Gô, in Sanscrit, also means a *voice*; almost all the derivatives from it adduced by Pictet are evident onomatopœias. Even in Chinese the animal is called *ngow, gü*, &c.

[3] These words mean the animal which makes the sound çû, kra, hin.

tiger? Can we see any other origin for *çvána*, *bhashaka*, and *rudatha*, names for the dog, from *kvan* to sound, *bhash* to bark, and *rud* to cry? In hañsa a goose (Lithuan. *'Zâsis*, Thibet. *ngangba*), and in the Persian *gigranah*, a crane, the same principle is indubitably at work, and in all these instances the onomatopœia, as it is indeed *incontestible*, is frankly admitted by M. Pictet,[1] the highest of authorities in everything which concerns the primitive Aryans, although he never admits such an explanation unless it is absolutely necessitated by the facts. Yet in the following cases also, where the Sanskrit root runs through the whole Aryan family of languages, he cannot avoid referring the names to simple imitation; nor can any candid reader avoid agreeing with him as a glance will show.

Bhéda. Ram; compare the Danish *beede*, &c.
Vatsa. Calf; from *vad* and *sar*, giving a voice, *i. e.* lowing.
Mênâda. He-goat, 'dont le cri est mê' (cf. $\mu\eta\kappa\acute{a}s$ and the Phrygian $\mu\hat{a}$ a sheep).
Makshika. Fly; from *maç*, to sound (musso).
Bha, Bhramara (cf. $\phi\rho\iota\mu\acute{a}\omega$, fremo, &c.). The bee.
Bambhara (cf. $\beta\acute{o}\mu\beta os$, &c.). The bee; like our childish word bumble-bee.
Indindira. Great bee (cf. $\tau\iota\theta\rho\acute{\eta}\nu\eta$).
Druna (probablement aussi une onomatopée). A drone.

[1] See Pictet, *Les Origines Indo-Européennes, ou les Aryas Primitifs*, i. pp. 330–535. We should certainly feel inclined to add many other words (e. g. sârispra, serpent, &c.), in spite of the often-strained and unlikely derivations suggested for them. If they were not originally onomatopœias, they have at least *become* so; and instances of this reflex tendency are hardly less important, as throwing light upon our inquiries, than names indubitably imitative in their *origin*.

Katurava. Frog (cri rauque); and Bhêka, frog; 'sans doute une onomatopée.'
Bhîruka (root bhr, cf. Pers. *bîr*, thunder). A bear.
Kurara and *Kharaçabda.* Eagle.
Kukkuta. A cock.
Grdhra. Vulture.
Krâgha (Pers.). Hawk (cf. *karaghah*, crow).
Krkavâku. Fowl in general; from krka, and vaç, to sound.
Uhîka, âlu, ghûka, gharghara, &c. Owls of different kinds.
Karaka. Crow. Kâka (cf. chough, &c.), 'évidemment une pure onomatopée.'
Kukûka. Cuckoo.
Koka. Swan; 'imitatif du cri kouk! kouk!'
Karatu. Crane.
Tittiri. Partridge.
Varvaka. Quail.
Pika. Woodpecker; 'cette racine n'est sans doute qu'une onomatopée.'

The list might be indefinitely multiplied; but let us now turn to the Hebrew, and see what analogous facts it offers. For the sake of English readers we will represent the Hebrew words in English characters also, that they may judge for themselves. Take, for instance, such distinctive imitative words as—

שָׁרַקְרְקָא *Scherakreka.* A pye; the Greek καράκαξα. Bochart, *Hieroz.* ii. p. 298.

זַרְזִיר *Zarzîr.* A starling. *Id.* p. 353.

שְׁפִיפוֹן *Schephîphoun.* The horned snake. Gesen. *Thes.* iii. p. 146.

אַרְיֵה *Aryéh.* The lion. The supposed derivations are very doubtful.

אִיִּים *Iyîm.* Lynxes. Nomen ὀνοματοποιητικόν. Bochart, *Id.* i. 845.

גּוּר *Gûr.* A whelp.

שַׁחַל *Shâchal.* The roarer. From an Arabic root = rugitus.

דּוּכִיפַת *Dûkîphath.* Lapwing (rather Hoopoe. cf. Copt. kukupha); Lat. Upupa.[1] Bochart, *Hieroz.* ii. p. 347.

צִיִּים *Tziîm.* Wild cats, &c.

לָבִיא *Lâbhîa.* A lioness; 'rugiendi sonum imitans.' Gesen. *Thes.* s. v.

סִיס *Sîs.* A swallow; compare Ital. zizilla, Lat. zinzulare, &c. Bochart, *Hieroz.* vol. ii. p. 62.

תּוֹר *Tôr.* A turtle-dove (*turtur,* &c.).

צְלָצַל *Tsilâtzâl.* A locust, from its shrill noise.

Again, if we take the ancient Egyptian language[2] we find such words as *mouee,* a lion; *hippep,* an ibis; *ehe,* a cow; *hepepep,* hoopoe; *croor,* frog; *rurr,* pig; *chaoo,* cat; *phin,* mouse.

We see then that, alike in the Semitic and in the Aryan families, onomatopœia supplies a *certain* and satisfactory etymology for the names of many animals; and if we add doubtful cases, where the suggested derivations are awkward and farfetched, we might say, without exaggeration, of *most* animals. We have seen similar onomatopœias in the ancient Egyptian, which is supposed to have affinities with both; and we have found them immensely prevalent in various sporadic

---

[1] Hence, the Greek legend about its cry,—that it was the transformed Tereus crying Ποῦ, ποῦ.

[2] *Prehistoric Man,* i. 71.

families, which some would call Turanian—a name which we may on some future occasion see very good reason to reject. In fact, in these Allophylian savage dialects, and the more so in proportion to the primitive character of the people who speak them, onomatopœia appears to be the rule, and terms derived from other relations or properties the rare exception. Without going any further, is it possible to doubt what *must* have been the *tendency* of animal nomenclature among the earliest men?

It has often happened in modern times that the extension of travel and commerce has thrown nations into connection with lands in which the flora and fauna are wholly different from their own. The instinctive procedure which they adopt to name these new objects will add new strength to our position. For here again one of these four processes takes place; either 1. They adopt the existing or aboriginal term, which they find already in use; or 2. They use a compound, expressive of some quality or resemblance, as in cat-bird, snow-bird, mocking-bird, blue-bird, &c; 3. They *misapply* some previous name of the animal most nearly resembling the one to be named; or 4. If they invent a new and original (indecomposible) term, *it is invariably an onomatopœia.*

1. The first procedure requires no illustration, as it offers nothing curious or instructive beyond the fact that the shorter and easier a native name is, the more readily is it adopted. The only reason why this practice is not more common is the inordinate length of the delicate imitative appellations in primitive languages.

2. The second process is not so common, and is only interesting as illustrating the *variety* of observed charac-

teristics by which a name may be suggested. For instance, the elephant has been called by names meaning 'the twice-drinking animal (*dvipa*), or the two-tusked (*dvirada*), or the creature that uses its hand (*hastin*); yet these different conceptions all represent one and the same object. Similarly the serpent is called in Sanskrit by names meaning 'going on the breast,'[1] or 'wind-eating.' Pictet furnishes us with many similar instances of this method of nomenclature, which is illustrated by the name duck-billed platypus, or 'beast with a bill,' for the ornithorhynchus of New Zealand, and the Dutch aardvark, or 'earth-pig,' for the Orycteropus capensis. 'Of everything in nature,' says Bopp, 'of every animal, of every plant, speech can seize only one property to express the whole by it.'

3. The third process deserves passing notice, because we shall see hereafter its importance. 'In the slow migrations of the human family,' says Dr. Daniel Wilson, 'from its great central hives, language imperceptibly adapted itself to the novel requirements of man. But with the discovery of America a new era began in the history of migration. . . . In its novel scenes language was at fault. It seemed as if language had its work to do anew as when first framed amid the life of Eden. The same has been the experience of every new band of invading colonists, and it can scarce fail to strike the European naturalist, on his first arrival in the New World, that its English settlers, after occupying the continent for upwards of three centuries, instead of

---

[1] *Les Orig. Indo-Eur.* i. 383. It is perhaps more common in the Zincali language than any other. Biondelli *Studii Linguistici*, p. 114, and in many argots, e. g. in the German Rothwelsch, goose is Plattfusz, hare = Langfusz, ass = Langohr, &c.—*Id.* 113.

inventing root-words wherewith to designate plants and animals, as new to them as the nameless living creatures were to Adam in Paradise, apply in an irregular and unscientific manner the names of British and European flora and fauna. Thus the name of the English partridge is applied to one American tetranoid (Tetrao umbellus), the pheasant to another (Tetrao cupido); and that of our familiar British warbler, the robin, to the Turdus migratorius, or totally different American [1] thrush.'

Mr. E. J. Eyre remarks that when an Australian sees any object unknown to him, he does not *invent* a name for it, but immediately gives it a name drawn from its resemblance to some known object. This is very true, but it is strange that he should have considered it as peculiar to Australians.[2] On the contrary, the fact has been observed from the earliest times, and is noticed by authors so ancient as Epicurus,[3] Aristotle,[4] and Varro. The latter[5] observes that in Latin the names of fish are usually borrowed from the land creatures which most resemble them, as *anguilla* (eel) from *anguis* (snake). Several similar instances occur among the Romans. The elephant, for instance, they called the Lucanian *ox*,

---

[1] *Prehistoric Man*, i. 62.

[2] 'Der Mensch stellt beständig Vergleichungen an zwischen dem Neuen was ihm vorkommt, mit Alten was er schon kennt.'—Pott. *Etym. Forsch.* ii. 139.

[3] Ὅθεν καὶ περὶ τῶν ἀδήλων ἀπὸ τῶν φαινομένων χρὴ σημειοῦσθαι.—Epic. ap. Diog. Laert. x. 32.

[4] Φυσικά. i. 1.

[5] 'Vocabula piscium pleraque translata a terrestribus ex aliquâ parte similibus rebus, ut anguilla.'—Varro, *De Ling. Lat.* v. 77. (Comp. ἔχις, ἔγχελος). Compare Amos ix. 3, where 'snake' is used for a sea-creature. By a very natural transference *anguilla* in later Latin means a thong for punishing boys—the Scotch 'tawse.'—Du Cange. s. v.

not being at first familiar with its name, and knowing of no animal larger [1] than the ox; the giraffe they styled *camelopardus*, from its points of resemblance to the camel and the leopard, and *ovis fera* [2] (or foreign sheep), from the mildness of its disposition; and they knew the black lion by the synonym of 'Libyan bear.' The Dakotas, we are told, call the horse *sungka-wakang*,[3] or spirit-dog; and Mr. Darwin[4] tells us that in 1817, 'as soon as a horse reached the shore, the whole population took to flight, and tried to hide themselves from "*the man-carrying pig*" as they christened it.' Some American nations call the lion ' the great [5] and mischievous cat.' In the Fiji Islands man's flesh is known as ' long pig.' When first they saw a white paper kite[6] they called it '*manumanu*' (a *bird*), having never seen such a thing before; and money from the same cause they called '*ai Lavo*,' from its resemblance to the flat round seeds of the Mimosa scandens. The Dutch could find no better name than Bosjesbok, bush-*goat*, for the graceful African antelope; and in the Spanish name alligator we see that they regarded that unknown river-monster as a large lizard.[7] The New Zealanders called the first horses they saw ' large dogs,' as the Highlanders are said to have called the first donkey which they brought to their mountains ' a large hare.' The Kaffirs called

---

[1] It is very doubtful whether in some Aryan languages there has not been a confusion between the names for *elephant* and *camel*. See Pictet s. v. *Le Chameau*.

[2] See Plin. viii. 17. Fera = peregrina.

[3] *Prehist. Man*, i. 72.

[4] *Voyage of the Beagle*, p. 408.

[5] Michaelis, *De l'Influence des Opinions sur le Langage*.

[6] Seeman, *Mission to Viti*, pp. 45, 377.

[7] El lagarto, the lizard. See Farrar, *Origin of Lang.* p. 119.

the first *parasol*[1] to which they were introduced 'a cloud.' To this day the Malays have no better name for rat than[2] 'large mouse.' This, then, is an important principle to notice in all theories respecting language.

4. If, however, *none* of these processes furnish a convenient name for animals hitherto unfamiliar to new colonists,—if the native name be too uncouth or difficult for adoption, and the animal offer neither a ready analogy, nor any very salient property, to provide itself with a new title,—then a new name *must* be invented; and in this case we venture to assert that there is not to be found in any country *a single instance of a name so invented which is not an onomatopœia*. Such names as whip-poor-will, pee-whee(*Muscicapa rapax*), towhee (*Emberiza erythroptera*), kittawake (*Larus tridactylus*), &c., may be profusely paralleled; and in some cases the onomatopoetic instinct is so strong that it asserts itself *side by side* with the adoption of a name; thus (as in the childish words moo-cow, bumble-bee) the North American Indian will speak of a gun as an *Ut-to-tah-*gun, or a *Paush-ske-zi-*gun. It has often been asserted that man has lost the power of inventing language, and this present inability is urged as a ground for believing that language could not have been a human invention. We have elsewhere[3] given reasons for disputing the assertion, and even if it were true, it would be beside the mark, seeing that the absence of all necessity of exercise for a faculty is the certain cause of its all-but-irretrievable decay. From the fact, how-

---

[1] Charma, *Or. du Lang.* p. 277, who refers to Condillac, *Gram.* ch. v.
[2] Crawfurd, *Malay Gram.* i. 68.
[3] *Origin of Lang.* p. 68 sqq. A very few instances of invented words, with some remarks upon them, may be found, *Id.* pp. 60, 61.

ever, that when men *do* invent new words they are almost invariably onomatopœias, *we see an index pointing us back with unerring certainty to the only possible origin of articulate speech.* For whatever may be true of abstract 'roots,' it is demonstrable, and will be shown hereafter, that roots which by their onomatopoetic power are the only ones capable of *explaining and justifying themselves,* so far from being the sterile playthings which Professor M. Müller represents them to be, have in them a fertility and a power of growth which can only be represented by the analogy of vegetable life, and which is as sufficient to account for the fullgrown languages of even the Aryan family as the germinative properties of an acorn are sufficient to account for the stateliest oak that ever waved its arms over British soil.

The history of colonisation, then, by reproducing some of the conditions of primitive man, enables us to see his linguistic instincts in *actual operation,* and those instincts undeniably confirm our theory by displaying themselves in the very directions which we have been pointing out. But we can offer yet another proof of the reasonableness of our view in certain languages of modern invention, to which we shall again allude. I mean the various Argots of the dangerous classes throughout Europe. These languages have to fulfil the opposite conditions of being distinct to those who use them, and unintelligible to the rest of the world. And how do they effect this? Partly indeed by generalising the special, and specialising the general; partly by seizing on some one very distinct attribute and describing it, if necessary, by periphrases; but also in great measure by *the obvious resource of direct sound-*

imitation. Thus the German thief, no less than the English, calls a watch a *tick,* the French thief calls it *tocquante*; the Italian thief speaks of a pig as *grugnante,* the German as *grunnickel,* the English 'the grunting,' the French as *grondin,* &c. These languages must, from their very nature, remain uncultivated, and the consequence is that they abound in onomatopœia. In the English slang, a pulpit is a *hum*-box; carriages and horses are *rattlers* and *prads.* In the French argot the heart is *battant*; a sheep is *bélant*; a grimace is *bobine*; a marionette is *bouis-bouis*; to die is *claquer*; a liar is *craquelin*; to drink a health is *cric-croc*; a skeleton-key is *frou-frou*; a glutton is *licheur*; a shoe is *paffe*; a soldier, by an onomatopœia which it would take too long to explain, is *piou-piou*; a little chimney-sweeper is *raclette*; a cab is *roulant*; a dog *tambour*; a noisy child *turabate*; and gendarmes, from the songs which soldiers like, is called *tourlouru.* These are but a few instances out of many, and it is impossible to deny that they establish the necessity of having recourse to onomatopœia when new words have to be invented. They therefore furnish a fresh support to the views here advocated.

When by strict etymological laws we have traced back a word through all its various changes, instructive and valuable as the process is sure to have been, we have done nothing to *explain* its origin or to account for its earliest history, *unless* we can point to its ultimate germ in some onomatopoetic or interjectional root; and perhaps in the *majority* of cases this can be done with a fair amount of probability; for the number of roots required for the formation of a language is extremely small; and that small number is amply supplied by the imitation of natural sounds, and by the instinctive utterances which all violent impressions produce alike in animals and in men. The reason why new words, except of an imitative kind, are *not* invented is because every word involves a long history from its sensational origin to its final meaning, and the result without the process is felt to be a contradiction and an impossibility. This is why all attempts to frame an artificial language have been a failure, and the ponderous schemes of Kircher, and Becker [1] and Dalgarno, and Wilkins, and Faignet, and Letellier can only move us to a smile, because they are based on a conventional theory of language which is utterly mistaken. This, too, is the reason why language is stronger than emperors, and Tiberius [2] could neither give the citizenship to a word, nor Claudius [3] procure acceptance even for a useful letter. A radically *new* word to have any chance of obtaining currency must of necessity be of an imitative character. It is a curious fact that some of the tribes [4] on the coast of New Guinea derive *even the names which they give to their children* from direct imitations of the first sounds or cries which they utter.

We are surely entitled then to draw secure inferences from the facts hitherto observed, and those inferences

---

[1] For an account of their systems see Du Ponceau, *Mém. sur le Syst. Gram. de quelques Nations Indiennes*, pp. 26-31, 320. Hallam, *Lit. Eur.* iii. 362; and Letellier, *Établissement immédiat de la Langue Universelle*.

[2] 'Tu enim Cæsar civitatem potes dare hominibus, verbis non potes,' said Capito to Tiberius.—Sueton. *De Illustr. Gram.*

[3] Claudius vainly tried to introduce into the Roman alphabet an antisigma Ɔ, with the value Ps. 'pro qua Claudius Cæsar Antisigma Ɔ hac figurâ scribi voluit, sed nulli ausi sunt antiquam scripturam mutare. —Priscian, i. *De Literarum Numero et Affinitate.*

[4] Salverte, *Hist. of Names*, i. 62. *Engl. Transl.*

may be summed up in the observation that animals were among the first objects to receive names, and that, in the absence of any previous words, they *could* not have been named except by onomatopoetic designations. This we have endeavoured to render strong and secure by many proofs, drawn both *à priori* from the nature of the case, and from the analogies presented by the methods in use among children and among savages; and *à posteriori* from the phenomena which have invariably recurred when, in the course of history, a condition of circumstances has been reproduced which in any way resembles that which must have existed in the case of primal man.

CHAPTER IV.

THE INFANCY OF HUMANITY.

Ἦν χρόνος ὅτ' ἦν ἄτακτος ἀνθρώπων βίος,
Καὶ θηριώδης, ἰσχύος θ' ὑπηρέτης.
. . . . . τηνικαῦτά μοι δοκεῖ
Πυκνός τις ἄλλος καὶ σοφὸς γνώμην ἀνὴρ
Γεγονέναι, ὃς . . .
. . . . τὸ θεῖον εἰσηγήσατο.
IGNOT. ap. SEXT. EMPIRIC.

As we have here arrived at a sort of landing-place, we may devote a separate chapter to consider the full bearing of the conclusions thus formed. In so doing, we are not digressing from the main point, but rather we are removing a groundless prepossession which would lie in the road of all further advance, and we are at the same time calling attention to one of those important facts which it is the object of philology to illustrate or discover.

For, obviously, if language was a human invention, and was due to a gradual development, there must have been a time in man's history when he was possessed of nothing but the merest rudiments of articulate speech; in which, therefore, he must have occupied a lower grade than almost any existing human tribe. This is a conclusion which cuts at the root of many preconceived theories. Thus, Lessing[1] remarks that God is too good to have withheld from his poor children, perhaps for centuries, a gift like speech; and M. de Bonald asks how we can suppose 'that a Good Being could create a social animal without remembering that he ought also from the first moment of his existence to inspire him with the knowledge necessary to his individual, social, physical, and moral life.' Such reasoners, therefore, reject the doctrine of the human origin of language as alike an injustice to God and an indignity to man.

In answer to such 'high priori' reasonings, it might be sufficient to say that we are content, for our part, humbly to observe and record what God *has* done, rather than to argue what He *ought* to do or ought not to do, incompetent as we are in our absolute ignorance 'to measure the arm of God with the finger of man.' Claiming for ourselves the character of observers only, and desirous to accept the results to which our enquiries directly lead, without any regard to system or prejudice, we might easily repudiate assumptions which rest on the mere sandy basis of systematic prejudice. It is childish arrogance in us to argue what plans are consonant to, and what are derogatory of God's Divine Power and Infinite Wisdom. Seeing that we have not the capacity for understanding that which *is*, it is preposterous in us to argue on any general principles as to what *must* have been. Perfect humility and perfect faith,—a faith in Truth which seems to have the least power in many of the loudest champions of a supposed orthodoxy,—are the first elements of scientific success. The problems and mysteries which encumber all our enquiries,—the

---

[1] *Sämmtl. Schriften*, Bd. x.

adamantine wall against which we dash ourselves in vain whenever we seek to penetrate the secrets of the Deity,—should at least prevent us from following Lessing and M. de Bonald in laying down rules of our own, in accordance with which we fancy that God MUST inevitably have worked.

Moreover, if language was a Revelation and not an Invention, at what *period* in man's life was it revealed? If, indeed, man was, according to the Chaldee paraphrast, *created* 'a speaking intelligence' (see p. 10), we get over this difficulty, though it is only at the expense of an absurdity, and by making the Bible contradict itself. But if not, there must have been a time, on any supposition, when man wandered in the woods a dumb animal, till God bethought Him of inspiring language. Surely such a view is even less pious than that of Lucretius himself. 'Any one,' says Steinthal,[1] 'who thinks of man without a Language' [or, he should have added, the *capacity for evolving* a language] 'thinks of him as one of the Brutes; so that any one who calls down the Deity as his teacher of Language, gives Him only an animal as a scholar.' In other words, unless man was *born* speaking,—(and it is apparent in Scripture that language was *subsequent* to creation),—then, even on this theory, man must have *once* been destitute of a language, and must, therefore, on this theory also, have emerged from a condition of mutism. Why then should a similar belief be held an insuperable objection to a theory so certain as the human discovery of language? It is forsooth an insult to the dignity of man and a slur on the beneficence of God to suppose that

---

[1] *Urspr. d. Sprache*, p. 40.

man appeared on this earth in a low and barbarous condition! But WHY is it? Do those who use such reasonings consider that they are thereby arraigning and impugning before the bar of their own feeble criticisms the *actual* dealings of God? If it be indeed irreconcileable with God's goodness to suppose that He would have created man in a savage state, is it *more* easy to believe that He would *now* suffer, as He *does* suffer, the existence of thousands who are doomed throughout life to a helpless and hopeless imbecility, and that for no fault of their own?—thousands in which the light of reason has been utterly quenched; thousands in whom it never existed, and who pass in helpless idiocy from the cradle to the grave, as irresponsible as the brutes who perish, without language, without religion, without knowledge, without hope? Facts like these ought to silence us for ever when we attempt beforehand to assign limits to the possible workings of God's Providence. We *know* that He is infinitely good and gracious, but we *cannot* know how His Providence will work.

If for many ages millions of the human race have been, and still are, born into a low and barbarous condition, why may they not have been originally so created? We know from history and from ordinary reasoning that existing savage races could not have *sunk*[1] into this condition, and there seems every ground for believing that they are morally, mentally, and physically incapable

---

[1] Archbp. Whately (*Preliminary Dissert.* iii. in the *Encycl. Britannica*) argues that savages can never, *of themselves*, rise out of degradation; it is as easy to show that they can never *sink* into such a condition. We do not believe that the primeval savages were in any way direct ancestors of the two noble races—the Aryan and the Semitic.

of rising out of it, since they melt away before the advance of civilisation like the line of snow before the sunlight. 'God,' says M. Jules Simon,[1] 'who suffers millions of savages to exist in three quarters of the globe, may well be supposed to have permitted in the beginning that which he permits at the present day.' What shall we say, for instance, of the tallow-coloured Bosjesman,[2] who lives for the most part on beetles, worms, and pismires, and is glad enough to squabble with the hyæna for the putrid carcass of the buffalo or the antelope? Of the leather-skinned Hottentot,[3] 'whose hair grows in short tufts, like a worn-down shoe brush, with spaces of bare scalp between,' and who is described as a creature 'with passions, feelings, and appetites as the only principles of his constitution'? Of the Yamparico, 'who speaks a sort of gibberish like the growling of a dog,' and who 'lives on roots, crickets, and several bug-like insects of different species'?[4] Of the aborigines of Victoria,[5] among whom new-born babes are killed and eaten by their parents and brothers, and who have no numerals beyond three? Of the Puris[6] of Brazil, who have to eke out their scanty language by a large use of signs, and who have no words for even such simple conceptions as 'to-morrow'

---

[1] *Rev. des Deux Mondes*, 1841, p. 536.
[2] Caldwell, *Unity of the Human Race*, p. 75.
[3] *Personal Adventures in S. Africa*, by Rev. G. Brown (a missionary), p. 7.
[4] Capt. Mayne Reid, *Odd Races*, p. 330 sqq.
[5] W. Stainbridge on the *Aborigines of Victoria.—Trans. of Ethn. Soc.* 1861, p. 289. Fern-roots, grubs, mushrooms, and frogs are their main diet; that of some other savages is too disgustful for utterance.—Greenwood, *Curiosities of Savage Life*, p. 15.
[6] Mad. Ida Pfeiffer, *Voyage round the World*.

and 'yesterday'? Of the naked, houseless, mischievous, vindictive Andamaner,[1] with a skull hung ornamentally round his neck? Of the Fuegians,[2] 'whose language is an inarticulate clucking,' and who kill and eat their old women before their dogs, because, as a Fuegian boy naïvely and candidly expressed it, 'Doggies catch otters, old women no'? Of the Banaks,[3] who wear lumps of fat meat, artistically suspended in the cartilage of the nose? Of the negroes of New Guinea,[4] who were seen springing from branch to branch of the trees like monkeys, gesticulating, screaming, and laughing? Of the Alforese[5] of Ceram, who live in trees, 'each family in a state of perpetual hostility with all around'? Of the forest-tribes of Malacca,[6] 'who lisp their words, whose sound is like the noise of birds?' Of the wild people of Borneo,[7] whom the Dyaks hunt as if they were monkeys? Of the cannibal Fans[8] of equatorial Africa, who bury their corpses before eating them? Of the pigmy Dokos,[9] south of Abyssinia, 'whose nails are allowed to grow long like the talons of vultures, in order to dig up ants and tear in pieces the flesh of serpents, which they devour raw'? Of the wild Veddahs[10] of Ceylon, who have gutturals and grimaces instead of

---

[1] Mouatt's *Andamaners*, p. 328.

[2] Darwin, *Voyage of a Naturalist*, p. 214. The boy who gave the philosophic defence of cannibalism, imitated, as a great joke, the screams of the poor old women, while being choked in the smoke.

[3] Hutchinson, *Ten Years' Wanderings*, p. 245.

[4] Crawfurd, *Malay Gram.* i. clxi.

[5] Pickering, *Races of Man*, p. 304 sqq.

[6] *Id.* [7] *Id.*

[8] Du Chaillu's *Equatorial Africa*. This has been denied.

[9] Prichard, *Nat. Hist.* i. 306. Norris's Note. Dr. Davy, *Researches*, ii. 177.

[10] Sir J. Emerson Tennent, *Ceylon*.

language; 'who have no God; no idea of time and distance; no name for hours, days, or years; and who cannot count beyond five on their fingers'? Of the Miautsee,[1] or aborigines of China, whose name means 'children of the soil,' and who, like the Malagassy, the Thibetans, and many African tribes, attribute their origin not to gods and demigods, not even to lions (as do the Sahos), or to goats (as do the Dagalis), but, with unblushing unanimity, to the ape? Of the Negrilloes of Aramanga, the Battas of Sumatra, the wild people of Borneo, the hairy Ainos of Jesso, the Hyglaus of the White Nile, the Kukies and other aborigines of India, even the Cagots and other Races Maudites of France and Spain? These beings, we presume no one will deny, are men with ordinary human souls. If then God can tolerate for unknown generations the perpetuation of such a state of existence as this,—the perpetuation of people with squalid habits, mean and deformed heads, hideous aspect, and protuberant jaws,—what possible ground is there for denying that he may also have suffered men at the Creation to live in what is called a state of nature, which is the name given to a state of squalor and ignorance, of savagery and degradation? Considering these facts, and believing with Schlegel that savage nations are savage by nature, and must ever remain so, some (and among them Niebuhr) have been Polygenists precisely *because* they thought

[1] Authorities for the facts mentioned in these two sentences will be found in Ritter, *Erdkunde, Asien*, ii. 273, 431 sqq.; Hope, *Ess. on the Origin of Man*; Virey, *Hist. Nat. du Genre Humain*, ii. 12; i. 190. Pickering, *Races of Man*, 175–179, 302–308; *Journ. Asiat. Soc. of Bengal*, xxiv. 206; Prichard, *Nat. Hist. of Man*, i. 250–274 (ed. Norris). Pouchet, *Des Races*, p. 59; Perty, *Anthropol. Vorträge*, p. 41; Michel, *Hist. des Races maudites*, &c.

it was more consonant with God's attributes to have created men in different grades of elevation than to have suffered them to degenerate in so many regions from a condition originally exalted.[1] The argument in this case may be as worthless as in the other; but what is the value of a method of reasoning from which two conclusions so opposite can be drawn!

It would be an error to suppose that 'the state of nature,' with its imperfect language, its animal life, its few natural wants, its utter ignorance, is necessarily a state so low as to render existence a misfortune or a curse. Nature, in all probability, provided as bountifully for her first-born as she does for many of his descendants; and if not, she at any rate 'makes habit omnipotent and its effects hereditary.' Even the Fuegian, in his land of cold and rain,—crawling from the lair in which he lies, unsheltered, coiled up like an animal on the wet ground, to gather at all hours, from morn till midnight, the mussels and berries, which are his only food,—does not decrease in numbers, and must, therefore, as Mr. Darwin observes,[2] be supposed 'to enjoy a sufficient share of happiness (of whatever kind it may be) to render life worth having.' It is hard to say how little is 'necessary' for man; and it is certain, both from Scripture and history, that not only the luxuries and ornaments of life, but even those things which we regard as indispensable, were the gradual inventions, or long-delayed discoveries, of a race which had received from God certain faculties in order that they might at once be exercised and rewarded by a perpetual progress in dignity and self-improvement. There can be no

---

[1] Pouchet, *Plural. des Races*, p. 105.
[2] Darwin, *Voy. of a Naturalist*, p. 216.

question that the systems of those Rabbis and Fathers,[1] and their modern imitators, who make Adam a being of stupendous knowledge and superhuman wisdom, are more improbable, as well as more unscriptural, than those of writers who, like Theophilus of Antioch among the Fathers, and Joseph Ben Gorion among the Jews, make his original condition a weak and inferior one. Philosophy, the arts, the sciences, the observations of the simplest natural facts, the elucidation of the simplest natural laws, required centuries to elaborate. We do not even hear of the first *kingdom* till some thousands of years after the first man. It is but as yesterday that man has wrung from the patient silence of Nature some of her most important, and apparently her most open secrets.

It is forsooth a degradation to suppose that man originated in an ignorant and barbarous condition! People prefer the poet's fancies:—

> One man alone, the father of mankind,
> Drew not his life from woman; never gazed
> With mute unconsciousness of what he saw
> On all around him; learned not by degrees:
> Nor owed articulation to his ear;
> But, moulded by his Maker into man,
> At once upstood intelligent, surveyed
> All creatures; with precision understood
> Their purport, uses, properties; assigned
> To each his place significant; and filled
> With love and wisdom, rendered back to Heaven
> In praise harmonious the first air he drew.

---

[1] Clem. Alex. *Strom.* iv. 25, § 173; 23, § 152. Buddæus, *Philos. Hebr.* 383-388, where he gives the Rabbinic fancies about Adam Kadmon. Suidas *s. v.* 'Αδμ. South, *State of Man before the Fall*, &c. On the other side see Clem. Alex. *Strom.* vi. 12, § 96; Greg. Naz. *Orat.* xxxviii. 12; and even Irenæus, *Adv. Hæres.* iv. 38.

> He was excused the penalties of dull
> Minority. . . . History, not wanted yet,
> Leaned on her elbow, watching Time, whose course
> Eventful should supply her with a theme.[1]

Fascinating and poetical, no doubt; the primal man, regarded as a being beautiful of body, gracious in soul,[2] filled in heart with virgin purity and sweetness, and discovering everything with exquisite and lightning-like spontaneity! Nevertheless, 'Science[3] banishes amongst myths and chimeras the fancy of a primitive man, burning with youth and beauty, to show us upon icy shores I know not what abject being, more hideous than the Australian, more savage than the Patagonian, a fierce animal struggling against the animals with which he disputes his miserable existence.' What support is there for the poetic hypotheses of those who love their own assumptions better than they love the truths which science reveals? In a handful of rude and bizarre traditions, in a few skulls of the very meanest and most[4] degraded type, in here and there a gnawed fragment of human bones, in a few coarse and pitiable implements of bone and flint, what traces have we of that radiant and ideal protoplast whom men have

---

[1] Cowper, *The Task.*

[2] The Bible tells us nothing of this kind; but it would take us too long here to examine fully the Biblical data. I believe that when fairly and thoroughly considered, they *sanction* the view here expressed. For a picture of frightfully degraded aboriginal races, see Job xxx. 1–8; Ewald, *Gesch. d. Volkes Israel*, i. 27; De Gobineau, i. 486.

[3] Aug. Laugel, *Rev. des Deux Mondes*, May 1, 1863; cf. De Gobineau, *De l'Inégalité des Races*, i. 228; Link, *Die Urwelt*, i. 84; Lyell, *Princ. of Geol.* i. 178; Laugel, *Science et Philosophie*, p. 270.

[4] It has even been suspected (most likely on insufficient grounds), from the position of the *foramen magnum*, that the head was not vertical on the neck. See *Ethnol. Trans.* p. 269, 1863.

delighted to invest with purely imaginary attributes, and to contemplate as the common ancestor of their race? But man, in his futile and baseless arrogance, must exalt the earliest representatives of his kind, though he cannot deny the infinite debasement of his cotemporary brethren. He refuses to see in his far-off ancestors what he *must* see in his living congeners, a miserable[1] population maintaining an inglorious struggle with the powers of nature, wrestling with naked bodies against the forest animals, and forced to dispute their cave-dwellings with the hyæna and the wolf.

Years pass before the infant can realise and express his own individuality; ages may have rolled away before those ancestors of man who lived in the dim and misty dawn of human[2] existence could in any way understand their own position in the yet untamed chaos of the ancient world. The recognition of the long and feeble periods of animalism and ignorance is no more degrading to humanity than the remembrance of the time when he was rocked and swaddled and dandled in a nurse's arms is a degradation to any individual man. Disbelieving, on the scientific ground of the Fixity of Type,[3] the Darwinian hypothesis, we should yet consider

---

[1] It is agreed on all hands that Gen. i. 26, has no bearing on this question, since it refers to the moral and intellectual nature of man—reason, liberty, immortality. 'Non secundum formam corporis factus est ad imaginem Dei, sed secundum rationalem mentem.'—Aug. *de Trin.* xii. 7. Obviously if all men—even Mundrucus and Ostiaks—are created in the 'image of God,' then the first men were so, however low their grade.

[2] It is a remarkable fact that native legends betray a reminiscence of the Elk, Mastodon, Megalonyx, Deinotherium, &c. Hamilton Smith, *Nat. Hist. of Human Spec.* pp. 104–106; Maury, *Des Ossemens humains* (*Mém. de la Soc. des Antiq.* i. 287), &c.

[3] I may perhaps be allowed to refer to my paper on this subject read

it disgraceful and humiliating to try to shake it by an *ad captandum* argument, or a claptrap platform appeal to the unfathomable ignorance and unlimited arrogance of a prejudiced assembly. We should blush to meet it with an anathema or a sneer; and in doing so we should be very far from the ludicrous and complacent assumption 'that we were on the side of the angels!'

Is it not indisputable that man's body—'all but an inappreciable fragment of its substance'—is composed of the very same materials, the same protein and fats, and salines, and water, which constitute the inorganic world,—which may unquestionably have served long ago as the dead material which was vivified and utilised in the bodies of extinct creatures,—and which may serve in endless metensomatosis [1] for we know not what organisms yet to come? Was there, or was there not, a time in the embryonic dawn of individual life, when every one of us drew the breath of life by means not of lungs but of a species of gills? Is this fact any disgrace to us, or will any pseudo-theologian have the dogmatic hardihood to deny it? Are we, in our gross and haughty ignorance, to assume that, because by God's grace we carry in ourselves the destinies of so grand a future, a deep and impassable gulf of separation must therefore divide even the material particles of our frame from those of all other creatures which find their development in so poor a life? What sanction have we for this assumption? Is it to be found in the future fate of

---

before the British Association this year, and now in the Ethnolog. Soc.'s *Transactions*.

[1] If the word, which has the authority of Clemens Alexandrinus, and which is now imperiously demanded by the wants of science, may be pardoned on the score of its necessity.

the elements of our body—destined, as we know they are, to be swept along by the magic [1] eddy of nature, to be transmuted by her potent alchemy into nameless transformations, and subjected by her pitiless economy to what we should blindly consider as nameless dishonour? or, looking backwards as well as forwards, is it to be found in the fact that there are stages in the earlier development of the human embryo, during which the most powerful microscope, and the most delicate analysis, can neither detect nor demonstrate the slightest difference between the [2] three living germs of which one is destined to be a wolf, the second a horse, and the third a man? If the question *is* to be degraded from scientific decision into a matter for teatable æsthetics and ignorant prepossessions, is this certain embryonic degradation or immaturity *less* oppressive than the admission of a bare possibility that, myriads of centuries ago, there may have been a near genetic connection between the highest of the animals and the lowest of the human race? It is not yet proved that there was; we believe that there was *not*; but, nevertheless, the hypothesis is neither irreverent nor absurd. Let those who love truth only consider what *are* the certain facts about our mortal bodies, and be still;—awaiting the gradual revelation of His own past workings which the All-wise Creator may yet vouchsafe, not assuredly to the clamorous, the idle, and the ignorantly denunciative, but to humble and studious enquirers,—to those loftier and less self-complacent souls, whom He has endowed with the desire, the wisdom, and the ability to search out the pathless mystery of

---

[1] Coleridge, *Aids to Reflection*; Huxley, *Lect.* pp. 15–19; *Hamlet*, v. 1.
[2] Karl Snell, *Die Schöpfung des Menschen*, p. 130.

His ways, through long years of noble and self-sacrificing toil.

It has, indeed, been asserted that the languages of some barbarous nations—for instance, the Greenlanders and the North American Indians—are of so rich, so perfect, and so artistic a structure, that they could not possibly have been achieved by them in their present condition, and furnish a proof that they have sunk into savagery from a state of higher culture. Du Ponceau [1] speaks in the most glowing terms of the genius displayed in the infinite variety and perfect regularity of those languages. Charlevoix calls attention to the beautiful union of energy and nobleness in the Huron, where, as in the Turkish, 'tout se conjugue.' Dr. James says that there are seven or eight thousand possible forms of the verb in Chippeway. Appleyard [2] tells us that 'the South African languages, though spoken by tribes confessedly uncivilised and illiterate, are highly systematic and truly philosophical;' that in Kafir there are a hundred different forms for the pronoun 'its,' [3] and that 'the system of alliteration maintained throughout its grammatical forms is one of the most curious and ingenious ever known.' Threlkeld [4] tells us similar facts about the Australian dialects; and Caldwell, [5] in his 'Comparative Grammar of the Dravidian Languages,' occupies many pages with the laws of euphonic permutation of consonants and harmonic se-

[1] Et. du Ponceau, *Mém. sur le Syst. Gram. de quelques Nations indiennes,* passim. A most valuable and brilliant work.
[2] Kafir Grammar, pref.
[3] *Id.* p. 66; p. 6, note, &c.
[4] Threlkeld; *Australian Gram.* p. 8.
[5] *Dravidian Grammar,* pp. 126–138.

quence of vowels, which exist both in those and in the Scythian languages. Instances of similar exuberance and complexity in savage languages might be indefinitely multiplied;[1] and the argument that they imply an intellectual power superior to what we now find in these races, and that they therefore prove a condition previously exalted, is so plausible that in a former[2] work I regarded it as convincing. Further examination has entirely removed this belief. For this apparent wealth of synonyms and grammatical forms is chiefly due *to the hopeless poverty of the power of abstraction.* It would be not only no advantage, but even an impossible incumbrance to a language required for literary purposes. The 'transnormal' character of these tongues only proves that they are the work of minds incapable of all subtle analysis, and following in one single direction an erroneous and partial line of development. When the mind has nothing else to work upon, it will expend its energy in a lumbering and bizarre multiplicity of linguistic expedients, and by richness of expression will try to make up for poverty of thought. Many of these vaunted languages (*e. g.* the American and Polynesian), —these languages which have countless forms of conjugation, and separate words for the minutest shades of specific meaning,—these holophrastic languages, with their 'jewels fourteen syllables long,' to express the commonest and most familiar objects,—so far from proving a once-elevated intellectual condition of the people who speak them, have not even yet arrived at

---

[1] Appleyard, p. 69; Du Ponceau, p. 95; Howse, *Cree Gram.* p. 7; Pott, *Die Ungleichheit d. menschl. Raçen*, p. 253; Steinthal, *Charakteristik*, p. 176; Maury, *La Terre et l'Homme*, p. 463.

[2] *Origin of Lang.* p. 28. See too Vater, *Mithrid.* iii. 328.

the very simple abstraction [1] required to express the verb 'to be,' which Condillac assumed to be the earliest of invented verbs! The state of these languages, so far from proving any retrogression from previous culture, is an additional proof of primordial and unbroken barbarism. The triumph of civilisation is not complexity but simplicity: and unless an elaborate Polytheism be more intellectual than Monotheism,—unless the Chinese ideography, with its almost indefinite number of signs, be a proof of greater progress than our alphabet,—then neither is mere Polysynthetism and exuberance of synonyms a proof of actual culture in the past, or possible progress in the future. If language proves anything, it proves that these savages must have lived continuously in a savage condition.[2]

I will here quote two high and unbiassed authorities in support of the same conclusion:—

'It has already been observed,' says Mr. Garnett,[3] 'that very exaggerated and erroneous ideas have been advanced respecting the structure of the class of languages of which we have been treating in the present paper. They have been represented as the products of deep philosophical contrivance, and totally different in organisation from those of every part of the known

---

[1] In American and Polynesian languages there are forms for 'I am well,' 'I am here,' &c., but not for 'I am.' In Elliot's Indian Bible 'I am that I am,' is rendered 'I do, I do' (compare the French idiom 'il fait nuit,' &c.). More than this, savage nations cannot even adopt the verb 'to be.' A negro says, 'Your hat no *lib* that place you put him in.' 'My mother done *lib* for devilly' (= is dead).—Hutchinson, *Ten Years' Wanderings*, p. 32.

[2] See among many other authorities Pott, *Die Ungl. der menschl. Raçen*, p. 86; Du Ponceau, *Transl. of Zeisberger's Lenni-Lenape Gram.* p. 14; Crawfurd, *Malay Gram.* i. 68; Adelung, *Mithrid.* iii. 6, 205.

[3] *Philological Essays*, p. 321.

world. The author of "Mithridates" regards it as an astonishing phenomenon that a people like the Greenlanders, struggling for subsistence among perpetual ice and snow, would have found the means of constructing such a complex and artificial system. It is conceived that there cannot be a greater mistake than to suppose that a complicated language is like a chronometer, or a locomotive engine, a product of deep calculation, and preconceived adaptation of its several parts to each other. The compound parts are rather formed like crystals, by the natural affinity of the component elements; and whether the forms are more or less complex, the principle of aggregation is the same.'

'In those which abound most in inflections,' says Mr. Albert Gallatin,[1] 'nothing more has been done than to effect, by a most complex process, and with a cumbersome and unnecessary machinery, that which, in almost every other language, has been as well, if not better performed by the most simple means. Those transitions, in their complexness, and in the still visible amalgamation of the abbreviated pronouns with the verb, bear, in fact, the impress of primitive and unpolished languages.'

Language, then, from whatever point of view we regard it, seems to confirm instead of weakening the inference to which we are irresistibly led by Geology, History, and Archæology—that Man,

> The heir of all the ages in the foremost files of Time,

is a very much nobler and more exalted animal than the shivering and naked savage whose squalid and ghastly relics are exhumed from Danish kjökken-möddings, and

---

[1] *Archæologia Americana*, ii. p. 203, quoted by Mr. Garnett.

glacial deposits, and the stalactite flooring of freshly-opened caves. These primeval lords of the untamed creation, so far from being the splendid and angelic beings of the poet's fancy, appear to have resembled far more closely the Tasmanian, the Fuegian, the Greenlander, and the lowest inhabitants of Pelagian caverns or Hottentot kraals. We believe that in Scripture itself there are indications that they appeared upon the surface of the globe many ages before those simple and noble-minded shepherds from whose loins have sprung the Aryans and Semites—those two great races to whom all the world's progress in knowledge and civilisation has been solely due.

CHAPTER V.

PSYCHOLOGICAL DEVELOPMENT OF DISTINCT THOUGHT.

Wenn ein unendlich Gefühl aufwogt in der Seele des Dichter's,
. . . .
O dann mag er ahnen von fern das Geheimniss der Sprache,
Wie in der Zeiten Beginn aus dem erwachenden Geist,
Da er sich selbst und die Dinge vernahm, das lebendige Wort sprach
Offenbarung und That, göttlich und menschlich zugleich.
GEIBEL.

LANGUAGE may with more accuracy be called a Discovery or a Creation, than an Invention of the human race. Undoubtedly the idea of speech existed in the human intelligence as a part of our moral and mental constitution when man first appeared upon the surface of the earth. In *this* sense we may call language a divine gift, and may apply to it, with perfect truth, the passage of Tertullian: '*invenisse* dicuntur necessaria ista vitæ, non *instituisse*; quod autem invenitur fuit, et quod fuit non ejus deputabitur qui invenit, sed ejus qui instituit. Erat enim antequam inveniretur.'[1]

But the germs may perish for want of development, and like the seeds in the diluvium, or grains of wheat in the hand of a mummy, may lie hidden for centuries before they meet with that combination of circumstances which is capable of quickening them into life. Yet we

[1] *Apolog. adv. Gentes*, xi.

do not agree with Lessing in supposing that *if* man discovered language by the exercise of his own endowments, *i.e.* if he merely evolved the speech-power which existed within him as an immanent faculty, *long centuries* would necessarily have been required for the purpose. The wants of primitive men, like the wants of infants, are few and simple,[1] and wholly sensuous. It is certain, by universal admission, that the ultimate roots of language are *few in number*; it is nearly certain that no language possesses more than a thousand, and that some have far fewer. These roots we regard as mere etymologic fictions; but if, with Max Müller, we suppose that they were ever used as words, there *must*, even on this theory, have been a period when men used but a *few* words; and consequently, since the notion of any revelation of these roots is expressly repudiated, there must have been a time, however short, in which man had *no* words, no articulate language at all, and in which significant gestures could have been his only way for communicating his thoughts. And this time, however short, must also be postulated even if, in defiance of Scripture, it be supposed that language was revealed.

But *why* should it be held impossible that man once existed with nothing but the merest rudiments of speech? There are whole nations *even now* which, if the testimony of travellers is to be accepted, possess very

---

[1] Prof. Max Müller traces back all language to 'roots,' and there he would stop, declaring the use of them to be an ultimate and inexplicable fact. Inexplicable indeed! yet the 'theory of roots,' 'phonetic types,' incapable of further analysis and, so far as appears, either wholly arbitrary, or else containing in themselves some mystic inherent fitness, is offered to us in the place of theories, so simple, so natural, and in part so *demonstrable*, as those which trace the rise and gradual growth of language out of onomatopœia and interjection.

little more. Nor, indeed, is it necessary to look to the remotest parts of the earth to find how very few are the words which are *necessary* to express the wants of man. Mr. D'Orsey mentions that some of his parishioners had not a vocabulary of more than 300 words; and although the assertion has been widely disputed, I should certainly be inclined to confirm it out of my own experience. I once listened for a long time together to the conversation of three peasants who were gathering apples among the boughs of an orchard, and as far as I could conjecture, the whole number of words they used did not exceed a hundred; the same word was made to serve a multitude of purposes,[1] and the same coarse expletives recurred with a horrible frequency in the place of every single part of speech, and with every variety of meaning which the meagre context was capable of supplying. Repeated observation has since then confirmed the impression. If this be so in Christian and highly-civilised England in the nineteenth century, what may not have been perhaps ten thousand years before the Saviour was born into the world?

If, then, man once existed with only the *germs* of speech and of understanding, to what was their development due? The question admits of distinct answer, and that answer is full both of interest and value.

The first men who ever lived must have learned for themselves those simplest lessons which have to be learnt afresh by every infant of their race. Confused, yet lovely, was the multitude of influences and appearances by which they were surrounded; how should they

---

[1] Just as in Chinese the same root may be a noun, a verb, and sometimes also a particle. Heyse, § 134.

thrid the all-but inextricable mazes of impressions so manifold? Over their heads the sun, and moon, and the infinite stars of heaven,[1] rose and set in endless succession; the heavens outspread their illimitable splendour; woods waved, and waters rolled, and flowers exhaled their perfume, and fruits yielded their sweetness, and the hours of day and night and the four seasons of the year encircled them in their mystic dance. Had man been created unintelligent, and merely receptive, the waves of this vast tide of being must have broken over him in vain; and, in the absence of a living spirit, the world must have continued to seem unto all save the Highest Being a formless chaos—no better, for all its lustre and loveliness, than if the darkness had still brooded over the void abyss. But that soul, 'created in the image of God,' whose birth is recorded in the book of Genesis, bore no resemblance to the statue-man of Condillac's famous *Traité des Sensations*. Had it been so, the senses could only have produced a jarring multitude of heterogeneous impressions, and man would have continued to be that mere organised sensitive mass which Saint Lambert supposes him to be at the moment of his birth until 'Nature has created for him a soul!' For unless there had also been in man the 'intellectus ipse' of Leibnitz, unless there had been the intelligence, as well as the *sensorium commune*, even sensation would be impossible,[2] seeing that in the complex act which we call sensation man opposes the internal action of his conscious individuality to the influence of external causes. Without this apperception, there could be no

---

[1] See a glorious passage of S. Chrysostom, *Or*. xii. 385, quoted by Lersch, i. 89; and Herbart, *Lehrb. d. Psychol.* p. 194.

[2] Herbart, *Psychol.* p. 108.

such thing as self-conscious sensation,[1] nor could mankind ever have arisen to any higher region than that of mere organic impressions.

But although at first the intellect be but a passive and dormant faculty, it is *there*, and it is the sole clue wherewith we disentangle the myriad-ravelled intricacy of sensuous impressions. And thus the senses become the gateways of knowledge; and a man born without the capacity for external sensations would also be of necessity soulless and mindless, because, though not the *single source* of all our thoughts and faculties, the senses are yet the necessary condition of their development. Thus it is that the senses, during the earliest days of man's existence, act the part of nursing mothers[2] to the soul, to which afterwards they become the powerful and obedient handmaids. They are the organs of communion between man and the outer world; they place him *en rapport* with it, uniting man to the Universe, and men to one another. Thus they baptize man as a member of the moral and physical cosmos,

---

[1] See Vict. Cousin, *Cours de Phil.* iii. passim. 'Sensation,' says Morell, 'is not purely a passive state, but implies a certain amount of mental activity. It may be described on the psychological side as resulting directly from the attention which the mind gives to the affections of its own organism. Extreme enthusiasm, or powerful emotion of any kind, can make us altogether insensible to physical injury.' Hence, a soldier, during the battle, is often unconscious of his wounds, and a general of the roar of cannon going on around him. 'Numerous facts of a similar kind prove demonstrably, that a certain application and exercise of mind, on one side, is as necessary to the existence of sensation, as the occurrence of physical impulse on the other.'—*Psychology*, p. 107. In point of fact, some nations are as pre-eminent for the keenness of their senses as for the meanness of their intellect, which could not be the case if the senses created the intellect.

[2] Heyse, *l. c.*

and awaken thereby the intellect, which would otherwise[1] remain infructuous, like an unquickened seed.

The first conception which man must learn is the conception of his own separate independent existence, and without this conscious distinction between the Ego and the Non-ego,—not indeed as a notion so clear and accurate as to admit of expression by the nominative of the personal pronoun, but as the general basis of all possible sensations,—he cannot advance a single step. And this lesson he learns by contact with the outer world, and mainly, beyond all doubt, from the organ of sight. At first he would regard himself (as all children do) rather as an object than a subject;[2] rather as 'me' than as 'I;' rather as ὅδε than as ἐγώ; rather in relation to others than as 'the machine which is to him, himself.' But even this elementary lesson is sufficient for the purposes of further education; and

> As he grows he gathers much
>   And learns the use of 'I' and 'me,'
>   And finds 'I am not what I see,
>   And other than the things I touch:'
>
> So rounds he to a separate mind
>   From whence clear memory may begin,
>   As thro' the frame that binds him in
> His isolation grows defined.[3]

---

[1] 'The earliest sign by which the Ego becomes perceptible is corporeal sensation.'—Feuchtersleben, *Med. Psychol.* p. 83, quoted by Fleming, *Vocab. of Phil.* p. 457.

[2] Mr. Browning, with that rare metaphysical accuracy which characterises him, no less than the other great poet of our age, chooses the *third* person as the only appropriate one for the meditations of the semi-brutal Caliban.

> 'Setebos, Setebos, and Setebos;
>   *Thinketh* he dwelleth in the cold grey moon,' &c.
>   *Theology in the Island.*

[3] Tennyson, *In Memoriam,* xliv.

The child, like the primal man, who has advanced thus far, learns with rapid and intuitive instinct to separate and discriminate between the many distinct and different impressions caused by physical contact with the outer world.

Thus, then, by means of an instinctive and reciprocal action, the senses develop the self-conscious individuality; and the self-consciousness, which contains indeed the germ of all intelligence, first quickens and then distinguishes, analyses, and combines, the impressions of those senses which have called it into life. And since two factors—the physical and the psychical—are indispensable to every true sensation, the two are so intimately related that, whereas without the psychical factor the physical could not exist, on the other hand, without the physical factor the psychical could not be developed. Speech is undoubtedly the product of the thinking spirit; but this spirit [1] received the first impulse of development from the impressions of the outer world and the needs of practical life.

At first, if we may trust the analogy of childhood, even sensuous influences must have been frequently repeated before they produced any definite impression. *Feeling*, which is a dull total impression, precedes sensation, to which indeed some of the lowest organisms

---

[1] Steinthal, *Grammatik, Logik, und Psychol.* 238 fg. Heyse, § 46. In this and the following remarks I have chiefly, though by no means exclusively, followed this wise and clear thinker. I fear that the unfamiliar words, intuition, representation, concept, &c., will render this tedious to readers unaccustomed to metaphysical enquiry; but I thought it better to adopt them than to confuse matters by that excessive looseness of English philosophical terms which we chiefly owe to the vacillating usage of Locke. I am greatly indebted to Fleming's *Vocabulary of Philosophy*.

can never attain at all; for, as we have seen already, an act of attention is required for every definite sensation, and it is not until after many sensations that we obtain a clear perception. 'Light[1] strikes on the infant retina; waves of air pulsate on the infant tympanum, but these as yet produce neither sight nor hearing; they are only the preparations for sight and hearing. . . . On the educated sense objects act so instantaneously as to produce what we call their sensations; on the uneducated sense they act only so as to produce a vague impression, which becomes more and more definite by repetition.'

It is not, however, *long* before the sensuous impression (*Sinnes-eindruck*) has kindled the electric fire of self-consciousness—in other words, the presentation soon becomes a perception or a sensation; for by a perception (*Wahrnehmung*) we mean a conscious presentation in reference to an object, and by a sensation (*Empfindung*) we mean a conscious presentation in reference to the modification of our own being. The impression on the senses, by calling into reciprocal action the two parts of our nature, produces a *sensation, i. e.* a certain conscious change in the state of our own minds; and these sensations rapidly give us a *perception, i. e.* they teach us something, which is at least subjectively true, respecting the qualities of matter.

But sensation and perception are common to man with the more intelligent animals, and the perfection

---

[1] Lewes, *Biog. Hist. of Phil.* p. 442. That attention is necessary even for a sensation, we may see from the fact that ordinarily (without a definite act of abstraction and observation) we are wholly unconscious of the numberless reflections of light, sound, smell, &c., which are playing on our senses. In fact, the phenomena of abstraction, reverie, preoccupation, *absence of mind,* &c., all point to this conclusion. See Sir H. Holland, *Chapters on Mental Physiology.*

of human reason enables us to advance further than this. Sensations tell us nothing about *objects*, but only about properties or attributes; we rise from sensations therefore to intuitions (*Anschauungen*),[1] which are a complex of all the sensations caused by an object. Sensations are analytical; they come to us from different senses, and tell us the shape, colour, sound, weight, hardness, &c., of an object: the intuition gives us the object itself as the synthesis of all these separable attributes, so that gradually we grow familiar with the sensuous perception, in its totality, as a 'collective impression,' or definite picture, 'presented [2] under the condition of distinct existence in space or time;' and this we call an *Intuition*, *i. e.*, according to the definition of Coleridge, 'a perception immediate and individual.'

And when this intuition has, by the power of abstraction, been raised into a complete picture, capable of being analysed into various elements, and is held fast in the consciousness as a permanent intellectual form, which may be banished and recalled *at will*, then we have a *Representation* (*Vorstellung*)[3]—the first permanent product of intellectual spontaneity, the first definite intellectual exertion of the will.

Lastly, by still higher processes of intellectual abstrac-

---

[1] Steinthal, *Gram. Log. und Psychol.* 261. His general outline of the psychological process differs in some particulars from Heyse's. Mr. Mill (*Logic*, i. 58 sq.) briefly touches on the same subject. He only alludes to perceptions as *acts* of the mind 'which consist in the recognition of an external object as the exciting cause of the sensation.'

[2] Mansell, *Proleg. Log.* p. 9. We mean, of course, an 'empirical intuition,' which, in the Kantian philosophy, corresponds to the representation of a sensible object. German, *Anschauung*.

[3] Steinthal calls this *Anschauung der Anschauung*, i. e. a power of regarding the intuition (v. supra) *as* an Intuition, which is firmly fixed in the consciousness and memory. *Grammatik*, p. 295.

tion, in which the judgment for the first time plays a part, we raise the representation into the sphere of generality, and then possess a *notion or concept* (*Begriff*). A concept [1] grasps an object as the synthesis of all its constituent attributes or properties; the Representation or image (*Vorstellung*) is subjective, and different people may have different images of the same object; but the notion is the objective conception of the species, and being independent of all accidental marks of the individual representation, is and must be the same for all men. The *representation* is due to the analytic activity of Abstraction, but is entangled with the sensuous accidents of the individual object; the notion (or concept) is the product of a higher creative activity of the thinking (logical) intelligence, and produces that ideal synthesis which enables us to think of a Genus or Species. It so far retrogrades to the concrete intuition as to reduce to unity a multitude of phenomena; but this unity is not that of the immediate object, but one ideally recognised by the synthetic activity of the intellect. The *representation* is arrived at by a merely material analysis of the Intuition; the *notion* [2] by a formal and logical analysis; and distinct knowledge is impossible without notions, which are thus the commencement of the development of pure logical thought.

---

[1] 'Conception' should more accurately be used of 'the *act* of the understanding, bringing any given object or impression into the same class with any number of other objects or impressions, by means of some character or characters common to them all' (Coleridge, *Church and State*, Prel. Rem.); *concept* of the *result* of the act.

[2] 'Notions, the depthless abstractions of fleeting phenomena, the shadows of flitting vapours, the colourless repetitions of rainbows, have effected their utmost when they add to the distinctness of our knowledge.' Coleridge.

Nevertheless, words correspond *not* to notions, but to images or representations. They mark the object of perception, *not* in the totality of its essential attributes, but by some single mark whereby the image may be conceived and fixed in the intelligence. In fact, the representation (*Vorstellung*), which in ordinary, although not in philosophical language, is called the conception, is a mere *empirical* notion, derived from familiarity with the external properties of the object (*Anschauungsbegriff, Erfahrungsbegriff*), and this is what every word expresses. The *logical* conception may be indefinitely more accurate and profound, but must yet employ the same word for its expression. Thus, to men in general, 'bird' simply means a creature with wings; nor would their rough definition of it exclude either butterflies or bats; yet the man of science has no other word than this (bird), to express the complex of essential characteristics involved in the accurate definition. And the philosopher uses the word 'man,' no less than the world in general; although the philosopher thereby expresses an idea which it exhausts his intellect to describe or to define, while the world merely implies by it the animal which Plato characterised as 'a featherless biped,' and which a modern philosopher has described as 'a forked radish with a curiously carved head.'

To illustrate this process: (i.) I see a bird flying, or a tree in bloom, and it makes a *sensuous impression* on my retina; but if I am absent or preoccupied, I may be wholly unconscious of this impression, which does not become even a sensation until my consciousness is excited. But when this is done, when my Attention is drawn to it, I have (ii.) a perception (*Wahrnehmung*). When I contemplate this perception as an inward picture, mirrored in my consciousness, I have (iii.) the intuition (*Anschauung*) of the flying bird and the blooming tree. If, by abstraction, I separate this individual phenomenon in its concrete totality into its several component elements, and range those elements under some definite intellectual form as an ideal possession of my consciousness, I then have (iv.) the representations (*Vorstellungen,* vernaculè 'conceptions') of 'bird,' 'flying,' 'tree,' 'blooming.' But the analytic activity of the intelligence proceeds still farther into particulars: it separates the elements of a representation, and apprehends them as so many independent representations. In the tree it distinguishes between leaf, twig, stem, root, and the properties of height, greenness, &c.—all of which furnish so many separate representations. It further distinguishes the species of a representation, such as tree, into oak, beech, pine, &c., each regarded as special representations, and recognised by specific signs; all of which I bear in mind when I use the word 'tree,' which thus, by material analysis, becomes to me (v.) an empirical concept (*Erfahrungsbegriff*), formed by a synthesis of observed characteristics, and expressing more or less adequately the nature of the object. Lastly, by still further acts of intellectual abstraction, I arrive (vi.) at the *logical notion* (*Verstandesbegriff*), which is no longer merely empirical or material, but which, by the synthetic activity [1] of the judgment, recognises the object as the sum-total of all those attributes (and those only) which constitute its essence.

Once more then. From passive receptivity I am

[1] Heyse, p. 86.

awoke by sensuous impressions into free, spontaneous, creative activity, whereby I pass through the stages of sensation and perception to that of Intuition, in which I first become independent of the immediate effect of the external object on my senses, and then free myself from the dominion of the senses, and possess an inward picture which I can contemplate without any assistance from them. Still advancing, my intellect *creates* representations for itself, no longer merely retaining the sensuous picture, but forming it to an ideal existence, and using it as its own possession and its own production.

Sensations, Perceptions, Intuitions are individual and special in their character; but representations are general, and no longer refer to that which is single and concrete, or to the individual object of perception. In this sense all words are Abstracta. The real world of appearances, in which everything is individual, is recreated [1] by the intelligence into an ideal world of general conceptions.

Thus, then, we have traced the psychological growth of the concepts, which may be represented by language. A word is a recognised audible sign for a special definite Intuition or concept. From the genesis of the *concept* we pass to the genesis of the *sound* which is accepted as its sign; and the questions which we have to consider are, How does the sound originate, and what is the connection, if any, between these two elements, the intellectual and the sensual, the concept and the sound? We need not fear that all such questions are insoluble. Speech is the expression of the free intellect, and if the

---

[1] Heyse, p. 88.

laws and processes of the intellect are capable of being conceived and understood, why should Speech,[1] which is nothing miraculous, arbitrary, or accidental, but which is the natural organ and product of the intellect, be deemed incapable of similar comprehension?

[1] Heyse, s. 20.

CHAPTER VI.

POSSIBLE MODES OF EXPRESSING THOUGHT.

He winketh with his eyes, he speaketh with his feet, he teacheth with his fingers.—Prov. vi. 13.

FROM what we have already observed, it is evident that every mode of expression serves only to describe internal sensations, not outward facts; it throws light on that which is subjective, not on that which is objective; it expresses *ourselves*, not the world around us; sensations, perceptions, intuitions, not external things.

But what is the *medium* of expression? Obviously it must have been one of the senses, which are the main gateways of knowledge, the portals of intercommunication between man and man, between men and the Universe around them.

It is *conceivable* that a language (*i. e.* a mode of communication) might have been invented which should use the medium of [1] the touch, the taste, or the smell. Yet such a language, in the case of the two latter, could not but be infinitely imperfect, difficult, and obscure, nor has the attempt ever been made. This is to a less degree the case with the touch. It is well known that among certain animals the touch *does* serve all necessary purposes of intercommunication. Bees, for instance,

[1] Heyse, p. 29; Charma, *Ess. sur le Lang.* p. 50.

to mention but one notorious case, communicate to each other the death of the queen by a rapid interlacing and striking together of the antennæ. Nor is a tactile language wholly unknown to man. For instance, the Armenian merchants, as we are informed by the traveller Chardin, are able to inform each other of any modification in their bargains, however complex, without the notice of the purchaser, by holding their hands together under their mantles, and moving[1] them in a particular manner. Yet a language which required for its possible development a constant contact, could never serve the purposes of so elevated a being as man.

The two highest and most ideal senses remain, and these, as they affect the soul more nearly and powerfully than the others, were clearly the best adapted for the expression of thought, which is a modification of the intelligent subject. We find accordingly that all actual language addresses itself to the eye or to the ear.

For in point of fact Art may be regarded as a language. We have read of a sculptor who conveyed, by means of a statue, the intense impression produced in his mind by the dawn of a summer day; and there is scarcely a thought, an emotion, or a fact that may not be conveyed by painting. Imitation—a fundamental principle on which rests the possibility of any communication between two sentient beings—may appeal as directly to the eye as to the ear. Philomela effectually reveals, by the mute tapestry, her woven tale:—

---

[1] *Voy. en Perse*, iv. 267, ed. Rouen. 'The finger extended means ten; bent it means five; the bottom of the finger is one; the hand, a hundred; the hand bent, a thousand. By similar motions of the hand they indicate pounds, shillings, and pence,—their faces all the while continuing to be expressionless and blank.'

> Os mutum facti caret indice. Grande doloris
> Ingenium est, miserisque venit solertia rebus!
> Stamina barbaricâ suspendit candida telâ,
> Purpureasque notas filis intexuit albis,
> Indicium sceleris.[1]

Shakspeare's mutilated Lavinia does not lack the means of revealing the authors of the outrage she has suffered. Pictures and hieroglyphics continue to this day among various Indian tribes, a sure method of reporting facts; and we know from history that a rude sketch first conveyed to Montezuma the ominous intelligence that men in strange vessels and of strange garb had landed on his shores. Nay, more, the mighty invention of a written alphabet has translated the sounds addressed to the ear into symbols for the eye; and one half at least of the thoughts of other men, whereof we become cognisant from day to day, is conveyed to us through the medium of sight.

How easy and how natural would have been a language of gesticulation, addressed solely to the eye, is proved by the large use of gestures to supplement the lacunas of a miserable speech among some degraded savage tribes; as, for instance, the Delaware Indians, who count by raising their hands a certain number of times, striking them as many times as there are tens. With savages generally, quot membra, tot linguæ; and of course for the deaf and dumb an eye language is the only one that can exist. To them the 'parole manuelle'[2] is the only possible or intelligible speech, as it undoubtedly would be to the whole human race if the sense of hearing were to become extinct. And that such a lan-

---

[1] Ov. *Met.* vi. 38 sqq.

[2] An expression of Jamet (*Mém. sur l'Instr. des Sourds-muets*, p. 15), quoted by Charma, p. 187. Condillac called it 'langage de la danse.'

guage would be most rapidly developed, and would be the same throughout the globe, appears certain from the fact that deaf mutes from different countries can at once converse together with freedom, when their speaking countrymen can hold no communication;—and that many signs, even some which apparently are quite arbitrary,[1] are mutually intelligible to the deaf mute and the savage. Ælian[2] relates an amusing instance of such a result. The tyrant Tryzus, that he might repress all possible means of conspiracy, published an edict that his subjects were to hold no communication with each other, either in public or in private. The order was at once rendered nugatory by an extraordinary development of the power of expressing thought by signs and gestures. When even this mode of intercourse was forbidden by the suspicious despot, one of the citizens went into the forum, and, without speaking a word, burst into a flood of tears. He was soon surrounded by a weeping multitude, who flew upon the tyrant and his bodyguard when he advanced to scatter them, and vindicated by his assassination their liberty of speech![3]

In truth, gesture is a most eloquent and powerful exponent of emotion, and may add almost incredible force to the utterance of the tongue. 'Every passion

[1] See some curious confirmations and instances of this in Marsh's *Lectures*, ed. Smith, p. 486.

[2] *Hist. Var.* xiv. 22.

[3] See some excellent remarks in Marsh's *Lectures*, pp. 486–488. 'The language of gesture,' he says, 'is so well understood in Italy, that when King Ferdinand returned to Naples after the revolutionary movements of 1822, he made an address to the lazzaroni from the balcony of the palace, wholly by signs, which, in the midst of the most tumultuous shouts, were perfectly intelligible to his public. And it is traditionally affirmed that the famous conspiracy of the Sicilian vespers was organised wholly by *facial* signs, not even the hand being employed.'

of the heart,' says Cicero,[1] 'has its appropriate look, and tone, and gesture; and the whole body of man, and his whole countenance, and all the voices he utters, reecho like the strings of a harp to the touch of every emotion in his soul.' 'What would you have said had you heard the master himself?' exclaimed Æschines to the admiring Rhodians, who had just heard him read the mighty oration of Demosthenes on the Crown; and Demosthenes has doubtless told us one great secret of that eloquence which

> Fulmined o'er Greece, and shook the Arsenal
> To Macedon, and Artaxerxes' throne,

when he defined gesticulation as the first, the second, and the third qualification of the successful orator. Who that in modern days has seen a Kemble or a Siddons, a Rachel, a Helen Faucit, or a Ristori, can be ignorant of what a language may be uttered by every motion and every look? Yet it is probable that even the first of our modern actors falls short in this respect of the skill of the ancient pantomimes, of whose 'loquacissimæ manus, linguosi digiti, silentium clamosum, expositio tacita,' Cassiodorus[2] gives so lively a description.

These may have been the considerations which led Isaac Vossius deliberately to give the preference to gesticulation over language, and to regret that the whole human race does not banish 'the plague and confusion of so many tongues,' and adopt an universal and self-evident system of signs and pantomimic expression.[3] 'Nunc vero,' he continues, 'ita comparatum est ut

[1] *De Oratore*, iii. 216.
[2] *Var.* iv. 51.
[3] Many an amusing story has been told of the facility with which by such means of expression Englishmen have travelled all over the continent with no fragment of any language except their own.

animalium, quæ vulgo bruta creduntur, melior longe quam nostra hâc in parte videatur conditio, utpote quæ *promptius et forsan felicius sensus et cogitationes suas sine interprete significent, quam ulli queant mortales* (!), præsertim si peregrino utatur sermone.'[1] Idle as the complaint may be, it is founded on the fact that gesture is in many cases more rapid and intense in the effect which it produces than words themselves. The sidelong glance, the drooping lid, the expanded nostril, the curving lip are more instantaneously eloquent than any mere expression of disdain;[2] and the starting eyeball and open mouth tell more of terror than the most abject words. M. Charma tells an anecdote of the actor Talma that, disgusted at the disproportion of praise which was attributed to the words of the poets, by which in the theatre he produced such thrilling effect, he one day, in the midst of a gay circle of friends, suddenly retreated a step, passed his hand over his forehead, and gave to his voice and figure the expression of the profoundest despair. The assembly grew silent, pale, and shuddering, as though Œdipus had appeared among them, when, as by a lightning-flash, his parricide was revealed to him, or as though the avenging Furies had suddenly startled them with their gleaming torches. Yet the words which the actor spoke with that aspect of consternation and voice of anguish formed but the fragment of a nursery song, and the effects of action triumphed over those produced by words.[3]

[1] Is. Vossius, *De Poematum Cantu*, p. 66, Oxon. 1673. It was the love of paradox, apparent in this passage, that led Charles II. to say of Voss that he believed everything *except* the Bible!

[2] See Charma (*Ess. sur le Lang.* p. 21), who has treated this subject admirably.

[3] Garrick on rare occasions used, as he called it, 'to go his rounds,'

It is, however, easy to see that gesture could never be a *perfect* means of intercommunication. Energetic, rapid, and faithful, it is yet obscure because it is sylleptic, i. e. it expresses but the most general facts of the situation, and is incapable of distinguishing or decomposing them, and wholly inadequate to express the delicate shades of difference of which every form of verbal expression is capable. The flashing of a glance may belie years of fulsome panegyric; a sudden yawn may dissipate the effect of a mass of compliments poured out during hours of simulated interest; an irrepressible tear, a stolen and smothered sigh, the flutter of a nerve, or the tremble of a finger, may betray the secret of a life which no words could ever have revealed.[1] The veiled and silent figure of Niobe may be more full of pathos than the most garrulous of wailing elegies. The wounds of the victor of Marathon, or the maimed figure of the brother of Æschylus, the unveiled bosom of Phryne, or the hand pointing to the Capitol which Manlius had saved, may have produced effects more thrilling than any eloquence; but such appeals were only possible at moments of intense passion, or under a peculiar combination of circumstances. The

i. e. to make his face and gestures assume in succession the aspects produced by the whole round of passions and emotions, from simple good humour to that of profound despair.

[1] ' Whereto the Queen agreed
  With such and so unmoved a majesty
  She might have seemed her statue, but that he,
  Low-drooping till he well-nigh kissed her feet
  For loyal awe, saw with a sidelong eye
  The shadow of a piece of pointed lace,
  In the Queen's shadow, vibrate on the walls,
  And parted, laughing in his courtly heart.'
  Tennyson, *Idylls of the King*, p. 208.

ancient orators, well aware of the power which lies in these mute appeals, made them gradually ridiculous by the frequency with which they employed them; and the introduction of a weeping boy upon the rostrum would produce but little weight when many of the audience knew that weeping may express a wide variety of emotions, and when an injudicious question as to the obscure cause of those moving tears might elicit the mal-apropos complaint '*Se ex pædagogo vellicari.*'[1]

In moments of extreme passion, then, a language of gesture, a language appealing to the eye rather than the ear, is not only possible but extremely powerful, and one which will never be entirely superseded. And possibly some natures may be so sensitive, some faces so expressive, that even during the most peaceful and equable moments of life the passing thought may touch the countenance with its brightness or its gloom. But this could never be the case with any but a few; and even with these, what attention would be found equal to read and interpret, without fatigue, symbols and expressions so subtle and so fugitive? Moreover, to the blind, and to *all* during the darkness, and whenever an opaque body intervened, and whenever the face was turned in another direction, such language would instantly become impossible. It is incapable of representing the distinctness and successiveness of thought; it is limited on every side by physical conditions; it requires an attention too exclusive and intense; it would reach a shorter distance,[2] and appeal to a less spiritual sense.

---

[1] 'Puer, quid fleret, interrogatus, se ex pædagogo vellicari respondit.' *Quint.* vi. 1. On the adoption of this trick before the dikasteria, see Aristophanes, *Vesp.* 568–571.   [2] Charma, p. 51. Heyse, 29.

For though *both* Sight and Hearing are ideal senses, as distinguished from the inferior ones of touch, taste, and smell, Hearing is more ideal in its nature, and reaches more nearly to the soul than Sight. It is the clearest, liveliest, and most instantaneously affected of the senses. That which is seen is material,[1] and remains in space, but that which is heard (although in reality as permanent and as corporeal) yet to our blunt senses has a purely ideal existence, and vanishes immediately in time. Hence sound is especially adapted to be the bearer; and the ear to be the receiver of thought, which is an activity requiring time for its successive developments, and is therefore well expressed by a succession of audible sounds. Juxtaposition in *space* appealing to the eye could only remotely and analogously recall this succession in time. Moreover, hearing requires but the air, the most universal of all mediums, the most immediate condition of life; whereas the eye requires light as well, and is far more dependent on external accidents. The fact that even a sleeper is instantly awoke to consciousness by the tremor of his auditory nerve under the influence of the voice, is a proof of the impressive and immediate adaptability of sound to the exigencies of the intellectual life. So that hearing is the very innermost of the senses, and stands in the strictest and closest connection with our spiritual existence. The ear is the ever-open[2] gateway of the soul; and, carried on the invisible wings of sound,[3]

---

[1] Heyse, 29; and see some beautiful remarks in Herder's *Abhandlung über d. Urspr. d. Sprache*, s. 101–108.

[2] Heyse, p. 31.

[3] Ἔπεα πτερόεντα, or (as Horne Tooke called his famous work) language not only the vehicle of thought, but the wheels.

there are ever thronging through its portals, in the guise of living realities, those things which of themselves are incorporeal and unseen. Wonderful, indeed, that a pulse of articulated air should be the only, or at any rate the most perfect means wherewith to express our thoughts [1] and feelings! Without its incomprehensible points of union with all that passes in a soul which yet seems so wholly dissimilar from it, those thoughts and emotions could perhaps have no distinct existence—the exquisite organism of our hearing would have been rendered useless, and the entire plan of our existence would have remained unperfected!

[1] Herder, *Ideen zur Gesch. d. Menschheit*, p. 190.

CHAPTER VII.

SOUND AS THE VEHICLE OF THOUGHT.

'Words are the sounds of the heart, and writings its pictures.'
YANGTSEE.

A GREAT part of the world around us is inanimate and dumb; yet such is the nature of all substances [1] that, by means of sound, we can interpret to the intellect their innermost peculiarity and constitution, even when light is absent, or the eye is most easily deceived. The inward shudder or oscillation of the component parts, even of lifeless objects, produced by any mechanical or external interference, betrays to us at once the degree of cohesion and homogeneity between the component particles, and some of their most general and necessary properties. There is, as might have been expected, a close analogy between the phenomena of Light and those of Sound. Thus *Sound*,[2] in general, corresponds to *Sheen*; Clear Sound to *Brightness*; *Echo* to *Reflexion*; *Noise*, a confused indistinct sound, to *Glimmer*; *Clang*, a steady, pure, homogeneous sound, to *Glow*; *Tone*, which is the element of music, and is derived from τείνω

---

[1] In the earlier part of this chapter I am mainly following the guidance of Heyse (*Syst. d. Sprachwissenschaft*, § 16), but I generally use my own words, because I have sometimes to amplify and more often to condense.

[2] Schall, Schein; Hall, Helle; Wiederhall, Wiederschein; Geräusch, Schimmer or Geflimmer; Klang, Glanz; Ton, Farbe.

G

because it depends on the greater or lesser tension by which it is produced, corresponds to *Colour*, and the relations between the different colours in a picture no less than those between the different intervals and harmonic relations of sound in music, are expressed by the word Tone.

All these kinds of sound are produced out of lifeless substances by mechanical influence; but they all differ from *articulate* sound, and from all sound which is the dynamic product of the animal organism. For sound, thus spontaneously produced, the Germans reserve the word *Laut*, for which we have no exact English equivalent, unless we choose a special sense of the word utterance.

Voice (*Stimme*) is the capacity of dynamic sound-production, but in English is chiefly used of man alone. The lower order of animals, which have no lungs, and fish, whose element is the water which is not a conductor of voice, are dumb. The higher animals have each their own utterance, by which they are recognisable, and by which they recognise each other. It has generally been asserted, and it is repeated by Heyse, that we cannot speak properly of a *language* of animals, because their utterances only express a general consciousness of existence, or at the best but a few sensations, a few longings and desires of the animal life (ψυχή), which, even in their highest possible development—even in the song of the nightingale—cannot attain to the expression of anything individual. With this conclusion, so like a thousand other hasty assertions [1] of human dogmatism, it is not necessary to agree, but,

[1] See a paper on 'The Distinction between Animals and Man,' in the *Anthropological Review*, No. 5.

in order not to break the continuity of the subject, I have relegated all further examination of it to another place.

Man possesses a voice,—a capacity for the dynamic production of sound,—as a mere animal Being in the yet dark and unconscious slumber of natural Life. The new-born infant enters the world with a cry, which is a mere natural sound, the expression of animal feeling, and is soon liable to various modifications for the purpose of expressing the different stirrings of life and sensation. These natural sounds are no more speech than the cries of animals are; no human intelligence is expressed by them; and the origin of rational language cannot be explained by them *alone*. They are inarticulate and involuntary; they are mere modifications of the breath, and do not express the thinking spirit. Nevertheless, they prove the possession of a high capacity, and this capacity is developed by man into significant speech, as the expression of his highest and innermost nature. His voice, independently of the words it utters, is capable, by natural flexibility, of expressing every variation of emotion, in all degrees of intensity; and by virtue of the penetrating nerve-shaking influence of sound upon the soul, it can convey to others a sympathy [1] with the same feelings, and the impression of a free activity. It instantly and involuntarily stirs the attention of the hearer by an energy which, like that of the soul itself, is to the highest

---

[1] The power of influencing by the *voice* is found in all, but in very different degrees. Few had it in greater perfection than Dr. Chalmers, who, we are told, moved a whole congregation to tears by the few simple words 'It was because God was very good to him.' Every one has experienced the effect of what Lamartine beautifully calls 'the gift of tears in the voice.'

degree varied, energetic, and effectual, yet is at the same time ideal and unseen. The voice, then, by a natural necessity, by an organic connection, is the organ of the understanding; and speech is the expression of the thinking spirit in articulate sounds. The union in speech of sound and sense, the combination of the phonetic and the intellectual elements into one organic unity, will be the subject of our enquiry hereafter. At present we must say a few words on the mechanical means by which the emission of the voice is rendered possible.

The voice of man is produced by a machinery far more exquisite [1] and perfect than that possessed by any other animal. The Larynx, with its cartilages and muscles, forms, in point of fact, a combination of musical instruments; it is at once a trumpet, an organ, a hautboy, a flageolet, and an Æolian harp. 'The air passing upwards and downwards through the larynx and trachea,[2] forms its analogy with the wind-instruments; the vibration of the *chordæ vocales*, its resemblance to the stringed.' 'The voice [3] is produced by the larynx, which is situated beneath the base of the tongue, and in front of the pharynx. The sides of the larynx are formed by the two large thyroid cartilages, which rest on the annular cricoid cartilage. On the upper surface of the back of the cricoid cartilage are mounted two small cartilaginous bodies, called the arytenoid, which are moveable in various directions by various muscles.

---

[1] Ladevi-Roche, *De l'Orig. du Lang.* p. 49; et ibi Bossuet, *Connaissance de Dieu et de soi-même*, p. 194.

[2] Hilles, *Essentials of Physiology*, p. 272.

[3] I have abridged this account from Dr. Carpenter's *Animal Physiology* (p. 528), generally using his own words.

To these arytenoid cartilages are attached two ligaments of elastic fibrous substance, which pass forward to be attached to the front of the thyroid cartilage, where they meet in the same point. These are the instruments concerned in the production of sound, and also in the regulation of the aperture by which air passes into the trachea; and they are termed *vocal chords*. By the meeting of these ligaments in front, and their separation behind, the usual aperture has the form of a V; but it may be narrowed by the drawing together of the arytenoid cartilages until the two vocal ligaments touch each other along their whole length, and the aperture is completely closed. In ordinary breathing the arytenoid cartilages are wide apart; but for vocal sounds it is necessary that the aperture should be narrowed, and that the flat sides rather than the edges of the vocal ligaments should be opposed to one another. When the ligaments are brought into position, by the contraction of certain muscles, the air, in passing through the larynx, sets them in vibration, in a manner very much resembling that in which the reed of a hautboy or clarionet, or the tongue of an accordion or harmonium, is set in vibration by the current of air made to pass beneath them. The *rapidity* of the vibration, and consequently the *pitch* of the sound, depends on the degree of tension of the vocal ligaments.' 'When we reflect,' says Mr. Hilles,[1] 'that the range of the human voice will extend, although rarely, to the compass of two octaves, and that in this range are included, in some singers, as many as 2,000 minor tones, we shall form some idea of the extreme delicacy of motion, of which the laryngeal muscles are capable when fully educated.'

[1] *Ubi supra*, p. 275.

The elementary sounds of which the voice is capable are about twenty in number,[1] and it is easy to see that the permutations and combinations of these sounds are amply sufficient to provide the world with an infinite variety of languages. The elements of articulate sound are three—1. The aspirate,[2] which is a mere strengthened expiration; 2. The vowel sounds, produced by a *continuous* stream of air passing through the trachea, and modified only by the form of the aperture through which they pass; and 3. The consonants,[3] for the utterance of which is required a partial or complete interruption of the breath in its passage through the organs in front of the larynx. These are of two kinds, viz. those[4] of which the sound can be prolonged, and the *explosive* consonants (b, p, d, t, g, k), which require a *total* stoppage of the breath at the moment previous to their pronunciation, and which therefore cannot be prolonged. The sound of the former is modified by the position of the tongue, palate, lips, and teeth, and also by the degree in which the air is permitted to pass through the nose.

[1] Harris, *Hermes*, ii. 2, 3rd ed. p. 325.
[2] Heyse, p. 74. In pp. 78, 79 Heyse traces what he supposes to be the natural connection of the vowels with various emotions; he admits, however, that language in its final stage confuses and neglects these primitive relations of sound to emotion, and makes the vowels mere signs in the service of the free understanding. Hence it is in interjections and other primitive words that we must study their original value. But alike for vowels and for consonants such enquiries seem to me both dubious and difficult.
[3] Hence it is in the use of consonants, speaking generally, that the sounds uttered by animals differ from the articulate human voice. Aristotle speaks of οἱ ἀγράμματοι ψόφοι οἷον θηρίων, *Probl.* xi. 57. They have but one or two consonants at most. *Id.* x. 39. R, for instance, is called 'litera canina.' 'Irritata canis quod rr quam plurima dicit.' Lucilius. 'R is for the dog.' Shaks.
[4] Carpenter, *l. c.*

Now, the natural sensuous life expresses itself in three kinds of natural sound, viz., Interjections, Imitations, and those sounds, expressive of some desire, which in imitation of the German *Lautgeberden*[1] we may roughly designate as vocal gestures. Aspirates and vowels are generally sufficient to express the mere passing emotions of the natural life; consonants are more the expression of the free intelligence. *Interjections* are the arbitrary expression of subjective impressions; *Imitations* advance a step farther, spontaneously reproducing something which has influenced the senses from without; *Lautgeberden*, though like interjections they have their source in the subject, are not a mere utterance of passive sensation, but an energetic expression of will, though as yet only in the form of desire.

At present, it will be observed, we are only dealing with the *elements* of articulate speech; the natural sounds out of which, by the aid of the understanding, perfect language is developed, and which in themselves are the mere expressions of animal feeling. In tracing the physical development of sound which corresponds to the psychical development of thought, we have not yet got beyond the means of finding vent for the sensuous impression, or at most the conscious perception. We have not even arrived at the *root*, which corresponds, in the development of sound, to the intuition (Anschauung) in the development of thought. The *word* which corresponds to the representation (Vorstellung) is beyond the vocal elements which we have yet reached. The further steps of the Process, which are as yet unexplained, will become evident as we proceed.

[1] Heyse, p. 71.

CHAPTER VIII.

INTERJECTIONS.

'Ως διδάσκει 'Επίκουρος—φύσει ἐστὶ τὰ ὀνόματα, ἀποῤῥηξάντων τῶν πρώτων ἀνθρώπων τινὰς φωνὰς κατὰ τῶν πραγμάτων.—Orig. c. *Cels.* i. 24.

THE theories of the interjectional and onomatopoetic origin of language *are not in reality different, and both of them might without impropriety be classed under the latter name*; for, in point of fact, the impulsive instinct to reproduce a sound is precisely analogous to that which gives vent to a sensation by an interjection. When we see a person laugh or yawn we can hardly help following their example, not from an instinct of imitation, but from a nervous sympathy; and the same nervous sympathy[1] forces a child to reproduce any sudden sound which is not beyond its power of articulation, as any one may see who cares to try the experiment. This result, no less than the utterance of a cry of joy or pain, arises from a purely physical cause, namely, the general influence on the nerves communicated to the delicate organs by which the voice is produced. The reason why children and savages are more given to imitative and interjectional sounds is because of the greater delicacy and sensibility of their

---

[1] Wüllner, *Ueber d. Urspr. d. Sprache*, p. 6, fg.; Poggel, *Ueber das Verhaltniss zwischen Form und Bedeutung*, § 5, .

nervous organisation. Nevertheless, while aware of this fact, I have preferred, for the sake of clearness, to treat separately of these two phonetic elements; and first of Interjections.

Interjections[1] are of two kinds; namely,

1. Those which are caused by some inward sensation, such as the cry of anguish, and the exclamation of joy; sounds of the voice, which are neither definite in origin nor distinct in articulation, but are perfectly vague both as to the form they assume and the source from which they arise; and,

2. Those which are evoked by some external impression, especially by perceptions of the ideal senses, sight and hearing. These stand on a higher stage than the last. They do not indeed, like imitations, express the *external* character of the thing perceived, but the inward excitement of the soul in consequence of the perception, whether it assume the form of astonishment, pleasure, surprise, disgust, or fear. In these the sound of the voice receives a more specific limitation, and vowels and aspirates are distinctly uttered.

We do not purpose to trace in the half-obliterated records of language the natural connection between particular vowel-sounds and particular sensations; but it seems clear that by the very constitution of man certain sounds *are* the natural and almost necessary exponents of certain conditions. There are certain 'inarticulate bursts of feeling not reacted on by the

---

[1] Heyse, p. 72, § 27. There is some meaning in the verse of Dr. King:
  'Nature in many tones complains,
  Has many sounds to tell her pains;
  But for her joys has only three,
  And those but small ones, Ha! ha! he!'

mind.'[1] This will appear at a glance if we compare the interjections of a Semitic with those of an Aryan language, and observe their almost complete identity. Thus, for instance, the הָהּ, אָהּ, and אֲהָהּ which occur in the Hebrew of the Bible (Ez. xxx. 2, vi. 11; Mic. ii. 7), are the same expressions of astonishment, fear, pleasure, or indignation which we find in the Latin hahe, aha, &c., and which in so many Aryan dialects are worn down to the mere O of the vocative case. The הוֹי is 'the obscure deep sound of seriousness, of threatening, or lamentation,' and is therefore like the Greek οὐαί, the Latin heu, eheu, væ in different circumstances.[2] The more definite expression of lamentation, הִידוֹ (Am. v. 16), offers an obvious analogy to the Latin ohe, while the אֲבוֹי (Prov. xxiii. 29), סַ (Ez. ii. 10), and אַלְלַי (Mic. vii. 1; Job x. 15), are almost identically the same with αἰβοῖ, papæ, phui, ἐλελεῦ, and even the Irish whilleleu! We find the same exclamations, Ha! ha! for surprise, Au-é! for sorrow, Abah! for disgust, among the New Zealanders;[3] and the Australian Ala! differs little either in sound or meaning from the English Halloo!

Latin is particularly rich in genuine interjections; and, besides this, Latin, Greek, English, and nearly all languages have a number of words which, although used interjectionally, are not really to be classed under this head, like the Hebrew חָלִילָה, μὴ γένοιτο, 'God forbid!' Such are the Latin malum! nefas! macte! amabo! age, sodes, sis, nae, profecto, &c., some of which are

[1] Ewald's *Hebrew Grammar*, § 440.
[2] See, too, Glass, *Phil. Sacr.* lib. iv. tract. 8.
[3] Ch. Miss. Soc. *New Zealand Gram.* p. 57. Threlkeld's *Austral. Gram.* p. 20.

verbs, and some are adverbs. Such too are the Greek ἄγε, φέρε, ἴθι, ἄγρει, δεῦτε, &c., and the English strange! hark! adieu! welcome! the deuce! Very many of such spurious interjections are explicable by some ellipse; they are in fact abbreviated sentences as much as the single letter O (or ὦ) for οὐ, 'not!' with which the poet Philoxenus[1] is said to have replied in writing to the tyrant Dionysius, who had invited him to the court of Syracuse. Under this head fall a large number of abbreviated oaths and exclamations, such as eccere, epol, mehercle, medius fidius, for per ædem Cereris, Pollucis; ita me Hercules, Dius filius, juvet, &c.[2]

The Greeks, not very accurately, reckoned interjections under the head of *adverbs*; the Latins, correctly observing that the interjection is, as it were, *flung into* the sentence (inter jacio), and is quite capable[3] of expressing some emotion even if no verb be added, placed them separately as a distinct part of speech. This classification has given rise to the most amusing vehemence of argument. The interjection, it is asserted,

---

[1] Egger, *Notions Élém. de Gram. Comp.* p. 103. It is curious to see how a spurious interjection like Alas! which comes from the exclamation *Ai lassa*, 'ah, me weary!' in the songs of the Provençal troubadours, is never used by the common people. They instinctively recognise its artificial and aristocratic origin, just as they substitute 'the Fall,' 'Harvest,' &c., for the only Latin name of a season, Autumn.

[2] Energetic brevity is indispensable to an interjection; hence, in all languages oaths assume a curt form, as morbleu = par la mort de Dieu; 'zooks,' by God's looks; 'zounds,' by God's wounds, &c.

[3] Priscian says, 'Interjectionem Græci inter adverbia ponunt,' and adds that the Roman grammarians separated the interjection, 'quia videtur affectum habere in sese verbi, et plenam motus animi significationem, etiamsi non addatur verbum, demonstrare.' xv. 7. Quintilian (*Instt. Or.* i. 4) mentions the rearrangement of the parts of speech by the Romans, who had no article,—and he adds, 'Sed accedit superioribus interjectio.'

is incapable of grammatical analysis, and belonging to the inarticulate cries and sounds of instinctive language it is also incapable of etymology, and stands in no syntactical relation to the rest of the sentence. Horne Tooke bewails that 'the *brutish inarticulate Interjection,* which has nothing to do with speech, and is only the miserable refuge of the speechless, has been permitted, *because beautiful and gaudy,* to usurp a place amongst words, and to exclude the Article from its well-earned dignity.' And when asked 'Why such bitterness against the interjection?' he replies, '*Because the dominion of speech is erected upon the downfall of interjections.* Without the artful contrivances of language, mankind would have nothing but interjections with which to communicate, orally, any of their feelings. The neighing of a horse, the lowing of a cow, the barking of a dog, the purring of a cat, sneezing, coughing, groaning, shrieking, and every other involuntary convulsion with oral sound, have almost as good a title to be called parts of speech as interjections have (!). Voluntary interjections are only employed when the suddenness and vehemence of some affection or passion returns men to their natural state, and makes them for a moment forget the use of speech; or when from some circumstance the shortness of time will not permit them to exercise it. And in books they are only used for embellishments, and to mark strongly the above situations. But where speech can be employed they are totally useless, and are always insufficient for the purpose of communicating our thoughts. And, indeed, where will you look for the Interjection? Will you find it amongst laws, or in books of civil institutions; in history, or in any treatise of useful arts or sciences?

No. You must seek for it in rhetoric and poetry, in novels, plays, and romances.'

Neither the energy of this passage, nor the endorsement of it by Professor Max Müller as 'an excellent answer to the interjectional theory,' move us at all.[1] Whether, indeed, grammarians choose to rank the Interjection as a part of speech or not, is a matter of great indifference, although the fact that they are regularly declinable in Basque[2] shows that their unsyntactical character is merely an accident of language. But at any rate, on the confession of the adversary, they do not deserve all this scorn. We do not assert that a mere interjectional cry has of itself attained to the dignity of language, but that, like the imitation of natural sounds, *it was a stepping-stone to true language, both by suggesting the idea of articulate speech and by supplying a large number, if not the entire number of actual roots.* I desire no better illustration of this than the one which Professor Müller has suggested. 'Even,' he says, 'if the scream of a man who has his finger pinched should happen to be identically the same as the French *hélas*, that scream would be an effect, an involuntary effect of outward pressure, whereas

---

[1] I cannot see *any* force in the objection that 'if the constituent elements of speech were mere cries, &c., it would be difficult to understand why brutes should be without language.'—Max Müller, *Lectures*, i. 355. Obviously, as has been observed a thousand times, the *mere power of articulation* is not the *source* of language (*Orig. of Lang.* pp. 79, 164). Half the arguments aimed at the interjectional and onomatopoetic theories altogether miss their mark by not observing that all which those theories profess to explain is the cause which guided man in the choice of *words* to express thought. There would be force in the objection if we held with Hamann that speech is the 'Deipara unserer Vernunft;' or with Shelley, that 'He gave man speech, and *speech created thought*.'

[2] Mentioned doubtfully by Mr. Marsh.—*Lectures*, ed. Smith, p. 197.

an interjection like *alas!* *hélas,* Italian *lasso,* to say nothing of such words as pain, suffering, agony, &c., is there by the free will of the speaker meant for something, used with a purpose, chosen as a sign.'

Precisely! but is that any reason why we should *despise* the word *hélas,* or ridicule the theory which points out that in the supposed instance *the interjection would have been the source, the root, the origin of the word?* Undoubtedly the cry of pain, *as such,* is not a word, but is a mere physical expression of pain due to the réflex action of the animal soul upon the organs of speech; but this cry, by the law of association, when repeated recalls the feeling itself; it becomes therefore first a symbol, and then a sign of the feeling; it stands for our subjective intuition (Anschauung) of the feeling, and thereby at once is elevated from a sound to a word, becoming, in fact, as much a word as any other, because it stands in precisely the same relation to the thing which it signifies. In fact, it stands, if anything, on a higher grade of dignity than any ordinary word, because its significance is more absolute and immediate. Let us, for instance, reject the purely artificial word 'alas!' and take the natural interjection ah! ach! and we have at once not merely the *probable,* but the absolutely *certain*[1] *root of a very large class of words in the Aryan languages,* such as ἄχος, achen, ache, *anguish,* anxious, *angustus,* and the word agony itself. When this fact is a little more widely expanded and illustrated, we have the interjectional[2] theory *proved.* Indepen-

---

[1] Cf. Wedgwood, *Etym. Dict.* i. p. xii. See a list of the derivatives from the root in Garnett, *Ess. on Engl. Dialects,* p. 64.

[2] M. Müller, *Lectures,* ii. 88. We see no *great* objection, and absolutely *no* ambiguity, in the words 'onomatopoetic' and 'interjectional';

dently of the many and wise students who have accepted it, it is a theory for which most important arguments may be adduced, and therefore is not one which either *can* be or deserves to be sneered out of notice by a mere nickname, such as that over which so many who are ignorant of the very rudiments of the subject have complacently chuckled.

Professor Müller himself admits that 'with interjections some kind of language *could*[1] have been formed;' and when we have shown at least the extreme probability that a very large portion of existing language *has* had such an origin, surely all *à priori* objections must fall to the ground. If the science of Comparative Philology is to do nothing more than

> To chase
> A panting syllable through time and space,
> Start it at home, and hunt it in the dark
> To Gaul, to Greece, and into Noah's ark;—

and if in that venerable receptacle for all ethnographic and philological theories we can only catch an archæological curiosity in the shape of some desiccated, never-spoken, lifeless 'root,' we cannot but think that it was hardly worth the trouble of being pursued! An etymology of this kind is no etymology at all. What are we the wiser for being told that a whole class of words comes from a root 'il,' to go, and another class from a root 'ar,' to plough? If this be all, one is somewhat weary of the information when it comes, unless, indeed, which of course often *is* the case, one has been rewarded during the search by the discovery or obser-

and we can assure Prof. Müller that, so far as we know, no one has accepted the word 'Imsonic' except the learned suggestor!

[1] *Lectures,* i. 353.

vation of other linguistic or phonetic laws. Still, if these be regarded as ultimate etymologies, they throw no light whatever on questions which we must regard as soluble, as interesting, and as important, viz. what is the origin of words? Why were sounds chosen as the signs of all things which can become the object of thought? and why were special sounds chosen in particular cases? To all these questions the interjectional and imitative theories are adequate,—up to a certain point,—to furnish us with intelligent and valuable answers; they throw a light on the germs and on the development of language, and they furnish a clear explanation of the origin and history of words in *so many* cases that we may fairly argue the existence of similar principles, even in the cases where the wear and tear of language have broken many important links in the chain of evidence. To refer words to some dry 'root,' which confessedly was never used in the intelligent speech of articulately speaking men, and to leave this root without any attempt at further explanation, is to offer us a *caput mortuum* as the prize of our researches, and to abandon unnecessarily, as beyond our reach, many of the deepest problems of language and of human history. If, for instance (to recur to previous examples),[1] a large class of words came from the root 'ach,' and another large class from the root 'dhu,' and if the former be an interjection, and the latter an onomatopœia, we have got at final facts which *give a new meaning and interest* to the history of the derivatives from these roots; but if we are told that a large family of words come from 'ar,' or 'gn,' or 'sal;' and if about

---

[1] *Origin of Lang.* p. 109.

'ar,' and 'ga,' and 'sal,' nothing more can be said, then what have we learnt? The roots are mere mysterious nonentities, which have taught us nothing and come from nowhere. The earth rests on the back of an elephant, and the elephant stands on a tortoise; but what does the tortoise stand upon?

But in point of fact it has repeatedly occurred to me that Professor Müller really does agree to a very great extent with the theories which he often seems to repudiate; in other words that the argument is in great measure due to mutual misapprehension. For in his new volume he *wishes to stand entirely neutral* with regard to the theory that all roots were originally onomatopœias or interjections (p. 92),[1] demanding only that the derivatives should be drawn according to the strictest rules of comparative grammar. If this be so, we entirely agree with him; so far from wishing to arrive at derivations *per saltum* and 'undo all the work that has been done by Bopp, Humboldt, Grimm, and others during the last fifty years,' the majority, at any rate, of those who hold the sneeringly termed Poohpooh and Bow-wow theories to be both valuable and true, have always felt the profoundest respect and gratitude to those great men, and the keenest appreciation of the immortal discoveries which have resulted from their labours.

The opponents of these theories constantly try to depreciate them by asserting that Interjections are purely animal, and Onomatopœias either vulgar or childish. Now, as applied to their primitive condition,

---

[1] Cf. also ii. 314, where he allows a possibly onomatopœic origin to the root Mar which he traces through so many stages.

their first stage, this language is capable of some sort of meaning. Nobody asserted that they *were* language, but only that they are the raw material of it. They are the steps by which man mounts to true language; they are

> the ladder
> Whereto the climber-upward turns his face;
> But when he once attains the utmost round,
> He then unto the ladder turns his back,
> Looks in the clouds, scorning the base degrees
> By which he did ascend.

If, as we are convinced, they helped to suggest the very idea of speech, and supplied man in part with the sounds which his tongue could modulate, and the plastic influence of his intellect could mould, it is surely ungracious to turn round and insult them as '*brutish and inarticulate.*'

And this, in the present instance, is the more unreasonable and inexcusable, because, as we have seen already, many interjections have passed *unaltered* into the domain of finished language.[1] They have their own province in the kingdom of speech, and if it be not universal, it is at least as noble as any other province. If they appear but seldom,—as Horne Tooke scornfully observes,—in Law or History or Science, they are yet capable of adding both power and beauty to rhetoric, poetry, and the drama, and are entitled therefore to a splendid position in the domain of literature. Feeling and passion, no less—perhaps we might say far more—than logic and abstract thought, demand their proper

---

[1] A long list of words—and words full of tragic grandeur—might be adduced which come *immediately and professedly* from interjections; such as οἰμώζω, αἰάζω, ὀλολύζω, ἀλαλάζω, ululo, ejulo, &c.

exponents in the Speech of Man, and it can hardly be correct to rank no higher than the purring of a cat, or the neighing of a horse, the expressions which give vent and utterance to the most passionate emotions in the instant of their most overwhelming power.[1] Mr. Marsh has reminded us that the interjections of Whitfield, 'his Ah! of pity for the unrepentant sinner, his Oh! of encouragement and persuasion for the almost converted listener, formed one of the great excellences of his oratory;'[2] and as in a former volume I endeavoured to redeem the onomatopoetic element of language from the charge of vulgarity by collecting many remarkable passages to show that onomatopœia often added a singular charm to the loftiest and loveliest passages of the greatest poets, so it would be easy to redeem Interjections from similar injustice by the same process. Take but passages like these:—'They shall not lament for him, saying Ah! my brother, or ah! sister. They shall not lament for him, saying Ah lord! or Ah his glory!'—or the passionate outbreak, 'Thus saith the Lord, the Lord of hosts, . . . *Ah!* I will ease me of mine adversaries.' And not to add many other Biblical apostrophes, who does not know Wordsworth's touching lines?—

> She lived unknown, and few could know
> When Lucy ceased to be,
> But she is in her grave,—and *oh!*
> The difference to me!

Any one acquainted with poetry will remember how many exquisite passages owe, to an interjection, their

---

[1] 'Écho des émotions profondes de l'âme, l'interjection traduit l'affection du moment, de la minute, plus fidèlement que toutes les descriptions ne pourraient le faire.' Chavée, *Les Langues et les Races*, p. 17.

[2] *Lectures*, p. 196.

beauty and their pathos. It was probably a lurking sense of some such truth that led Horne Tooke to say that they were 'beautiful;' what he means by the qualification that they are also 'gaudy,' I can but dimly conjecture.

Sanctius[1] loftily relegates Interjections from the region of speech with a dictum of Aristotle that 'all parts of speech must be originated by convention, not by nature.' Now Interjections, he says, are *natural*, because they are found among all, resembling in fact the cries of birds and animals. Passing over for the present the arrogant assumption, which runs through such vast portions of human reasoning, that everything pertaining to man must differ in *kind* no less than in *degree* from its analogon among brutes, we may observe that the *naturalness* of interjections,—their independence of what Horne Tooke calls 'the artful contrivances of language,'—their truthfulness, and simplicity, and freedom from the degraded conditions by which language is made subservient to the concealment of thought,—is in fact one of their chief glories. Another of their remarkable properties, 'which not[2] only vindicates their claim to be regarded as constituents of language, but entitles them unequivocally to a high rank among the elements of discourse,' is the inherent and independent expressiveness, by which we may condense into a single ejaculated monosyllable all, and more than all, of a whole sentence;—condense it too with an impressiveness which no mere sentence can emulate. And again, the interjection is 'subjectively connected with

---

[1] Sanctius, *Minerva*, i. 2. See Harris, *Hermes*, ii. 5. Horne Tooke, *Div. of Purley*, i. 5.

[2] Marsh, *Lectures*, p. 194.

the passion or sensation it denotes, and is not so much the *enunciation or utterance* of the emotion, as *symptom and evidence of it,*'—in other words it is subjective not objective, expressive not descriptive, and therefore may be rightfully considered as 'the appropriate language, the mother-tongue of passion.' Regarded from this point of view, it stands on a higher rather than a lower grade than the other constituents of human speech.

If we look to savage nations as displaying to us a picture of the infancy of man, we shall expect to trace some of the earliest and most important facts of speech exemplified in their languages. We have seen already how prominent a part Onomatopœia plays in those languages; nor is Interjection less predominant. The exclamations used by the excitable Indians, the Kafirs, or the New-Zealanders, are beyond all comparison more rich and varied than those used by more advanced nations. It is undoubtedly one of the effects of civilisation to diminish the impressionable excitability of untutored races; and as excitability finds in interjections its most natural utterance, we naturally expect to find them more numerous among primitive races, and we may reasonably suppose that at the dawn of humanity the interjectional element provided a larger[1] number of roots than it now could do.

The ancients had some remarkable stories which show how fully they felt that utterance is the spontaneous and almost *inevitable* means for the expression of emotion. For instance, Herodotus[2] and other historians

[1] The very words *Sprechen, sprache* are etymologically connected with *brechen* (cf. *fragor, frangere,* ῥήγνυμι), and like the phrases ῥῆξαι φωνήν, rumpere vocem (Herod. i. 85; Virg. *Æn.* ii. 129), imply the interjectional outburst of speech. See Heyse, p. 114.

[2] Herod. i. 85. Cic. *Div.* i. 53, &c.

tell us how the dumb son of Crœsus burst out with an articulate voice for the first time when he saw a soldier on the point of assassinating his father. Aulus Gellius relates a story that Ægles, a dumb Samian athlete,[1] seeing that he was being cheated by a deceitful lot in a sacred contest, cried out with a loud voice, and from that time recovered the power of speech. Pausanias has a similar anecdote about Battus of Cyrene, who first got over his impediment of speech in consequence of the horror caused by suddenly catching sight of a lion in the African desert. We are inclined to consider that these stories are not wholly fabulous, and at any rate we have heard a perfectly authentic instance of a lady, who for years had lost her voice, and who recovered it in consequence of the shock caused by a sudden emotion. She had been riding up a hill in Ireland, and being in advance of the rest of the party, came suddenly and unexpectedly on an exceedingly glorious view. Turning round eagerly to signify her delight, she found that the sudden effort had restored loudness and clearness to her voice, and from that time forward experienced no difficulty in speaking, although for a very long period she had only been able to use an inarticulate whisper. *Expression*, then, by a law of nature, is the natural and spontaneous result of *impression*; and however merely animal in their nature the earliest exclamations may have been, they were *probably the very first* to acquire the dignity and significance of reasonable speech, because in their case more naturally than in any other the mere repetition of the sound would, by the association of ideas, involuntarily recall the sensation of which

---

[1] Aul. Gell v. 9. Val. Max. i. 8.

the sound was so energetic and instantaneous an exponent. In the discovery of this simple law, *which a very few instances would reveal to the mind of man*, lay the discovery of the Idea of Speech. The divine secret of language,—*the secret of the possibility of perfectly expressing the unseen and immaterial by an articulation of air which seemed to have no analogy with it,*—the secret of accepting sounds as the exponents and signs of everything 'in the choir of heaven and furniture of earth,'—*lay completely revealed in the use of two or three despised interjections!*[1] To borrow a simile from the eloquent pages of Herder, they were the sparks of Promethean fire which kindled language into life.

[1] The objection 'Why, then, did not animals also discover language?' rises so often from the grave where it was long since buried, and appears to be endowed with such inextinguishable vitality, that we must *again* repeat that it was not the *mere* possession of these vocal cries that enabled man to invent a language, but that, the Innate Idea of language being already in his mind by virtue of his divinely-created organism, the possession of these natural sounds taught him how, and supplied him the materials wherewith, to develop the Idea into perfect speech. We entirely agree with the remark of Wilh. von Humboldt, ' Die Sprache liesse sich nicht erfinden, wenn nicht ihr Typus in dem menschlichen Verstande schon vorhanden wäre.' *Ueber d. Verschied. d. menschl. Sprachbaues*, p. 60. The same thing has been said from the beginning. τὸ δὲ τοῖς οὖσι σημαντικὰς φωνὰς ἐφευρίσκειν καὶ προσηγορίας, τῶν ἀνθρώπων εἶναι τῶν τὴν λογικὴν δύναμιν θεόθεν ἐν ἑαυτοῖς κεκτημένων, κ.τ.λ. Greg. Nyss. *Contra Eunom.* xii. p. 848.

CHAPTER IX.

LAUTGEBERDEN, OR VOCAL GESTURES.

'Isis et Harpocrates digito qui significat st!'
Vet. Poeta *ap.* Varr. L. L. iv. 10.

So far as I am aware, Professor Heyse, in his 'System der Sprachwissenschaft,' was the first to distinguish accurately between interjections which are the signs of individual emotion beginning and ending with the utterer, and which are in fact a concentrated soliloquy, and those which, like visible gestures, convey meaning to some other person, and generally intimate a desire or command. It was certainly Heyse who first[1] called the latter by the expressive and picturesque name of Lautgeberden or Begehrungslaute, vocal gestures or sounds of desire, like *st! ps! sch!* and to animals *brr!* He called them by this name both because they are often connected with gestures, and because they can be represented by them; as *st!* by the finger on the lips, &c.[2] Such in English are tush! pish! pshaw! pooh! which are expressive of contempt or aversion, and can only be conceived of as addressed to another; hush! hist![3] mum!

---

[1] See *Syst. der Sprach.* p. 29. '*Die Lautgeberden.* So *nenne ich* solche, zum Theil consonantische und dabei nicht syllabische Laute,' &c.

[2] Compare the French *zest* 'interjection, qui ne se prend que dans cette acception proverbiale, "*entre le zist et le zest*,"' i. e. 'middling.'

[3] M. Nodier observes that it would hardly be supposed that etymologists could be found who derived st! from '*silentium tene.*' 'Cela est

hark! halloo! hip, &c.; and of this nature are many of the exclamations addressed to animals. 'Among them,' says Mr. Marsh,[1] who does not however refer to Heyse, 'are all the isolated, monosyllabic, or longer words by which we invite or repel the approach, and check or encourage the efforts of others; in short, all single detached articulations intended to influence the action or call the attention of others, but not syntactically connected with a period.'

This class of interjections rises, in three respects, above those previously noticed;—first, because they are mainly consonantal, and therefore approach more nearly than the others,—in which consonants play a very subordinate part, — to the complicated articulations of human speech; secondly, because they have for their object, not merely *expression*, but *communication*; and thirdly, because they do not originate in a mere passive feeling, but are, as has been already noticed, the energetic utterance of desire or will, and are spontaneous rather than involuntary. They hardly attain to the dignity of Language because they express no thought, and are the utterance rather of the feeling life than of the thinking spirit; yet they, in common with the other natural sounds which we have mentioned, correspond to a new step in the development of the human intelligence. The Interjection corresponds to the dawn of sensation; the mere Imitation is an analogon of the word into which it almost immediately passes; the Vocal gesture is an analogon[2] of the sentence, especially of the imperative sentence (compare st! with the Latin

---

cependant vrai, car il n'y a point d'idée bizarre dont ce genre d'érudition ne puisse offrir un exemple.' *Dict.* p. 87.

[1] Marsh, *Lectures*, p. 196.   [2] Heyse, p. 73.

sta!). And thus in the sphere of the natural life, the three chief steps in the development of Intellect and Language are foreshadowed or represented.

To recapitulate a little. Impressions affecting the senses produced a physical effect on the organs of sound, and thereby provoked interjectional *expressions*; the repetition of these expressions recalled, by the law of association, the impressions of which they were the utterance, and recalled them not only in the mind of the speaker but also of the hearer. Hence the Interjection served as a sign, and could be recalled by the intellect, no less than the impression by the memory. Here, then, we are at once furnished with all the elements or requirements of speech, namely impressions producing sensations, sensations becoming representations (Vorstellungen), and representations expressed by signs. Thought receives its life from Sensation, and Language receives from the interjectional elements its capability of being intuitively understood. Is any other origin of speech conceivable?[1] Speech results from the combined working of the Intellect and the Senses, and no part of speech more directly and immediately illustrates this united activity of the Senses and the Intellect than the Interjection. Is it then strange that Interjections should become as it were the tap-root of all Language? If we extend the meaning of 'Interjection' to embrace the imitations of all spontaneous sounds expressive of physical conditions,—not only the natural sounds of wrath, horror, disgust, &c., but those which express the sounds of yawning, sneezing, licking, heavy breathing, shuddering, &c.,—then the words *im-*

---

[1] See on the whole subject F. Wüllner, *Ueb. d. Urspr. d. Sprache.* Münster, 1838 (*passim*).

mediately reducible to this origin may be counted by hundreds; and if to these we add their derivatives, they may perhaps be counted by thousands. And this is equivalent to saying that they *alone* can form a language; for be it remembered that even the Bible itself says all that it has to say by the help of 10,000 words.

And as we shall say no more on the Interjectional origin of Language, we will add what has long been a puzzle to us. While arguing against such an origin, Professor Müller appears to us to accept what is the same thing in other words. If, as is probable, he also seems to have at least modified his originally strong hostility to Onomatopœia, we may yet perhaps live to see a change of view as complete, though less marvellous, than that of Herder. I allude to the *only* passage in which I can from his writings discover the faintest gleam of light on the question, 'What was the origin of roots?' Now if he confessedly gave up this question as insoluble, there would be no more to say; but this he does not do. He rejects utterly and distinctly the *miraculous* origin of language, yet he says that *phonetic types* 'exist as Plato would say by nature, though with Plato we would add that when we say by nature, *we mean by the hand of God.*' He rejects and nicknames the Interjectional theory of Language; yet on a page (i. 370) which, in spite of the generally matchless clearness of his style, gives me none but the very vaguest and most uncertain conception of his fundamental belief on the matter, *unless it be a complete acceptation of the Interjectional theory*, he says, referring to Heyse, 'There is a law which runs through nearly the whole of nature, *that everything which is struck rings.* . . . It was the same with man, the most highly organised of nature's works.' In the note he says that this fact 'can of course be used as an illustration only, and not as an explanation.' Yet he adds, 'The faculty, peculiar to man in his primitive state, by which every impression from without received its vocal expression from within, must be accepted as a fact.' And in the text he continues, 'Man ... was endowed not only, *like the brute*, with the power of expressing his sensations by Interjections, and his perceptions by onomatopœia. He possessed likewise the faculty of giving *more articulate expression* to the rational conceptions of his mind.' This was 'an irresistible instinct;' 'the creative faculty which gave to each conception, as it thrilled for the first time through the brain, a phonetic expression.' Now what explanations have we here? Language was not revealed, yet 'phonetic types' 'exist ... by the hand of God.' Language did not arise from Interjections or Imitations, yet it came from these *plus* an irresistible instinct whereby man gave 'more articulate expression to the rational instincts of his mind.'[1] I leave the explanation as I find it. The postulated additional instinct is either a mere development of the Interjectional faculty, or I can only repeat of it, 'Entia non sunt multiplicanda præter necessitatem. Frustra fit per plura quod fieri possit per pauciora.'

[1] Long after this passage was written I met with an almost verbally identical criticism of this passage in Steinthal, *Philologie, Geschichte, und Psychologie* (Berlin, 1864), p. 21. He ends, 'd. h. obwohl hier der Ursprung der Sprache erklärt sein sollte, so bleibt er doch eben völlig unerklärt.'

CHAPTER X.

VOCAL IMITATIONS.

'Ο γὰρ 'Επίκουρος ἔλεγεν ὅτι οὐχὶ ἐπιστημόνως οὗτοι ἔθεντο τὰ ὀνόματα, ἀλλὰ φυσικῶς κινούμενοι, ὡς οἱ βήσσοντες καὶ πταίροντες καὶ μυκώμενοι καὶ ὑλακτοῦντες καὶ στενάζοντες.—PROCLUS, p. 9.

EPICURUS, if he be correctly reported by Proclus, in the often-quoted passage which stands at the head of this section, espouses the views of the Analogists who argued for the *natural* origin of language, against the Anomalists who regarded it as the result of convention. Thus much, at least, is certain:—the *sounds* to which language gave distinct meaning and regular articulation were all of them readily supplied by nature,[1] partly as the involuntary expressions of feeling or desire,—under which heads fall the Interjections and Lautgeberden,— partly as the instinctive imitations of an external world of sound.

The instinct of imitation has a far deeper foundation than is usually supposed, and plays a most important part in the history of human progress. There is hardly a branch of art, there is hardly a mechanical invention which has not originated in the observation and copying of some process or phenomenon of nature. The instinct,

---

[1] τὰ ὀνόματα καὶ τὰ ῥήματα φωναί, αἱ δὲ φωναὶ φύσει, τὰ ἄρα ὀνόματα καὶ τὰ ῥήματα φύσει. Alex. Aphrodis. *Schol. in Arist. de Interpr.* p. 103, in Lersch, i. 89.

as Herder observes, is common to men and to the higher animals, and is by no means the result of intelligent reflection, but an immediate product of organic sympathy. As one string sounds in unison with another,— as a lute laid on the table echoes the tune played upon the lute in the performer's hand, — so the human organism is a musical instrument strung into such exquisite harmony with nature, that it vibrates in sympathy with all external influences. The imitative instinct is in fact a kind of intellectual assimilation. We have already seen how powerfully it has worked among all nations in the nomenclature of animals, which were probably the earliest objects to acquire a name. At present, however, we are speaking only of natural sounds, and simple imitations which have not yet reached to the position of *language*, but are the childish instinctive echoes of sensuous perceptions, or the playful reproductions of animal cries and other sounds. The main object of language is communication; but these imitations, in their earliest stage, convey nothing to the hearer, and are merely the result of an inherent tendency to imitate and reproduce, which is found also among birds and animals, and in which a child at a very early stage of his existence finds spontaneous amusement.

It is however important to observe that the imitation is purely subjective;—in other words the imitative sound represents rather the impression produced than the *sound* which produced it.[1] The sounds of nature,

---

[1] 'Man vergesse nicht, dass ursprünglich nicht von Nachahmung des Lautes der Aussenwelt die Rede sein kann, so dass gleichsam ein Wetteifern mit der Natur stattgefunden hätte; sondern dass der Mensch *durch den Eindruck des äusseren Lautes eine bestimmte Empfindung erhälte*, und dass sich diese unmittelbar, ohne Reflexion, durch einen

for instance, are inarticulate; but by the very nature of the human voice, as used for purposes of speech, the *imitation must* be more or less articulate, and must require consonantal sounds for its production. It is true that caw-caw, bow-wow, βρεκεκεκὲξ, κοὶ κοὶ, &c., are not *words*; but nevertheless they are imitative utterances which stand much nearer to words than the mere unarticulated emission,—which is quite within the range of the human voice,—of the sounds which are actually uttered by the rook, the dog, the frog, or the pig. A child can with a little practice imitate with tolerable accuracy the crowing of a cock, and this imitation merely exercises one capacity of his voice; but if he says 'cock-a-doodle-doo,' the imitation is subjective, and merely reproduces in a conventional but very simple manner the *impression* caused by the cock's noise; the child has not yet got to a *word* properly understood, but he is on the high road which leads directly to it. Some inkling of this fact must be lurking in the curious story of Phædrus about the buffoon who received the plaudits of a crowded theatre for his very successful imitation of the squeaking of a pig. As he had begun by bending down his head into the bosom of his robe, the multitude believed that he had a pig concealed there, and redoubled their applause when he shook out his robe and showed them that it was empty. An envious rustic exclaimed that he could excel the exhibitor, and next day both of them appeared on the stage. The buffoon, pretending to have a pig hidden in his robe, repeated

Laut äussert,' &c. Wüllner, *Ueber die Verwandschaft des Indogerm.*, &c. § 3. 'The imitative nature of language consists in an artistic imitation not of *things*, but of the *rational impression* which an object produces by its qualities.' Bunsen, *Outlines*, ii. 103.

his exhibition of the previous day to the delight of the populace; the rustic, going through the same pantomime, pinched the ear of a real pig which he had brought in with him, and which naturally squeaked its sincerest and best. The people exclaimed that the buffoon's imitation was much the more natural of the two, and ordered the rustic to be kicked out!

> At ille profert ipsum porcellum e sinu,
> Turpemque aperto pignore errorem probans,
> En! hic declarat quales sitis judices![1]

'Nevertheless,' says Perrault, 'the people was in the right; for the comedian who imitated the pig had studied all its most marked and characteristic sounds, and, collecting them together, came closer to the notion which all the world has of a pig's grunts.'[2] The story is too curious not to be true, and the explanation too ingenious not to be correct!

The same fact as to the *nature* of linguistic imitations explains the vast diversity in the articulated attempts of various nations to reproduce one and the same sound. This subject has been already illustrated fully,[3] and little more need be added upon it. Who would assert that *kiao kiao* in Chinese, and *dchor dchor* in Mandshu, cock-a-doodle-doo in English, and Gœkerdihœ in Franconian, are not onomatopœias for the crowing of a cock,

---

[1] Phædrus, *Fab.* v. 5.
[2] *Parallèle des Anciens et des Modernes*, iii. 216. Charma, p. 253.
[3] See Lobeck, *Aglaophamus*, i. 779. *Origin of Lang.* pp. 81–85. The fact, however, that the actual sounds imitated are often *really* different in different countries has often been overlooked. *Ding-dong* represents the tone of a large church-bell, but *bilbil* or *tintinnabulum* of a little hand-bell. So פהק represents the laughter of an Oriental, *cachinnus* of an Italian, &c. Compare, however, לבלב with γελάω, *lachen*, Gothic *hlahjan*.

because on paper they look so different? or that '*bang*' is not an onomatopœia for the sound of a gun, because it is wholly unlike the '*Pouf*' of the French? or that Screech-owl is not as onomatopoetic as ulula? or that *taratantara* is not as much an imitation of the trumpet as the Hebrew Chatzôtzrah (חֲצוֹצְרָה), or the German Kling-klang as the Hebrew (צְלָצַל) Tziltzâl, though they have not a letter in common? The Greeks used both κόγξ and βλώψ (compare our '*flop*') to imitate the sound of the Clepsydra, for which sound Nævius invents the word '*bilbit* amphora.' Yet a Latin poet says '*glut glut*[1] murmurat unda sonans,' and from this derives the word 'glutton;' and Varro[2] makes 'puls' (our *pulse*) to be an onomatopœia of similar meaning! A comparison of the sounds of animals, as represented in different languages, will illustrate the fact most clearly. Coleridge speaks of the nightingale's 'murmurs musical and sweet *jug-jug*,' while Tennyson writes in the person of a peasant-woman,

Whit, whit, whit, in the bush beside me chirrupt the nightingale,

and the Turkish poet, still trying to reproduce the same sound, calls the bird a *bulbul*. How then is this remarkable diversity to be explained?[3] The reason of it is, that

---

[1] 'Percutit et frangit vas; vinum defluit, ansa
  Stricta fuit, *glut glut* murmurat unda sonans,
  Credit glutonem se rusticus inde vocari.'
  Anthol. Lat. ii. 405. Burm.

[2] Varro, *L. L.* iv. 22. For κόγξ, βλώψ, κύξ, &c., see Eustathius, p. 768, 12.

[3] In the fanciful and often absurd *Ornithophonia* of Bœrius one may see how manifold are the ways of representing our impression of a bird's note. Parts of it are quoted in Nodier's *Dict. des Onomatop.* p. 283; and he also gives at length Bechstein's amazing analysis of the song of the nightingale.

man does not attempt to make the *identical* sound which he hears, but *artistically* [1] to reproduce it or the impression it has made, just as a painter often purposely deviates from the actual colours of nature because they would not produce the same effect on the mind under the limited conditions of his art. In fact the *mind* no less than the sense contributes its share to the imitative result. It is not a dull passive echo, but an ideal reflection. The mind, like the magic glass of Cydippe, *modifies* every image which it reflects. It is, as has been proved repeatedly, an absurdity to say that there is any resemblance between the impression and the phenomenon or object which produces it. The former is of course a coefficient of the latter, but as the relations between them are utterly unknown, any comparison of the two involves an inherent absurdity.

Imagination then plays no small part even in the production of these imitative sounds, and it is probable that among primeval races imagination, as exercised in the appellative faculty, was far more delicate and active than it now is; indeed, we may at once infer that such was the case by noticing its workings among savage tribes. Language, be it remembered, was not fashioned at the writing-desk or in the close study of the philosopher. 'If we would follow its track,' it has been said, 'we must place ourselves under the broad free heaven, in the fresh life-exuberant Youth of Mankind, in the age of overweening strength, fermenting vigour, overflowing plenty. . . . The whole deeply-felt necessity which urged the primitive men from one step of language to another must come out before us in most

---

[1] See Benloew, *Recherches sur l'Origine des Noms de Nombre*, p. 91.

living reality, and penetrate our whole being with its inward and primitive force. So possibly may we succeed in finding once more the long-obscured traces of past millenniums.'[1]

The manifold forms which words may assume, which are yet all directly inspired by the imitative principle, are perhaps best shown in the names for thunder,— although the word thunder itself, and its cognates, tonitru, donner, tonnerre, &c., are believed to have had a different origin,[2] and merely to have been subsequently moulded into onomatopoetic semblance by an unconscious feeling of congruity. Two treatises have been written on the subject,—one by Grimm (*Ueber Namen des Donners*, Berlin, 1855), and another by Pott (*Ueber Münnichfaltigheit des sprachlichen Ausdrucks*).[3] From the latter of these (which the author did me the honour to send me with a most kind letter) I select a few only of the names for thunder. Such are Sanskrit *garǵi*, distant thunder; *vaǵraǵvala*, a clap of thunder; Gaelic *tàirneanach*; Bohemian *hr̆mêng*, *hromobitj*; Albanian βουμβουλίτ; Wallachian *trësuetu*; Icelandic *thruma*. Who does not see the imitative instinct here at work? Yet the results are as different as are the individual impressions, which even differ in the same person with the mood in which they find him at any particular time. Nay, more, our impressions are often

---

[1] Drechsler, *Grundlegung zur wissenschaftlichen Konstruction des gesammten Wörter- und Formschatzes zunächts der semitischen, versuchsweise und in Grundzügen auch der indogerm. Sprachen*, p. xxi. Can no one influence the German writers to remember that life is too short for such intolerably long-winded titles to their books?

[2] I have examined, further on, the connection of τείνειν and tonitru. Pott, *ubi infra*, p. 208. Heyse, p. 93.

[3] Printed in the Journal of Steinthal and Lazarus.

purely conventional in their origin. Ancient writers for instance, and nearly all writers down to the time of Milton, make the song of the nightingale 'most melancholy,' and fancied they caught in it the echo of a bereaved mother's wail. But in modern days we have long been agreed that it is

> the *merry* nightingale
> That crowds and hurries and precipitates
> With fast thick warble its delicious notes.

What the eye sees and the ear hears depends in no small measure on the brain and the heart. The hieroglyphics of nature, like the inscriptions on the swords of Vathek, vary with every eye that glances on them; her voices, like the voice[1] of Helen to the ambushed Greeks, take not one tone of their own, but the tone that each hearer loves best to hear.

So far then we have examined (1) the development of 'representations,' as the objects of distinct thought; and (2) the natural sounds out of which can alone be framed the language which expresses thought. It still remains to catch a glimpse, so far as is possible, of the further process of development which weds the sounds of language to its sense. But even so far as we have yet proceeded we may see that Speech was not produced either by purely arbitrary or by distinctly conscious processes. The human organism evolved it as an integral part of its own life, by an unconscious necessity which resulted from its inmost constitution.[2] There was no need to *search* for the sounds which should

---

[1] Vid. *Od.* iv. 278. ἐκ δ' ὀνομακλήδην Δαναῶν ὀνόμαζες ἀρίστους πάντων 'Αργείων φωνὴν ἴσκουσ' ἀλόχοισιν.

[2] Drechsler, *ubi supra*, p. 10.

correspond with and paint the sensations they expressed; Instinct supplied them, in the form of Interjections and Imitations, far more powerfully and swiftly than could have been done by the wavering process of conscious selection. 'As the artist fashions the symbol in which his Idea is reborn, not by conscious consideration, but, like nature, by unconscious science;—as the heart stirred by joy or sorrow, still, without search or hesitation, immediately, unconsciously, but surely and appropriately, utters the sound which truly paints the colour of the passion,—so it is in all language.' To develop Language was the appointed task for the youth of humanity, and its work, as is ever the case with the work of the inspired artist, is inconceivable to the uninitiated, and wonderful to all.

It is a curious and interesting fact that even among uncivilised nations we find what appears to be a trace, mythologically expressed, of this same conception, viz. that it was the mighty diapason of nature which furnished man with the tones which he modulated into articulate speech. The Esthonian [1] legend of the kettle of boiling water which 'the Aged one' placed on the fire, and from the hissing and boiling of which the various nations learned their languages and dialects, mythically represents the Kesselberg, with its crests enveloped in the clouds of summer steam, which they regarded as the throne of the thunder-god; and the Languages which it distributes are the rolling echoes of Thunder and Lightning, Storm and Rain. They have another and still more beautiful legend of a similar character to explain the

---

[1] Grimm, *Urspr. d. Sprache*, p. 28. The explanations are given by Steinthal, *Gesch. d. Sprachwissenschaft bei den Griechen und Römern*, p. 10.

origin of Song or Festal-speech. The god of song Wannemunne descended on the Domberg, on which stands a sacred wood, and there played and sang. All creatures were invited to listen, and they each learnt some fragment of the celestial sound; the listening wood learnt its rustling, the stream its roar; the wind caught and learnt to reecho the shrillest tones, and the birds the prelude of the song. The fish stuck up their heads as far as the eyes out of the water, but left their ears under water; they saw the movements of the god's mouth, and imitated them, but remained dumb. Man only grasped it all, and therefore his song pierces into the depths of the heart, and upwards to the dwellings of the gods.

The legends of savages, and their mythical attempts to express a dim philosophy of speech, are so *extremely* few that it is interesting to observe in them this tendency. The following legend of the Australian aborigines appears at first sight to be meaningless. They say that there was an old woman named Wururi, who went out at night and used to quench the fires with a great stick. When this old woman died the people tore her corpse to pieces. The Southern tribes coming up first ate her flesh, and immediately gained a very clear language. The Eastern and the Northern tribes, who came later, spoke less intelligible dialects. If Steinthal [1] be right in seeing in Wururi a personification of the damp Night-wind, then at the root of this legend also, lies the notion that the Imitation of Nature helped largely to furnish the material of speech.

[1] *Gesch. der Sprachwissenschaft*, p. 9.

CHAPTER XI.

FROM IMITATIVE SOUNDS TO INTELLIGENT SPEECH.

Μεγάλη τούτων ἀρχὴ καὶ διδάσκαλος ἡ φύσις, ἡ ποιοῦσα μιμητικοὺς ἡμᾶς
καὶ θετικοὺς τῶν ὀνομάτων, οἷς δηλοῦται τὰ πράγματα.
DION. HAL. *De Comp. Verb.* p. 94.

THE Intelligence plays but a very subordinate part, and finds no adequate expression,[1] in the Natural Sounds which tell of sensation and sensuous impression.

Reasonable speech begins when the mind has arrived at those immediate individual perceptions which we have called Intuitions,[2] and which correspond to the German *Anschauungen*. These intuitions are expressed, in the parallel development of sound, by Roots.

The Representation is a development of the Intuition, by means of Abstraction; and in the same way the Word is a development of the Root by a formal limitation of the merely material meaning of the root into a determinate object of thought, which also externally assumes a determinate and limited Sound.

[1] Throughout this brief section I generally follow Heyse, p. 88 sqq.,—except where otherwise indicated; I do not however translate him, frequently preferring other forms of expression or arrangement of sentences, and frequently interweaving my own comments or illustrations.

[2] 'Every act of consciousness of which the immediate object is an individual thing, state, or act of mind, presented under the condition of distinct existence in space or time.' Mansel, *Proleg. Log.* p. 9, in Fleming, p. 272.

Just as the intuition (*Anschauung*) melts into the representation (*Vorstellung*) without acquiring any permanent fixity, so in actual speech the Root vanishes into the Word. It has no independent existence; but can only be separated into its elements by an analysis of Language in its finished state.

The production of the word is necessarily coincident with the production of the 'representation.' For in consequence of man's double nature, partly corporeal partly spiritual, he cannot firmly grasp a 'representation' otherwise than by means of the word which is its sensuous sign. The creative Spontaneity of the Intellect in the production of the 'representation' must express itself in a corresponding spontaneous effort of the physical organism. The representation must receive an objective form. In order to grasp and retain the representation in his own intellectual possession, man must necessarily likewise clothe it in a palpable form, for himself, and—since his life is essentially social—for others also. In order to master an object and appropriate it to himself for his own mental purposes, he must give it an Ideal existence instead of its real one, and even this Ideal existence must have its sensuous form in order that it may be exhibited and expressed. He cannot be thoroughly conscious of the representation, as of something which he definitely possesses, without giving it *some* form of expression,[1] and the most perfect and natural form, as has been shown already, is furnished by Sound.

We have arrived then at that point in the Rise of

---

[1] Similar reasoning may be found in Humboldt, *Ueber d. Verschied. d. menschl. Sprachbaues*, p. 68. See p. 51 of the Analysis of this work by M. Tonnellé.

Language at which man must develope those Natural Sounds which he possesses as a part of the animal creation, into meaning and appropriate words, so specialised as to become the signs of distinct conceptions. What we have yet to try and understand is the reason why *particular* sounds should have been attached to particular conceptions; or in other words we must try and discover whether there are any principles on which we can establish a natural, organic connection between words, regarded as sounds, and the meanings which we attach to them.

Now unless we take refuge in miracle or mysticism,— unless we shield ourselves behind a plea of lazy ignorance, which simply means a refusal to enquire, or hide that very ignorance under the exploded jargon of a pseudo-metaphysical science by talking of occult causes, —we must admit that there *must have been an original connection between sound and sense.* 'The word,' as Steinthal observes, 'belongs not only to the speaker but to the hearer,' and 'comprehension [1] and speech are only different effects of the same power of Language.' Now a root, or a word, could be practically neither root nor word if it were unintelligible to the hearer; it would be as meaningless as the babble of an idiot. How then could such a sound be intelligible? It is too late in the day to talk of the possibility of *Convention* being the origin of the meaning attached to sounds. Against *such* a theory alone applies with full force the celebrated dictum of Humboldt that 'man is man only by means of language, but that without language he never could have invented language.' Now as the connection be-

---

[1] Steinthal, *Urspr. d. Sprache*, p. 11. Humboldt, *Ueber d. Verschied.* p. 70. Heyse, p. 13. Becker, *Organ d. Sprache*, § 3.

tween sound and sense was not arbitrary, and was not miraculous, it must have had a definite reason. Any sound therefore which would at once express and convey even the simplest sensation, must necessarily be a spontaneous *natural* sound; i. e. it must be either imitative or interjectional. The living, feeling, observing Child of Nature, without deliberation, influenced only by sensation or the imitative instinct, produces a sound to represent his conceptions; and this sound, so originated, is instantly intelligible, by virtue of its natural force, to a fellow-man, similarly organised, standing on the same step of mental development, and surrounded by precisely the same conditions, circumstances, and climatic influences. The nearer men stand to the natural life, the more they resemble one another.[1] Individuality is evolved by dawning civilisation. The whole life of the savage in all its external indications, is the life rather of a species than of an individual, and consequently it is dominated over by certain natural necessities rather than by the freedom of the Intellect. Hence among uncultivated races, far more than among civilised races, the *sound* uttered by each individual would with extraordinary rapidity be accepted and understood as a *sign* by the entire nation. Thus there would be in the Origin of Language nothing either capricious or mystical, but the harmonious and perfect working of laws and instincts inseparable from the very nature of mankind; and it may confidently be asserted that if the explanation thus offered as to the original union between sound and sense be not correct, it is at any rate

---

[1] It has been said that the members of savage tribes are, even in countenance, so exactly like each other that no passport system would be possible among them.

an explanation that naturally suggests itself,—it is one which has been accepted by many profound and eminent philologists,—it is one which may be supported by many powerful and valuable arguments, and *no other worth considering has ever been offered in its place.*

We say ' *no* other;' for the theory of ' phonetic types ' stops short of this question altogether. There must have been a *reason* why a ' phonetic type ' *was* a type,— and this is the reason which, as being deeply interesting as well as most important, we try to discover. For if the ' phonetic type ' was ' an accidental label stuck on to a thing ' there is an end to *the Science* of Language, and words are but the accidents of accidents. Is not such a view of words an instance of the very fault which the author of it reprobates,—the fault of preferring the unintelligible which can be admired to the intelligible which can only be understood?

We must now consider yet more closely the growth of natural sounds, and especially Imitations, into Language,—which together with a defence and explanation of the results arrived at will occupy the two next sections.

CHAPTER XII.

ONOMATOPŒIA.

'Ονοματοποιΐα δέ ἐστι φωνῆς μίμησις πρὸς τὴν ποιότητα τοῦ ὑποκειμένου ἤχου.—SUID. s. v. σίζω.

IF we consider on the one hand the different kinds of natural sound, and on the other the stock of words which belong to intelligent speech, we shall find many close points of contact and transition between the two.[1] We find, in fact, in Imitations and Interjections two concurrent points of origin for the two main classes of words. All the words of language may be classed under two great divisions, which may be called Matter-words and Form-words. To the former class belong Nouns [2] and Verbs, which supply the main materials of Thought and Speech, and signify perceptible objects or distinct actions; to the latter belong pronouns, particles, &c., which express our perceptions as modified by numerous relations of Space and Time. Now as a general, though far from invariable rule, all matter-words of whose origin we can give any account at all spring from imitative sounds; and form-words from interjections, especially from what have been called Vocal Gestures.

---

[1] Heyse, p. 90.
[2] A somewhat similar division is found in Aristotle's φωναὶ σημαντικαί (ὄνομα, ῥῆμα) and φωναὶ ἄσημοι (σύνδεσμος, ἄρθρον).

In the primitive language indeed, parts[1] of speech had no recognised existence; the very genius of language was holophrastic, and a sound stood for a sentence,[2] the same sound having many meanings according to its position or pronunciation. Nevertheless there must have been from the first a traceable distinction between nominal and pronominal roots. 'A rigorous analysis of the Indo-European tongues,' says Mr. Garnett, 'shows, if we mistake not, that they are reducible to two very simple elements: 1. Abstract nouns,[3] denoting the simple properties or attributes of things. 2. Pronouns, originally denoting the relations of Space.' We shall hope to show reasons for believing that nouns had, for the most part, their direct origin in imitative sounds; and considering that in the origin of language the distinction between parts of speech is only of the slightest and most rudimentary character,[4]—if we can trace the genesis of nouns, we have solved the problem before us.

[1] 'Die Sprache ist nicht stückweis oder atomistisch, sie ist gleich in allen ihren Theilen als Ganzes und demnach organisch entstanden.' Schelling, *Einl. in die Philos. d. Mythologie*, p. 51. On the primitive speech-cells, which have as yet no special organs for the functions of distinct parts of speech, see Schleicher, *Die Darwinische Theorie und die Sprachwissenschaft*, p. 23. This is an ingenious pamphlet showing the light which the Darwinian hypothesis throws upon language.

[2] 'Les inventeurs des langues n'étaient pas des grammairiens comme Condillac, Adam Smith et tant d'autres, *qu'on croirait avoir dîné avec nos premiers parents*, tant ils sont bien instruits de la manière exacte et précise dont le premier langage a été formé.' Du Ponceau, *Mém. sur le Syst. Gram. des Langues de l'Amérique du Nord*, p. 15.

[3] It is impossible to speak of the *priority* of nouns or verbs; both originate together, as specialisations of the original vague elements of speech. See Schleicher, *Compend. d. vergl. Gram.* p. 412.

[4] Every lingua franca presents a picture of what the primitive languages must have been, by reducing language to its simplest elements and by the almost complete elimination of grammar. See Appleyard, *Kaf. Gram.* p. 10. Latham, *Var. of Man*, p. 320 sqq. Here for in-

An imitative sound, gives expression to an auditory perception, and therefore has a necessary and obvious relation to the object which causes the perception. The *sound*, perceived and reproduced, gives to the Intellect a fixed mark of the *object* perceived. How then could man more naturally name the representation of an object which he has grasped in his intelligence, than by the copy of its characteristic mark? Now when the Imitative natural sound is firmly held as a sign of, and then as a name for the representation, it becomes a Word; and this method of forming words is named Onomatopœia.

First of all man names the *perceived sound itself* by the natural imitation of it, e.g. a croak, a shriek, βοή, &c.; next the producing of the sound, as croaking, shrieking, βοάν, &c.; and finally the object from which the sound emanates, and which the repetition of it recalls before the mind, as crow, βοῦς, cuckoo, &c.

Now those who attack the Onomatopoetic theory invariably leap to the conclusion that we mean by it to describe Language as due *solely* to the Instinct of Imitation, and that as other animals have this instinct and yet do not possess language the theory breaks down. Possibly indeed such a notion may arise from want of sufficient precision in our statements of the theory; but as we have repeatedly protested against it before, so we

stance is a negro crier's version of the notice that 'Pigs without rings in their noses are to be shot.' 'I say—suppose a pig walk—iron no live for him nose!—gun shoot! kill *im* one time.' Hutchinson, *Ten Years' Wanderings*, p. 32. And here is a specimen of the Chinese 'pigeon' (i. e. 'business') English. 'My chin-chin you, this one velly good flin (=friend) belong mi; mi wantchie you do plopel pigeon (=proper business), along he, all same fashion along mi,' &c. *Prehistoric Man*, ii. 428.

here again caution the student that this is not our view, and that to argue as if it were is not to refute but to misrepresent. A *mere* capacity for sensuous imitation would end, as it does with the jay and the mockingbird, in a mere collection of natural sounds. But here the intellect steps in, and makes the imitation a means for the satisfaction of its higher needs. In itself the mere imitation is a natural sound expressive of a sensuous impression, and nothing more; but the mind seizes upon it as a means for its own culture, reproduces it at will as the *sign* of a fixed representation, as the name of that representation, and so as a WORD.. And when the Sound has become a Word, it has a far richer and at the same time more abstract meaning, inasmuch as it no longer signifies or even calls attention to the imitated Sound, but stands for the whole conception. Nobody for instance in using the word cow [1] dreams of its *primeval* significance as the creature that *lows* (in North Country dialect ' coo '), but as a most useful domestic animal, possessing numberless familiar attributes.

Now, as far as the mere outward form is concerned, there may be only a single step from the natural Sound to the Word; nay more the two may be *phonetically*

---

[1] Is it conceivable that any one can, with this explanation before him, prefer to derive it from the Sanskrit root *gu, to go*? Would any human being have fixed on *going* as a special attribute, a characteristic mark, of the cow!—so characteristic as to be selected out of a host of attributes to suggest the animal's name! See Pictet, *Les Orig. Ind.* i. 331, who very sensibly admits the onomatopoetic origin. See too T. Hewitt Key's able pamphlet, *Quæritur*, p. 8. I take this opportunity of apologising to Professor Key for my inadvertence in attributing to him the derivation of 'vivo' from 'bibo,' which he never in any way sanctioned (*Orig. of Lang.* p. 105). I have already explained to him by letter the origin of my mistake.

coincident; but between the inner meaning of the two lies the entire chasm which separates the natural life of sense from the free intellectual life,—the entire chasm which separates the sensation from the concept.

It is true that in finished language the pure and obvious onomatopœias are *mainly* those which express the actual sounds imitated, or verbal forms derived from them; to roar,[1] buzz, whizz, crack, clang, screech, hiss, rustle, &c.; and more rarely substantives, such as crow, cuckoo, peewit, &c., because when the Intellect pierces deeper into the nature of things, it often rejects the crude imitation which is no longer *a necessity*, and proceeds to the naming of objects by deeper-lying and more significant characteristics,—which are often expressed by words in which all traces of original imitation have disappeared for centuries.

So far Heyse; with much that he proceeds to add, we disagree, and we shall incidentally give reasons for doing so in the following part of the chapter. On one point however we are *entirely* of his view, in regarding the onomatopoetic principle as *a starting-point of Language*; we do not however think with him that the advancing intellect of mankind *soon* dispensed with it, and still less that it had but a trifling influence in

---

[1] It would be easy to produce a very long and striking list of such verbs in Hebrew. Greek is also rich in them, as ὀλολύζειν, ἀλαλάζειν, μηκᾶσθαι, μυκᾶσθαι, βρυχᾶσθαι, ῥοίζειν, χρεμετίζειν, συρίζειν, σίζειν, κλαγγαίνειν, κ.τ.λ. Latin ululare, balare, mugire, rugire, stridere, hinnire, sibilare, &c. See Egger, *Notions Élémentaires de Gram. Comp.* p. 155. The little poem *Philomela*, by Albius Ovidius Juventinus, is a string of such onomatopœias, mostly of his own invention. It deserves a passing glance, though its value is purely philological. Many of these imitations with others may be seen in the fragment of an old glossary, 'Ex regula Phocæ.' Mai, *Auct. Class.* vi. 600.

liberating the intellect from mere sensuous impressions. The fact that it is still seen so conspicuously at work in the language of children and savages seems to us to refute such conclusions. I venture to disagree from Heyse only in the small degree of importance which he attaches to the principle. Granting that he is correct in considering the Sound to be a mere means, or element, or 'moment' in the development of the Word, just as the perception is in the development of the concept,— granting that the Word never, or very rarely, continues to be a *mere* Echo or Reflex of the sensuous impression —still without this means, without these mere echoes, it seems to us certain that language could never have existed. They were the appointed instrument to develope the latent germ, or Idea, of Speech, and we believe that they suggested the vast majority of actual roots.

Perhaps a consideration of the objections to the theory will enable us to understand it more clearly. They will at any rate leave the reader more in a position to judge for himself, and will show our desire to avoid mere *ex parte* statements and reasonings. I have searched for these objections and refutations far and wide, and not consciously shirked any one of them; and in order to give them the best possible position, I shall quote them, as often as I can, from the pages of Professor Max Müller. It will, I think, be seen that the only ones which are at all insuperable are aimed not at the theory rightly understood, but at mere misapprehension of it.

CHAPTER XIII.

OBJECTIONS TO THE IMITATIVE THEORY — ASSERTED PAUCITY OF ONOMATOPŒIAS, EVEN IN ANIMAL NAMES.

> 'Gallorum cantus, et ovantes gutture corvos,
> Et vocum quidquid bellua et ales habet,
> Omnia cum simules ita vere ut ficta negentur,
> Non potes humanæ vocis habere sonum.'
> <div align="right">Auson. <i>Epig.</i> lxxvi.</div>

1. THE first objection to the theory that the imitation of natural sounds was the chief starting-point of language, and the source of most nominal roots, is that '*the certain onomatopœias in our language are few in number.*'

'Though there are names in every language formed by mere imitation of sound, yet these constitute [1] *a very small proportion of our dictionary.* They are the playthings, not the tools of language, and any attempt to reduce the most common and necessary words to imitative roots ends in complete failure.'

So wrote Professor Müller in his first series of Lectures (i. p. 347); but it is fair to hope that his view has been a little modified, because in his second series

---

[1] A similar objection is urged by Egger: 'Si l'on compare à l'immense richesse des langues grecque, latine et française, le petit nombre des mots dont il peut rendre compte, on se convaincra que l'étymologie ne doit pas accorder à l'onomatopée une trop grande importance.' *Notions Élémentaires*, p. 155.

he writes (ii. 92), 'There is one class of scholars who derive all words from roots according to the strictest rules of comparative grammar, but who look upon the roots in their original character as either interjectional or onomatopœic.' With regard to this theory, which is the only one which I am maintaining, he says, '*I should wish to remain entirely neutral,* satisfied with considering roots as phonetic types till some progress has been made in tracing the principal roots not of Sanskrit only, but of Chinese, Bask, the Turanian, and Semitic languages, back to the cries of man or the imitated sounds of nature.'

Our reply to the objection is this: That if the proposed etymologies be correct, 'the words formed by mere imitation of sound' do *not* constitute by any means 'a very small proportion of our dictionary.' Perhaps the meaning is however that the *obvious, certain, and indisputable* onomatopœias are few in number. Indeed we conceive that this must be the meaning because elsewhere it is admitted 'that each language possesses a *large stock* of words imitating the sounds given out by certain things.'[1] The word 'few' then is a very relative word, and if any one will examine for himself with patience a fair portion of a Greek, Hebrew, or English Lexicon, he will find that even the *certain* onomatopœias, with their derivatives, furnish him with a very long list; and that the number of words which have so much of the onomatopoetic element in them as most plausibly to be referred to a similar origin (especially as any other account which can be given of them is *at least* equally questionable), is *very large in-*

---

[1] *Lectures,* ii. 89.

deed. In French and in English the student will find the task ready performed to his hands by Charles Nodier in his *Dictionnaire des Onomatopées,* and by Mr. Hensleigh Wedgwood in his *Dictionary of English Etymology.* The former is full of errors which were perhaps inevitable at the time when it was written; and every student will find a good deal from which he must withhold his consent until further proofs are adduced. But even with this deduction a candid consideration of M. Nodier's and Mr. Wedgwood's labours can hardly fail to convince him that the objection as to the paucity of actual onomatopœias is one which is wholly without weight. Only, in looking for onomatopœias he must remember that there is an immense gap between articulate and inorganic sounds,[1] and that he is looking, not for *imitations,* like bow-wow, but for human *words* adopted into rational speech, and therefore framed by the Intelligence of man from mere raw echoes to artistic articulated sounds in accordance with the processes which we have already endeavoured to trace. He must remember too that in the course of ages, Words (to borrow the frequent similitude) are tossed and rolled and chipped[2] out of

---

[1] And, for this reason, 'in the imitative synonyms of the same or cognate tongues, we must expect only to meet with *resemblances of a very general nature.*' Mr. Wedgwood, in *Phil. Trans.* ii. 118. It is most necessary to enforce this observation. Onomatopœia is not so much the imitation of sounds, as the instinctive and quasi-imitative reproduction of *the impressions made by sounds.* Wüllner, *Urspr. d. Sprache,* s. 28. We must not therefore expect to find them either uniform or exact. They may range over wide phonetic differences, and yet be onomatopoetic in origin.

[2] Similarly, in ideographical characters which were once pictorial, 'that the resemblance should be in many cases so exact as in itself to *demonstrate* the object, is scarcely to be expected.' Marshman, *Chinese Gram.* p. 17. And Ewald (*Hebr. Gram.* § 135) says of the Hebrew alphabet,

shape like the pebbles which are perpetually tumbled by the sea-waves upon a shingly beach, and that therefore a word, once distinctly imitative, has often lost every possible external trace of its sensuous origin. It is now an established fact that every abstract word has acquired its meaning by derivation and metaphor from other words expressive of mere sensation,[1] yet how long and difficult, in some cases how uncertain or even impossible, it is to point out the intervening stages; and to the flippant and the ignorant how ridiculous is the apparent inadequacy of the origin to produce the result! Yet the fact has now been demonstrated, and we only ask the same patience and unprejudiced learning in the endeavour to trace the physical origin of all our words from natural sounds. And as we are confirmed in our conviction of the sensational origin of all our abstract words by observing that the more primeval and uncultivated a language is, the more numerous are its sense-words, and the fewer its abstractions, so we are confirmed in our conviction about onomatopœia by observing its extreme prevalence and vividness in the tongues which have least been subjected to the influences of civilisation. 'That portion of the vast growth of language,' says an ingenious writer,[2] 'which can be traced to a directly mimetic root may remain a small fraction of the whole; but *if it be the only portion whose structure is intelligible to us*, we shall readily believe that the

---

'The signs have been for the most part very much altered, because in writing they retained the dead traces only from habit, without thinking of their meaning according to the intention of the first discoverers.' This is, *verbatim*, true of language also.

[1] 'So hat auch keine Sprache ein Abstractum, zu dem sie nicht durch Ton und Gefühl gelangt wäre.' Herder, *Abhandl.* s. 122.

[2] In *Macmillan's Magazine*.

working of this principle is limited by our ignorance and not by its own nature. The progress of all science consists in the destruction of these phantasmal limitations which, like the circle of the visible horizon, we project upon the outward world. . . . The study of language, we doubt not, is destined to achieve an analogous triumph over the weakness of our imagination, teaching us, in the imperfect accents of the child or the savage, to recognise the working of that principle which has perfected for us the instrument of thought.'

Let us take a parallel case. It is now admitted by all competent scholars that all alphabetic writing derived its origin from pictorial and ideographic signs which originated from systems invented in Egypt, in Mesopotamia, and elsewhere. The analysis of the whole body of speech into its elementary sounds, and the representation of these sounds to the eye by figures on a plane surface, is so marvellous a discovery,—hardly less marvellous than the discovery of speech itself,—that, like speech and no less erroneously, it has been attributed to direct inspiration, and ascribed by Jews and Christians to Moses, Abraham, Seth, or Noah,[1] as by the ancient Egyptians to the god Thoth. Yet it is now established that writing was a gradual human discovery, and that the secret of it, like that of speech, was suggested by the instinct of imitation. Now this has been proved by precisely similar steps of induction to those [2]

---

[1] Voss, *De Arte Grammatica*, pp. 39-43. He truly says that on this topic 'multi multa tradiderunt et fuse, et confuse.'

[2] In fact the processes are *strictly analogous*. The alphabet originally presented pictures, i. e. copies or imitations, to the eye, and when the secret of such representation was once learnt, the pictures rapidly became conventional and unrecognisable: so language presented copies or imita-

which we have followed in referring all roots to an onomatopoetic origin; and if the steps of the argument have been in the one case universally accepted as conclusive and satisfactory, why should they not be similarly accepted in the other? Just as we have proved that imitative words are most common in savage languages; that they are more numerous and distinct in primitive than in modern languages; that many of them are confessedly and clearly traceable; that they supply us with a *vera causa* or adequate explanation; that the steps of the progress are thus simple and natural; and that no other theory has been seriously attempted;—so we show that picture-writing *has* prevailed and *does* prevail among various uncultivated races; that it is the most obvious principle which could have been adopted; that it explained itself; that in all traceable instances the picture was the origin of the letter; and that for instance in Egyptian [1] writing the Demotic or enchorial system is a corruption of the Hieratic, which is a degeneration of the Hieroglyphic, which is but a modification of the pictorial. With these clues we take any alphabet; and as the Aramæan is the most important, and may most probably, as tradition asserts, have been the origin of the Phœnician, and through that of the Greek, and through that of the Roman alphabet and of our own,—and as the Hebrew alphabet is one of our oldest approximations to the Aramæan,[2] let us take that alphabet, and see how it was

tions to the ear, which imitations were rapidly modified out of mere echoes into definite words by the action of well-defined physical and psychical laws.

[1] See for details the admirable article on Hieroglyphics by Mr. R. S. Poole in the 8th ed. of the *Encycl. Britannica*.

[2] According to Ewald it was not invented by the Phœnicians (*Luc.*

arrived at. We find then at once *that the name of each letter is the name of some object, and the form of the letter a rude representation of the form of the object.* Thus:—

    א Aleph = an ox; originally ∀ an ox's head.[1]

    ב Beth = a house; sometimes ∩ a tent (nearly as in Chinese).

    ג Gimel = a camel; the form representing its neck or hump.

    ד Daleth = a door; Greek Δ a tent-door.

    ו Vau = a tent-peg, or hook.

And so on in nearly every case; so that in the doubtful instances, such as ה He, and ס Samech,[2] we are entitled at once to conclude a similar parentage, though not with certainty discoverable. If we take other letters from the Greek alphabet, which were not among the original φοινικήϊα γράμματα of Cadmus, some curious origins are suggested to us. Thus Simonides, the legendary inventor of the letters ξ, ψ, and ω, is said to have invented the figure of the first because it resembles a saw of which its sound is an imitation, and the second because *'ps'* recalls the whistling of an arrow, which the letter roughly represents. Of Υ and Φ, both of which are mythically attributed to Palamedes, tradition tells us

Phars. iii. 220), but by the Aramæans (Plin. *Nat. Hist.* vii. 56). The name of each letter begins with the letter for which it stands.

    [1] See Ewald's *Hebr. Gram.* § 135-140.

    [2] The word *samech* possibly means 'a prop;' but may not its *form*, no less than that of the letter ס, the Greek σ s, and the English S, represent the chief sibilant animal, the serpent? If we remember the curious fact that the Hebrew letters are arranged according to the meanings, and not on any scientific principle (e. g. ז and ח (weapon and scrip), י and כ (hand and hollow of hand), ע and פ (eye and mouth) come together), then samech, if it ever stood for 'serpent,' comes appropriately after נ (a fish). Cf. Amos ix. 3.

that one represents the flight of cranes,[1] and the other a crane standing on one leg. These last are but illustrations, and *very* doubtful ones; but our argument is this. Supposing that the forms of the Hebrew letters had lost even the remotest resemblance to the things which they once represented,—and that the *names* of the large majority of them had been phonetically corrupted, so as to have lost all trace of their original significance,— supposing, too, that other historical links in the chain of evidence had been broken,—still, if we could only *in two or three cases* have distinctly proved that in spite of these corruptions the alphabetic signs certainly had such an origin, would any one have hesitated about accepting the explanation as an adequate one for the entire series of letters? Would any one have hesitated, even if *all* direct *proof* failed, and the explanation were merely suggested as possible? Surely not; and the *à priori* simplicity and naturalness of the explanation would help, as in the case of language, to give it immediate weight. In both cases we have direct proof to a considerable extent; but even an hypothesis, resting on no direct proof, deserves attention, and sometimes even inspires conviction, if it be clear, adequate, and intrinsically probable, particularly if it be only rivalled by theories which rest their claims on 'elementary unintelligibility' or which begin by abandoning the problem altogether. But onomatopœia, as a theory of the formation of language, is something more than an hypothesis; it rests on the basis of a large induction; and it furnishes

---

[1] 'Turbabis versus, nec litera tota volabit,
    Unam perdideris si Palamedis avem.' Mart. xiii. 75.
i. e. they no longer represent the letter, if one crane be removed.
    'Hæc gruis effigies Palamedica porrigitur Φ.' Auson. *Idyll.*

a remarkably close analogy to other processes of the human mind.[1]

So that we are not disturbed when our opponents tell us that we can produce few direct and indisputable imitations in illustration of our theory. In the first place it is not a fact that we can produce only a *few* even of these. We can produce more than enough for the purpose; and more even than might have been expected because the very theory as we have stated it admits for the rapid tendency of language to *become* mechanical by corruption.[2] At first, as we have said already, people hate to use a word which is a *mere* sound to them, alike strange and unmeaning. Their *own* language they will use all their life without the vaguest consciousness of the etymology or original meaning of any one of its words, because it is familiar to them, and they are as indifferent to its obliterations as they are to the blurred and dinted surface of a piece of money in their own coinage. But they will not use a foreign or strange word, until, like a coin, it has been, to use the technical term, *surfrappé* with an image and superscription which they understand. If a foreign word be introduced they will either not use it at all, or

---

[1] Words whether written or spoken are *signs*; to convey an impression to others we must imitate either the sound or the shape of that which produced it. 'L'onomatopée est donc le type des langues prononcées, et l'hiéroglyphe le type des langues écrites.' Nodier, *Dict. des Onomatopées*, p. 11.

[2] *Origin of Lang.* pp. 57–61, where numerous instances are given from the names of horses, of ships, and of flowers. Prof. Müller gives some from the names of inns (ii. 530 sqq.). Many are supplied in *Philolog. Trans.* v. 138 (by Dr. Whewell), and by Mr. Isaac Taylor in his admirable work on *Words and Places*, pp. 409 sqq. Steinthal also mentions a few, *Gesch. d. Sprachwissensch.* s. 6: e. g. Vormund, Leumund from *Munt* protection, not from *Mund* mouth; Zanktüffe for Xanthippe, &c.

CH. XIII. OBJECTIONS TO THE IMITATIVE THEORY.

not until they have twisted it into some shape which shall explain itself to them. Let any one try to introduce such a word,—not being in any sense imitative,—and he will find himself fail as egregiously as the Emperor Tiberius. We see then, from watching the laws and instincts still at work, that *words not self-explicative* would have had no chance of obtaining currency at the dawn of language, and that therefore the most vital and powerful roots must have been not arbitrary but self-explaining, i. e. imitative; and also that the process of phonetic corruption is such as to lead us to expect *à priori* that but few words, compared with the whole number, would retain a positive and unmistakeable trace of their primitive origin, precisely in the same way as, and for the same reason that, only a few letters in the Alphabet have retained their original and significant shape.[1] But if the words which retained such a trace were even far fewer than they are, we

---

[1] Let us take an instance; we assert the imitative origin of language, and some one objects 'But the word horse is not imitative of a neigh;' and if we answer 'Yes, it ultimately was so,' people laugh. Yet horse is derived from the unquestionable onomatopœia *hrésch* 'to neigh,' though one cannot always bring so distinct a proof at once. Now assert the imitative, pictorial origin of the alphabet, and some one objects that *Mem* means 'water,' and the sign ם does not in the least resemble water. Good; but the original sign (much as in our own cursive character) was like the Chinese ∩∩∩, and represented *waves*. It would greatly assist those who really wish to arrive at truth on this subject, if they would bear these analogies constantly in mind; and that is my reason for dwelling on them here. But the majority of those who know nothing about the matter content themselves with the refutation implied by a stolidly self-complacent smile;—just as for years people used to refute the theory of the world's diurnal revolution on its axis. This στρατιωτικὴ ἀλογία is no new thing:

'Dixeris hæc inter varicosos Centuriones,
Continuo crassum ridet Vulfenius ingens;
Et centum Græcos curto centusse licetur.' Pers. v. 189.

should still be entitled to believe that they revealed to man (as has been previously explained) the great and wonderful discovery which lies at the root of all language —the discovery that the physical and spiritual worlds with all their phenomena are capable of analysis, of expression, and of communication by a world of vocal sounds.

2. It is another, and perhaps it will be considered a more telling form of the same objection, that ' we [1] speak of a cow, not of a *moo*; of a lamb, not of a *baa*. . . . If this principle of onomatopœia is applicable anywhere, it would be in the formation of the names of animals. Yet we listen in vain for any similarity between goose and cackling, hen and clucking, duck and quacking, sparrow and chirping, dove and cooing, hog and grunting, cat and mewing, between dog and barking, yelping, snarling, or growling.'

To say nothing of the fact that this aggressive sentence supplies us for its construction no less than twelve confessed onomatopœias, I may perhaps refer to the entire answer to the previous objection, as well as to the whole of my second chapter 'On the Naming of Animals,' as a sufficient proof that we *do find the principle most remarkably at work* in the large majority of animal names, especially in those languages in which we should be most reasonable in expecting it, such as Sanskrit, Hebrew, Chinese, and the languages of savage tribes. Before entering on the argument we may oppose assertion with assertion and say with M. Nodier: [2] 'La plupart

---

[1] *Lectures*, i. 344–351, 1st ed. I have not shirked a single argument, or shadow of an argument, which I could find in these Lectures, or in the writings of Pott, Steinthal, &c.

[2] *Dict. des Onomatopées*, p. 38. Cf. Pott, *Doppelung*, pp. 29. 51 sqq.

CH. XIII. OBJECTIONS TO THE IMITATIVE THEORY. 141

des animaux sont caractérisés par l'onomatopée.' Even were it true, which we shall see good reason to doubt, that in this handful of selected names, there is no trace of imitation, there are *hosts* of names in which there *is* such a trace, and these would be enough to prove the real point for which alone we have been contending. Such, for instance, are horse, buck, hog, cow, ai-ai, agouti, lion,[1] kooloo-kamba, cuckoo, crow, crane, crake, quail, peewhit, chough, owl, buzzard, sandpiper, pigeon,[2] daw, tit, finch, whip-poor-will, cricket, &c.

That there are numerous instances where the ultimate name has been derived from some other attribute of the animal is only what we should expect in the growth of language. Although the names here urged against us *are* mostly onomatopoetic, it would be quite easy to select as many that are not. The selection of such instances as a disproof of our principle would be analogous, as an argument, to the inference that the names of animals in the Romance languages are not derived from Latin because renard, blaireau, belette, mouton, crapeau, hochequeue, moineau, have no connection with vulpes, meles, mustela, ovis, rana, motacilla, or passer; or that the names of birds are not generally onomatopoetic—though even the ancients[3] had observed this fact,—because redbreast, wagtail, eagle, vulture, falcon, may not be. 'The most immediate and the most naïve sensations of a people always end,' says M. Nodier, 'by

---

[1] Hebr. לָבִיא, 'rugiendi sonum imitans,' Gesen. Thes. *s. v.* Cf. Germ. Löwe; and the old Egyptian *mouee*. The name agouti is from its cry *couy*.

[2] From the onomatop. *pipi*, pipire. Vid. Diez, *s. v.* Piccione.

[3] Σχέδον γὰρ τὰ πλεῖστα τῶν ὀρνέων ἀπὸ τῆς φωνῆς ἔχει τὴν σημασίαν. Athen. ix. 392. This is especially the case in Latin: grus, gracculus, bubo, strix, buteo, &c. Pott, *Doppelung*, p. 51.

disappearing before its illusions.' For instance, almost every name given to the species of the genus Goatsucker is an onomatopœia (*Churn*-owl, Night-jar, Spinner, Jar-owl, &c.), of which an Australian variety is called More-pork, an American variety Whip-poor-will, and another (Caprimulgus Lyra) Chuck Will's Widow, each of these names being crude analogies from its cry: yet over these natural and distinctive names how constantly prevails the name Αἰγοθήλης, caprimulgus, tête-chèvre, Ziegenmelker, Russian *kozodoi*, *goatsucker*, &c., from a stupid superstition as old as the time of Aristotle (*Hist. Anim.* ix. 30, 2), which is not even yet extinct.

I will not however rest on any of these general considerations, but will at once come still more closely to the point and examine each of the words *which Mr. Max Müller has himself chosen* to disprove our theory; taking his argument sentence by sentence from the beginning. Nearly every paragraph will show whether there is any ground for his allegation that 'most of these onomatopœias vanish as we trace our own names back to Anglo-Saxon and Gothic, or compare them with their cognates in Greek, Latin, or Sanskrit.' Reversing this sentence, we should be inclined to say that on the contrary *it is only by such tracing and comparing* that we can, in many cases, prove the imitative nature of the word.

'*We speak of a cow, not of a moo.*' A strange instance this! since 'cow,' as we have seen already, is *unquestionably* imitative in origin, and is admitted to be so, if one must quote an authority, by M. Pictet himself. Yet simply because the imitation is not *obvious*, a child has to learn how to get at the word cow, by crossing to it over the onomatopœic stepping-stone 'moo.'

'*Of a lamb, not of a baa.*' Yet the Sanskrit word for a ram is *bhêda*, as the Danish is *beede*, and the French *bélier*; and all three come from baa! The derivation of 'lamb,' like that of several names for sheep, is uncertain, so we will say nothing about it, only as before calling attention to the consequent necessity for the imitative stepping-stone baa-lamb, and to the fact that if 'lamb' be not imitative, many words for lamb in other languages are, e. g. the Swiss baageli, the Swedish *bagge*, the Malay *biri-biri*.

'*There is no connection between goose and cackling.*' Are we so sure of this? Almost certainly there *is*. Mr. Wedgwood mentions that in Lithuania *guz-guz* is a cry to call geese; but setting this aside, and accepting the Aryan and non-interjectional origin of the word, it is derived from the Sanskrit *hañsa*; Greek χήν; Lat. *anser*; Germ. *gans*, &c.[1] And what is the derivation of hañsa? Let M. Pictet, always anxious to avoid an onomatopœia when he can, tell us: '*La racine est probablement has, ridere, par allusion au cri peu mélodieux de l'oiseau et à la manière dont il ouvre son bec pour le pousser*' (*Les Aryas Primitifs*, i. 388). 'Goose' then is a word which, so far from having 'no connection with cackling,' is *doubly* imitative, and is solely suggested by cackling![2] And this its imitative character is further established by the fact that a similar root for the name is discoverable all over the world, from Iceland to Japan, not only

---

[1] The French *oie* is from *avicula*, an interesting instance of the use of the general for the special, and a proof of the value attached to the bird; compare our 'birds' for 'partridges.'

[2] It is connected with many other onomatopœias, such as χαίνω, yawn, *gackern*, *gingrire*, &c. Wüllner, *Urspr. d. Sprache*, s. 27. The name of the bird is almost always imitative—Swedish *gaas*, Danish *gaas*, Mexican *Halacatl*, &c.

in Aryan, but even in the remotest allophylian languages![1] Moreover in other instances the name given to the bird is an unconcealed onomatopœia, as for instance in the Scotch *claik* or *clake*.

'*There is no similarity between hen and clucking.*' To expect '*similarity*' is to misunderstand the conditions of the problem, as already explained. Nevertheless the name 'hen' (Sanskrit *Kânaka*, Persian *Kank*, German Hahn, Huhn, Henne) is as certainly imitative as is cock, and expresses clucking distinctly enough. Of the Sanskrit *Kuhkuta*, Pictet says: 'C'est là une onomatopée que l'on retrouve dans l'ancien Slave kokoshu, &c.' *Kukkubha* is 'un autre nom imitatif.' *Krkavâku* is still more remarkable, being formed from *vâku*,[2] the creature that cries *krka*, 'un mot par lui-même imitatif du cri guttural' (Pictet, i. 396). Even Professor Pott, who is always *most* cautious in admitting an onomatopœia, sees it without hesitation in the word cock, quoting the verb *cucurire*,[3] a distinct invention for the purpose, adopted by the author of 'Philomela:'

'Cucurrire solet gallus, gallina gracillat,' l. 25.

'*There is no similarity between a duck and quacking.*' As we have already proved and illustrated, the

---

[1] It is curious to observe that Varro—knowing of course nothing whatever about the origin of the word—*did* instinctively find a 'similarity between goose and cackling;' for he says, '*De his pleræque ab suis vocibus*, ut hæc: upupa, cuculus, corvus, hirundo, ulula, bubo; item hæc: pavo, ANSER, gallina, columba.' *De Ling. Lat.* v. 75.

[2] Formed on the exact analogy of the African kooloo-kamba, the creature which cries *kooloo* (Du Chaillu's travels); and the Galla *dadagoda*, for which see Wedgwood, i. v.

[3] See his paper *Zur Culturgeschichte* (on the names of fowl and goat). I do not know where it appeared. Professor Pott was so kind as to send me a copy of the paper.

objective repercussion of a subjective impression in many cases neither aims at nor pretends to 'similarity' even in the first instance, and much less after the phonetic modification of centuries. And next, the name 'duck' is derived from the same root as the German 'tauchen,' from the animal's habit of diving; but duck, tauchen, dab, dive, &c., are imitative in origin, although here the imitation is not from the sound which the bird makes. Yet from this sound we have the name πάπια a duck in modern Greek, which Diefenbach compares with the Italian *papero* a gosling, and the Spanish *parpar* to quack.[1]

'*Between sparrow and chirping.*' Sparrow is a very doubtful word, but if we compare such cognate forms as *sprew, spreuve, sparavière,* &c., it is impossible to *assert* that it was *not* originally mimetic; and we fully believe it was.[2] And if we hear no chirp in the word 'sparrow,' we do in the names of many other birds which twitter and chirp, as, for instance, σπίγγος, σπίζα, pinson, finch, fringilla,[3] linnet, pipit, tit, &c.

'*Between dove and cooing;*'—but there is a direct similarity between cooing and the *synonyms* for dove, turtle, culver, pigeon (from pipi, v. ante), and cushat,[4]

---

[1] Wedgwood, i. 497. The names anas, νῆσσα, the French *canard*, the Mongol *ngusun*, &c. are *probably* imitative. Wüllner, *Urspr. d. Sprache*, s. 27.

[2] May it not be connected with the Greek ψάρ 'a starling,' an imitative word from ψαίρω, *I scrape*? The mere confusion between starling and sparrow is nothing, because instances of much more startling interchanges of name may be adduced, as in vulpes '*fox*' and wolf, &c.

[3] The Sanskrit bhrnga, which also means a bumble-bee; 'ce qui ne laisse aucun doute sur son caractère d'onomatopée.' Pictet, i. 486.

[4] Which Pictet derives from *cû* cow, and *sceotan* to rush—the bird that rushes to cows!!!. He makes the Anglo-Saxon *culufre,* 'culver,' mean *cow-lover*; surely it would be even better than this to connect it with the

L

so that out of five names *four* are from the bird's murmuring voice. But besides this, 'dove' is connected with dive, dab (cf. *dab*-chick, *tap*, &c.), from the very remarkable characteristic which it has of ducking [1] the head, whence too is derived the Latin columba (cf. κολυμβάω); and therefore dove no less than duck is imitative, though not from the bird's voice.

'*There is no similarity between hog and grunting.*' Surely a most unfortunate assertion, as will be very apparent from Mr. Wedgwood's note on the word. 'Hog. Breton, *hoc'h houc'h*, swine, from *houc'ha* to grunt. So Lap. *snorkeset* to grunt, *snorke* a pig, &c.' Moreover, 'grunter' is in English an actual synonym for pig, as Mr. Tennyson shows us:—

> If thou be he, or draggled mawkin thou
> That tends her bristled *grunters* in the sludge.
> *The Princess.*

With the Italian *ciacco*, the French *cochon* and *goret* (cf. χοῖρος), the Russian *cushka*, or,—not to quote the invariably imitative name in other Aryan languages,— the Sanskrit *sûkara* (qui fait sû, son imitatif pour grognement,' cf. *swine*, &c.) before him, it is strange that Professor Müller should have hazarded this instance.

'*There is no similarity between cat and mewing!*' Not in English, at first sight, but in the most ancient of tongues—the Chinese—a cat is 'Miau!' The word 'cat' is traced back by Pictet to an African origin, and so it is impossible to say whether or no its original form was imitative. That it was so seems very probable

---

Sanskrit *kalarava*, 'l'oiseau dont la voix est un murmure.' The analogies of goatsucker and *bergeronette* for wag-tail, and Pferdehüter for a Peruvian bird, and *Vyaghrâta*, tiger-goer, for lark, &c. are not to the point, since there is no connection between pigeons and cows.

[1] Cf. Pictet, i. 400. Wedgwood, s. v.

CH. XIII. OBJECTIONS TO THE IMITATIVE THEORY. 147

from the imitative forms which several developments of the word take, of which the most striking is the German *Katze*, which, I must repeat (whatever may have been its origin), 'obviously catches an echo of the animal's remarkable spit,' as is rendered nearly certain by a comparison of the Wallachian *mëtzë*,[1] *pisicë*; unless indeed it be from the sound made in calling the animal, like the Polish *kic kici*, and the English *puss*. If so, then in this case, as in the cries made in calling a pig (*cushu cushu, chig chig*, &c.), we see the various points of possible origin for an onomatopoetic word; it is one of the many instances which connect a *Lautgeberde* with an imitation. In other words we see that the sound made by an animal is often instinctively adopted as the sound to invite or repel its approach, and so passes into the animal's name.

Lastly, '*there is no similarity between dog and barking, yelping, or snarling.*' Is it certain? The Icelandic '*doggr*' at any rate looks very like a growl;[2] and, if not, the synonyms Hound, German *Hund*, Greek Κύων, Canis, the Sanskrit *Çvan*, are distinctly imitative, and are recognised as such by Pictet, who adds that, except on the imitative principle, it is impossible to account for the wide similarity between the names for the dog among various nations. A name bow-wow *might*, indeed, have been invented, 'yet, strange to say, we hardly ever find a civilised language in which the dog

---

[1] Diez, s. v. *Gatto*; and Wedgwood, *Et. Dict.*
[2] To say nothing of the fact that the dog furnishes to language his full share of onomatopœias; such as the words βαΰζω, baubari, ὑλακτεῖν, *beller, aboyer*, ῥύγχος, knurren, &c. In some Canadian languages the dog is called *gagnenon*.

L 2

was so called' (ii. 312). True, and for this perhaps *a very sufficient reason* may be given. Although as far back as history carries us the dog has been a domesticated animal, yet it must at one time have been wild, and it may probably have received a name, or some of its names, while in this condition. Now it is at least doubtful *whether the bark is a dog's natural utterance*, and whether in its original state the dog *did* bark. For whole races of dogs, and perhaps it may be said *all* wild dogs, do not know how to bark,—for instance the Esquimaux dogs, and those which run wild in the Pampas, in Chili, and in the Antilles, which only howl. Indeed Prichard,[1] who notices this fact, mentions the conjecture that the dog's bark '*originated in an attempt to imitate the human voice!*' If this conjecture, however apparently ludicrous, be correct, then men will have contributed more to the language of dogs, than dogs to the language of men; for, as Dr. Daniel Wilson[2] observes, the words bark, yelp, howl, snap, snarl, whine, whimper, are 'words directly derived from the dog language!' At any rate it is certain that the dogs left by the Spaniards on Juan Fernandez to destroy the goats on which the pirates fed, had, when found thirty years afterwards by Don Antonio Ulloa, *forgotten* how to bark, and only imitated very awkwardly the bark of other dogs. It is known too that some puppies brought by Mackenzie from Western America were unable to bark, though their puppies acquired the power. There would be a reason then why *bow-wow* should not be *the*

---

[1] Prichard, *Nat. Hist. of Man*, p. 33 (ed. Norris). *Rev. des Deux Mondes*, Feb. 1, 1861.

[2] *Prehistoric Man*, i. 83. Many German words, as *winseln, heulen,* &c., might have been added.

particular form assumed by any onomatopoetic name of the dog.

'What really took place was this,' says Professor Müller rather dogmatically. 'The mind received numerous impressions from everything that came within its ken. A dog did not stand before it at once properly defined and classified, but it was defined under different aspects,—now as a savage animal, now as a companion, sometimes as a watcher, sometimes as a thief, occasionally as a swift hunter, at other times as a coward or an unclean beast. From every one of these impressions a name might be framed, and after a time the process of natural elimination would reduce the number of these names, and leave only a few or only one, which like *canis* would become the proper name of the dog' (ii. 312). Now, would it not be amazing if the *most* obvious aspect of all,—the noise made by the animal, which would be the first thing noticed about it, as it is the first thing noticed by all children,—should *not* have contributed one of the characteristics which suggested a name? Secondly, observe that the name which in the Aryan family *did* prevail was the one derived from the onomatopœia *çvan*. Thirdly, observe that out of *five* Sanskrit names for dog, *three* are imitative, viz. *çvan*, *rudatha* from *rud* (rudire) 'l'animal qui hurle et gémit,' and *bhacha* 'the barker' from the root *bhach*, to bark! Do not these facts speak for themselves?

Surely therefore, even when we meet Professor Müller on ground selected by himself, we can abundantly vindicate the applicability of our theory,—throwing, we trust, some further light on the *nature* of the theory in the course of our enquiry. *We* have dwelt upon it in detail because *he* does so, being desirous, from his well-merited authority in all matters of philology, to give full consideration to all the arguments on the subject which we could find in his writings, and to state the reasons why they do *not* carry conviction to our minds. To us the answer appears complete and convincing.

CHAPTER XIV.

FERTILITY OF ONOMATOPOETIC ROOTS.

'Sed cunctas species animantum nemo notabit,
Atque sonos ideo dicere quis poterit?'
Alb. Ov. Juventinus, *Philomel.* 68.

In his second series of Lectures, the Professor returns to the attack with undiminished vigour, and as though he felt the insecurity of the outpost which we have just been trying to carry by assault, he entirely abandons it, and retreats behind another which is presumed to be more strongly fortified. In point of fact he cedes by implication his previous position; '*Ibi omnis effusus labor!*' Nevertheless, as the cession is only apparent, we do not regret the trouble we have taken to secure our ground; and so we proceed to the new points of attack and defence.

'The onomatopœic theory,' he says (*Lectures,* ii. 91), '*goes very smoothly as long as it deals with cackling hens and quacking ducks*; but round that poultry-yard there is a dead wall, and we soon find that it is behind that wall that language really begins.'

So far as this means merely that natural imitations are *not* in themselves language, but only *the materials of it, and the stepping-stones to it*, we not only agree with such a view but have from the first been asserting and illustrating it. If however it means that out of the sphere of animal names the imitative principle is excluded from its immense share in the elements of language, then we must once more emphatically dissent. For the meaning will then be the same as that which has so often been asserted in other forms, and which we will consider as the third objection, viz. that

3. Onomatopœias are 'like artificial flowers without a root. They are *sterile*, and are unfit to express anything beyond the one object which they imitate.'

Professor Müller illustrates this by saying that there are but few derivatives from the root ' cuck,' which is found in cuckoo, and cock, and that ' cuckoo stands by itself like a stick in a living hedge.' Heyse implies the same (s. 92) by his remark that many onomatopœias are not 'old fruitful roots of language, but modern inventions which remain isolated in language, and are incapable of originating any families of words, because their meaning is too limited and special to admit of a manifold application.'

There is a certain *primâ facie* truth in this remark, but it seems to us wholly immaterial to the question before us, which is merely this, ' Did language *originate* from interjectional and imitative roots?' With the reasons urged against the interjectional origin we have already dealt; and it is surely no refutation whatever of the imitative origin of another great division of language to say that *some* imitative roots (and especially modern ones) are infructuous, or nearly so. The *paucity* of the original roots of Language is an admitted fact, and if the difficult combination of c's or k's in ' cuckoo ' be a root of which little use is made we cannot be surprised, although even from this root, as Professor Müller himself admits, various words have been derived, and the list of derivatives might be largely increased;[1]—but at any rate there are plenty of other roots which we believe to be imitative, and *some which every one will admit to be so*, which so far from being sterile are 'the mothers of thousands.' On the very page from which we have been quoting, Professor Müller supplies us with one,—the root *ru* or *kru*, which passes through all kinds of fruitful metamorphoses, and 'has ever so many relations from a rumour to a row.' But this, says the Professor, 'is derived from a root which has a general predicative power. It is not a mere imitation of the cry of the raven; it embraces many cries from the harshest to the softest.' Here apparently we are at issue. For whether the root was originally suggested by the cry of the raven or not,—and this is a matter on which dogmatism is impossible,—it is most certainly a natural sound, a sound caught from nature, an *imitative* sound, and *therefore the words formed from it were formed in strictest conformity with the Imitative theory*. 'It might have been applied to the nightingale as well as to the raven,' says Prof. Müller. In the absence of any proof we should hold this to be very questionable, but if so it only shows how exquisitely delicate were the nuances which a word might receive by differences of pronunciation. Every one will admit that crow and croon are onomatopœias; yet the one is used of the harsh caw of the rook, and the other of the soft moan of doves. Every one will admit that these names of the grasshopper in different languages—Sanskrit *çiri*, Armenian *dzghrid*, Greek γρύλλος, Cymric *grilliedyz*, Basque *quirquirra*, Mahratta *râlra*, Chinese *sirsor*,

---

[1] The verb to cock, cog, cockade, coquet, coxcomb, &c.; in short, so many that even this root *cannot* be called a sterile one.

Hebrew *tslätsâl*, and many more which might be adduced [1]—are all imitative:—yet how immensely are they varied by the fantasies of imitation! How is this to be explained? Simply by the fact to which it is so often necessary to recur, that words are not mere imitations but subjective echoes and reproductions—repercussions which are modified both organically and ideally—which have moreover been immensely blurred and disintegrated by the lapse of ages. *Kôka* in Sanskrit is a confessed onomatopœia, and it means a goose, a cuckoo, a frog, a lizard, and a wolf. How wide then must be the differences expressed by one and the same imitation! But we leave it to the reader whether it is more reasonable to suppose that the root 'kru' was a 'phonetic type,' having 'a general predicative power,' arrived at by abstraction from the combined influence of all sorts of noises from the murmur of rivers, and the barking of dogs, to the songs of nightingales,—or to suppose with us that it was an imitative root, the echo of *some one* distinct sensuous impression, which subsequently was modified to suit other sounds, and which passed through a whole cycle of meanings by the working of processes which we shall hereafter consider? Which of the two suppositions is most in accordance with common probability, and with the remarkable feebleness of the power of abstraction among all uncivilised men?

But we shall perhaps best refute the asserted sterility of imitative roots, by producing a few instances of the

---

[1] Pictet, i. 528. Our blunted senses can no more realise the original delicacy of the appellative faculty than they can attain to the keen perfection in which they still exist in the savage. Lepsius, *Paläogr.* p. 21, quoted by Pott, *Etym. Forsch.* ii. 261.

vast range of conceptions which they have been made to express. If, in a few traceable instances, an onomatopœia be found to fructify so far as to convey notions and impressions which might be thought to be *infinitely* removed from the possibility of even a metaphorical expression by sounds borrowed from the outer world, we shall see that these sounds, raw and vulgar as they may originally have been, were the natural sound-cells [1] in which thought was quickened and developed into perfect speech. Whether the earliest origin of a word can be definitely *proved* or not, let it be considered that the choice rests in every case between an ultimate imitation or interjection—and *nothing*. Most etymologists when they have got to a root stop there, at the most interesting point of the enquiry, pretending to offer no explanation whatever of the root itself, although if they could do so they would obviously be throwing a flood of light on the whole history of the word, and would also be inevitably illustrating the influence of certain primary psychological laws, the observation of which is of the utmost importance both to philosophy and history. It is true that the Mimetic School (if I may be allowed such a term in treating of a subject in which the nomenclature is as yet cumbrous and only tentative) must often stop short of what they believe to be the final step of Etymology; but this does not detract from the value of their actual results, nor diminish their belief in the principle on which they rely. The principle indeed is one which requires the less proof, because we see its

[1] The prominence recently given to Mr. Darwin's theories naturally suggests this metaphor. Since writing it I have met with Aug. Schleicher's pamphlet (previously referred to) on the bearings of Language upon the hypothesis of development.

daily-working and powerful effect even on living languages, and especially in the process of their earliest acquisition.

Let us look at the history of one or two imitative roots, and I think that we shall definitely *prove* how little they deserve the charge of sterility.

For instance, let us take some of the simplest and earliest roots,—beginning with *ma*. From the fact that it is among the most facile, and therefore among the earliest sounds uttered by children, we have it (and cognate sounds) first applied in almost all languages to name the simplest and tenderest and earliest known of relationships,—'motherhood.' This is not an *hypothesis* but a *certainty* ;[1] it is one of those linguistic discoveries which must be accepted as established facts from which to start in all enquiries about the origin of language. 'It is impossible to doubt,' says M. Pictet, 'of their nature,—purely phonetic and imitative of the earliest infantile syllables,—when one finds them reappear among the most diverse nations. The reduplications papa, mama, so familiar to our European ears, have astonished more than one traveller who discovered them among the negroes of Africa, no less than among the savages of America and Oceania.'[2] For a comparative list of such terms we must refer to the interesting and ingenious essay of Buschmann *Ueber den Naturlaut*. In it he points out that this identity of terms is due to the fact we have mentioned, and is no proof whatever

---

[1] Lists have often been published. Among others, see Nodier, *Dict. des Onomatopées*, pp. 18–21 (taken from De Brosse).

[2] Pictet, ii. 348. The fact that in Sanskrit and most Aryan languages they are attached to a verbal root in no way detracts from their imitative origin.

of the connection or relationship of Languages. It is one of the merits of the Imitative theory that it explains, not in this case only but many others, the similarity of a few words in languages which, as may be easily proved, are neither genetically nor historically connected with each other, but which have probably been separate from the very dawn of human life.

But the root *ma* (or *am*,[1] which is the same thing) does *not* remain sterile. We get from it at once,—as we should expect alike from the limited range of a child's experience and his limited command of articulate sounds—a name for other relations,—as the Latin *amita* aunt, the German *amme*[2] a nurse, the Spanish and Portuguese *ama* a housewife, *amo* master of a house, *amma* screech-owl from its supposed affection for its young (cf. stork from στέργω),—and, indeed, in all probability the root 'amo'[3] I love, with all its immense stream of derivatives.

Then by an easy and natural transference we get the Latin *mamma*, the breast, which is also found with the same meaning all over the world; and the Dutch

[1] Cf. Hebr. אם = mother, grandmother, &c. It is strange that Plato does not in the *Cratylus* notice this syllable, which would have afforded so singularly strong an illustration of the point contended for (viz. the intrinsic meaning and appropriateness of certain consonants) in sections 91-94. C. Lenorman sees in this reticence 'une réservation conseillée par la gravité religieuse de cette syllable μυ, qui est le nom même des mystères.' *Comment. sur le Cratyle*, p. 275.

[2] Diez, ed. Donkin, s. v. *Ama*; and cf. Pictet, ii. 350.

[3] We say 'in all probability.' If any one prefers to suppose that '*amo*' is from the Sanskrit *am* 'to rush forward,' he may; and he will have Professor Müller on his side. (*Lectures*, ii. 91.) Let me here observe that the mere production of some analogous Sanskrit form as the derivation of a word is by no means a refutation of its imitative origin. I have already called attention to many admitted Sanskrit onomatopœias.

moeder the womb, &c. And so by simple laws of association we get to the English *mammet*,[1] Swiss *mämmi* a doll, German *memme* a coward, and *memmerei* poltroonery. So widely and so rapidly does the ripple spread on the surface of language!

Equally universal, equally fruitful, and equally rapid in its development is the cognate root *pa*. In Greek alone we have πατήρ a father, πάππος a grandfather, παππάζω to wheedle and to prattle, πάππος the first down on the cheek of youth, παππoσπέρματα the bearded seeds of the dandelion, παππώδης woolly. In Latin we have *papparium* (the English pap), and *papilla* the bosom (cf. mammilla). In Sardinian *papai* to eat, in Italian (and Russian) *pappo* bread; in Spanish and Portuguese (connected with papilla) we have *papo* a dewlap, or anything fat and puffy. Then from Papa as a title of respect, we get Pope, Papist, Papistry. In German we have *Pappe* in the sense of paste, pasteboard.

Thus from some of the most obvious derivatives of two very simple imitative roots we at once and without any shadow of difficulty get meanings so different, and apparently so much beyond the range of onomatopoetic representation, as aunt, owl, breast, doll, coward, dandelion-seed, bread, a fatty protuberance, the Pope of Rome, and pasteboard! Who after this shall assert the sterility of imitative roots?

From *ta* and *da*, two other of the earliest sounds, we get to *dade*,[2] an old English word for teaching a child

---

[1] Not to be confounded with Mawmet (from Mahomet). See Wedgwood, ii. 372.

[2] Vide Diez (ed. Donkin), s. vv. *Dandin* and *Tartagliare*. Wedgwood, s. v. *Dade*.

CH. XIV. FERTILITY OF ONOMATOPOETIC ROOTS. 159

to walk; to *toddle,* to *dawdle,* to *dandle*; the French *dandin* a simpleton; the Italian *dandolo* a toy, and *tartagliare* to stutter; the Dutch *tateren* to stammer; the Icelandic *totta* to suck, teat, &c. (cf. τίτθη, &c.)

Again, from *ba,* to mention only a few out of many, we have in Latin *babiger,*[1] *bubulus,* and *baburrus* stupid (Gloss. Isid.), *babœcalus* a trifler (Arnob. iv. 141), *basium,* buss, a kiss; in Greek we have βαβάζω, βαμβαλίζειν, I stammer; in Hebrew בלל confundere, בבל Babel,[2] Babylon. In the Romance languages *babbo* a father (Ital.), *babbuino* baboon, *beffa* a scoffing (shooting out the *lips*), *babbeo* a blockhead, *bambino* a doll, *bava*[3] slaver (cf. *Bavieca* the name of the Cid's charger), Spanish *babosa* a slug, *badare* to gape; then through the Scotch word 'abeigh' to stand gazing or gaping at a thing, we have 'abeyance,' and 'to stand at bay,' &c. In French we have *babines* large lips, *beyer, bavardage, babiller, babiole,* &c.[4] In English babe, babble, baboon, baffle, &c. We have not nearly exhausted the list, and indeed the fertility of this root may perhaps form the excuse or apology for those very bold theorists who have erroneously supposed that the letter B is a picture of the closed lips requisite for the enunciation of this important labial.[5]

Again, from *ta* and *ba* as emblematic of early, confused, inarticulate sounds we get such national names as Tatars, from *ta-ta* the Chinese onomatopœia for a barbarian,

---

[1] See Forcellini, *Lex. Tot. Lat.* s. vv.
[2] Ἑβραῖοι γὰρ τὴν σύγχυσιν Βαβὲλ καλοῦσι. Jos. *Antt.* i. 5. Compare our 'babble.'
[3] Diez, Wedgwood, Nodier, Scheler, &c.
[4] Nodier, *Notions de Linguistique,* p. 24.
[5] For the odd notion of Pierius Valerianus, see *Orig. of Lang.* p. 75.

whose language sounds to them like a mere collection of meaningless noises,—and the word barbarian [1] itself from the Sanskrit *varvara* a jabberer or confused talker. Of similar origin is the name Zamzummim,[2] applied by the Hebrews to one of the primitive tribes of Palestine, and transferred, from an instinctive sense of its derivation, as a nickname to the fanatics in the seventeenth century who pretended to speak with tongues, precisely as St. Paul applies the word βάρβαρος in 1 Cor. xiv. 11. Possibly the word Hottentot, and certainly the word Wälsch (from Sanskrit *mlêch*), and the Hebrew לֵעֵג (from לָעַג to stammer, Ps. lxiii. 1), illustrate the same curious fact,—of which, indeed, we see daily instances,—that ignorant people of all races and ages regard the language of foreigners as an unmeaning babble. For the surprisingly numerous developments of this word *bar* through almost every shade of meaning we must refer our readers to the pages of Diez, Wedgwood, and other etymologists.

Ohe jam satis! we imagine that we hear the reader sigh; nevertheless for the sake of the argument we must detain him a little longer. From the imitation then of inarticulate sounds we get such words as πάτος, πατεῖν; French *patte* a foot, *patin* a skate, *patois* a dialect; English *patten* (cf. pittle-pattle, pit-a-pat). From the labial *m* attached to various vowels to reproduce low sounds we get to hum, to mutter, muzzle,

---

[1] κατ' ὀνοματοποιΐαν ἐπὶ τῶν δυσεκφόρως καὶ τραχέως καὶ σκληρῶς λαλούντων, Suid. See the Author's article on 'Barbarian' in Dr. Smith's *Dict. of the Bible*, i. 166; and cf. *Types of Mankind*, p. 560; Pictet, *Orig. Ind.* i. p. 55; Renan, *Langues Sémitiques*, i. 35; and Mr. Is. Taylor's *Words and Places*, pp. 67, 87.

[2] See Mr. Grove, s. v. *Zamzummim*, *Dict. of the Bible*.

mute, and to be *mum* for to be silent, whence come mummery, and mumble, and mumps; from the same root come the French *mot* a word, and *motto*, as we see from the line of Lucilius, 'Non audet dicere *muttum*;' the Latin *mussare*, *muse*, and *music*, and amuse; *musca* a fly, and musket,—for which latter word and its curious history we must refer to Diez and Scheler,—the Greek μύζω, and mystery with all its cognates. Beyond such a word as this language can hardly proceed;—it dashes itself in vain against the 'flammantia moenia mundi,' the adamantine barrier which separates the temporal from the spiritual, the unseen from the seen. It is one of those words which, as Iamblichus says, 'being more excellent than every image is yet expressed by an image.' Yet to this distance Language attains by barely a single stride from the simple imitation of the sound naturally produced by closing the lips. Mr. Müller derives *mutus* from the Sanskrit *mû* to bind, and contemptuously refuses to give up either it, or many other words for which we should claim an imitative origin, 'to the Onomatopœic School.' In this we are convinced that he will find *very few* followers. That μῦ (like *mum*) is simply a natural sound made by closing the lips, and that from it come first μύω, then μυέω, then μύστης, then μυστήριον, and a number of derivatives of every shade of meaning from μῦσος 'hatred' to μυχός 'a corner,' μύκος 'phlegm,' and μύκης 'a mushroom,' seems to us a fact which can hardly be seriously denied. Dr. Liddell and Dr. Scott collect no less than forty-six such derivatives under the word μύω, and that number might very easily be doubled in Greek alone. So much then for the sterility of onomatopœias!

Perhaps if any one class of words could be chosen as presenting an insuperable obstacle to the endeavour to trace them from an imitative origin, it would be the class of *numerals*, the existence of which is due to one of the greatest efforts of analysis and abstraction—an effort in fact such, that to this day many savage tribes have not attained to it. Even Plato [1] argued that the existence of numerals at any rate must depend on custom and convention, since it was impossible that there could be any resemblance between the name of a numeral and the number which it indicated. In modern times the progress of comparative philology has thrown a flood of light on the origin of the numerals; it has shown the pronominal origin of the first, second, and third numerals, and it is most probable that all three sprang from interjectional or imitative elements; for instance the Sanskrit *êkas*[2] one is etymologically connected with *aham* 'I,' in which there is nothing fanciful in supposing that (as in the Hebrew היה) we catch a very natural reproduction of *the act of respiration*. There is however one numeral which comes from an onomatopœia *pur et simple*. It is the word 'myriad,' which is undoubtedly connected with the root μύρω, I roll or flow. 'The derivation of the idea of a large number from the sight of water falling in infinite drops is too obvious,' says Dr. Donaldson,[3] 'to require any remark.' No one, we hope, will now deny the con-

[1] ἐπεί, ὦ βέλτιστε, εἰ θέλεις ἐπὶ τὸν ἀριθμὸν ἐλθεῖν, πόθεν οἴει ἕξειν ὀνόματα ὅμοια ἑνὶ ἑκάστῳ τῶν ἀριθμῶν ἐπενεγκεῖν, ἐὰν μὴ ἐᾷς τι τὴν σὴν ὁμολογίαν καὶ συνθήκην κῦρος ἔχειν τῶν ὀνομάτων ὀρθότητος πέρι. Plato, *Crat.* p. 435.

[2] Bopp, *Vergl. Gram.* §§ 309 sqq. Donaldson, *Crat.* § 154, &c.

[3] *Cratylus*, § 163, where he also supposes a relationship between χέω flow, χιλός fodder, and χίλιοι thousands.

CH. XIV.   FERTILITY OF ONOMATOPOETIC ROOTS.   163

nection[1] between μύρω and the obvious onomatopœia *murmur*. The connection between a multitude and sound, and the extremely natural metaphor of waves to describe the roar of a crowd (*unda salutantum*, Virg.; *turba fluctuantis populi*, Aul. Gell.; ῥεῦμα φωτῶν, Æsch.), show us how probable such a derivation is. Tempting as it is to derive μύρμηξ 'an ant' from this root, we fear that Benfey's attempt to do so is scientifically untenable.[2] But if even a *numeral* can be so easily and directly traced to an imitative sound, there is little reason to doubt the wide applicability of this principle of word-formation.

So that by taking *the very first and simplest illustrations that came to hand*, we have shown that imitative roots are *not* sterile; that, on the contrary, almost every one of them produces so numerous and diverse an offspring as to show the possibility of expressing by their means every possible conception that Language is capable of expressing at all. And, with all these proofs before us, we say with Steinthal[3] that it is *inconceivable* to us that any one should be hardy enough to deny that Onomatopœia was the primeval tendency of language which has furnished us with all elementary words. Those who do so must abandon all attempts to see any connection between sound and meaning, except such as

[1] Benfey did so on the very insufficient ground that the υ in μύρω is long, and in murmŭro short. *Wurzel-lexicon*, i. 16. See the admirable pamphlet *Sur l' Origine des Noms de Nombre*, by Louis Benloew, Giessen, 1861.

[2] The Sanskrit *vamri*, *vamraka*, the Latin *formica*, and the form βύρμαξ preserved in Hesychius, seem to render it possible that the root is *vam* = vomere, from the formic acid which the insect throws from its mouth.

[3] *Gram. Log. und Psychol.* p. 309.

was due to the most absolute and unmeaning chance. Without the aid of imitation the earliest communications of mankind must have been a meaningless jabber of arbitrary sounds, and such, from the very nature of the case, they must always have remained.

CHAPTER XV.

DIGNITY OF ONOMATOPŒIA.

'*Ὀνοματοποιΐα*, id est, fictio nominis, Græcis *inter maximas habita virtutes*, nobis vix permittitur. Et *sunt plurima ita posita ab iis, qui sermonem primi fecerunt*, aptantes affectibus vocem.'
QUINCTIL. *Instt. Or.* viii. 6.

CONDILLAC complained that to suppose man to have learnt his language from imitation would be to place him below the animals, and this was why he favoured the Interjectional origin rather than the Onomatopoetic. We have seen already that *both* points of origin are requisite, and that neither can be separated from the other; but independently of this, Condillac's objection, which is perfectly worthless as an argument, was founded on the common misconception of supposing that *animal cries* offered the *only* materials for imitation. On the contrary *every* sound of nature contributed its element to human speech,—the rustling and whispering of her forest leaves, the howling of her storms, the booming of her seas, the rush of her cataracts, the rippling sequacious murmur of her rivulets. That there must be an intimate connection between nature and language is shown by the manner in which the sound of a language is often a reflex of the geographical conditions by which the people who speak it are surrounded—by the strident hirrient roughness of

Northern tongues (for instance) compared with the soft[1] musical vowelled undersong of the sunny South. It was suggested by Nodier that the presence or absence of the more remarkable and difficult articulations of language is always explicable by the existence or non-existence of certain animals in the countries where they are spoken, and that the tiger and the rattlesnake have suggested the click of the Hottentot and the rough sibilant of the North American Indian. This may be true or not; but, as we have shown,[2] onomatopœia rests on a far wider basis than this, and reproduces ideally and articulately that ringing shiver caused by the oscillation of material particles which results from every possible impact. Yet if it were probable that man had been taught to speak by listening to the animals alone, it would be absurd to reject such a conclusion solely in consequence of that *à priori* assumption of human exaltation which has stood so often in the path of science, and which has so often prevented men from reaching the Gate of Honour by making them refuse to pass under the Gate of Humility.

4. It has however been urged, with more of plausibility, that the most obvious and intentional onomatopœias are generally modern and often undignified, and that onomatopœia could never therefore have been a leading principle of Language.

We reply briefly that pure imitations are the only words now open for us to invent, and therefore that many such words are *apparently* modern. Whether they are, in any case, really so may be doubtful when, to

---

[1] Greek, removed to the enervating climate of Asia Minor, becomes the soft Ionian.
[2] *Origin of Lang.* 76.

give but one instance, we learn that the Laplanders have the onomatopœia 'to *slam*' in the very same sense as ourselves, although 'countless ages must have elapsed since their ancestors and ours parted from a common stock.'[1] Probably there are not many words which have thus for ages preserved their *exact form* in the mass of *detritus* of which modern languages are composed; but all we have asserted is the traceable existence, often even to the latest moment of a word's history, of the original imitative element. And the fact that an onomatopœia is the only word whose invention is still admissible, is an additional proof of our proposition. For what is the reason of this fact? Simply because an onomatopœia is the only word formed in obvious accordance with the earliest principle of language, the only one which is immediately intelligible, the only one which possesses an inherently graphic power, the only one which can add the beauty of novelty and delighted surprise to the effects produced by existing language, the only one which has any chance of a permanent currency. The fact, then, that new words are mostly imitative is so far from furnishing an argument against us that it tells distinctly in our favour. It tends to prove that the only words which can be invented on any reasonable principle are onomatopœias; and therefore points back to onomatopœia as the necessary principle of all language at its commencement.

In the present stereotyped condition of language, in which it has been so largely modified and its spontaneous development checked in so many ways by the influence of writing and literature, we can hardly be astonished

---

[1] Wedgwood, i. p. iv.

to find that a *direct* sound-imitation, particularly if it be rude and inartistic, is probably too special and limited in significance to give birth to a family of words. Yet the fact that the greatest and most popular poets[1] of every age and nation, from Homer to Tennyson, from Ennius to Göthe, from Archilochus to Bürger and Lamartine, have employed these Echoes of Nature freely, and that the passages in which they have done so have attracted constant attention, is at least sufficient, as I have previously shown,[2] to redeem these words from the position of 'illegitimate pretenders to the dignity of language.' The timid rhetoricians of the Silver Age, and the desiccated pedantic grammarians of a later period, might not venture to use such a privilege,[3] but they could at least point with admiration to the λίγξε βιός, and the σίζε δ' ὀφθαλμός, and the

κάρκαιρε δὲ γαῖα πόδεσσιν
ὀρνυμένων ἄμυδις

of Homer; they could catch the hurtling of battle in

σκέπτετ' ὀϊστῶν τε ῥοῖζον καὶ δοῦπον ἀκόντων,

and a murmur of the 'hollower-bellowing ocean' in

ἐξ ἀκαλαρρείταο βαθυρρόου Ὠκεάνοιο.

---

[1] οἱ χαριέστατοι ποιητῶν τε καὶ συγγραφέων τὰ μὲν αὐτοί τε κατασκευάζουσιν ὀνόματα, συμπλέκοντες ἐπιτηδείως ἀλλήλοις τὰ γράμματα, καὶ τὰς συλλαβὰς δὲ οἰκείως, οἷς ἂν βούλωνται παραστῆσαι πάθεσι, ποικίλως φιλοτεχνοῦσι. Dion. Hal. *De Comp. Verb.* p. 94. Steinthal, *Gesch. d. Sprachwissensch.* p. 340.

[2] *Origin of Lang.* pp. 91-96.

[3] Quinctilian says, '*Minime nobis concessa est ὀνοματοποιΐα*,' and he goes on to say that, were it not for the authority of the ancients, they could hardly even venture to use such words as *hinnire* and *balare!* (*Instt.* i, 5, 72.) He adds in another place that it was more permissible to the Greeks; and in two places he admits that it was a primitive principle of language. 'Non aliâ libertate, *quam quâ illi primi homines*

Further study and the comparison of more languages would have shown them that there is no poet worthy of the name who does not *abound* in imitative expressions; that these are in fact the most appropriate, the most simple, the most passionate, the most picturesque; and that 'poetry reproduces the original process of the mind in which language originates. The coinage of words is the primitive poem of humanity, and the imagery of poetry and oratory is only possible and effective, because it is a continuation of that primitive process which is itself a reproduction of creation.'[1]

There are whole poems,—like the *Paradise Lost*,— and whole languages—like the Hebrew—which are, one may boldly say, an onomatopœia from beginning to end. An imitative harmony runs throughout them, and their very sounds bear the impress of the thoughts they breathe. Often this is due to the number of vigorous and appropriate imitations which they contain, as in Homer:—

> 'Par quel art le chantre d'Achille
> Me rend-il tant de bruits divers?
> Il fait partir la flèche agile
> Et par ses sons s'ifflent les airs.
> Des vents me peint-il le ravage?
> Du vaisseau que brise leur rage
> Éclate le gémissement;
> Et de l'onde qui se courrouce
> Contre un rocher qui la repousse
> Retentit le mugissement.'[2]

---

rebus appellationes dederunt' (viii. 3, 30); and 'et sunt plurima ita posita ab iis, *qui sermonem primi fecerunt,* aptantes affectibus vocem' (viii. 6, 31).

[1] Bunsen, *Outlines*, ii. 135.
[2] Racine (le fils), *Ode sur l'Harmonie*.

But often it results from a certain inward inexplicable harmony which makes sound the coefficient of sense,[1] and by virtue of which thoughts are often welded into an apparently indissoluble union with the language in which they are expressed.

---

[1] On the whole subject, which cannot here be pursued, see L. Quicherat, *Traité de Versification Française*, pp. 144–176. Pobel, *Grundzüge einer Theorie des Reims*. The question of Assonances, Rhymes, Alliterations belongs to this part of our enquiry, but may safely be passed over. It is curious to find a powerful euphonic concord (a sort of Umlaut) running through the South African dialects. In Kafir, for instance, the adjective varies its prefix ten or twelve times, according to the prefix of the governing noun. Appleyard, *Kaf. Gram.* p. 6.

CHAPTER XVI.

SUPPOSED ILLUSORINESS OF THE SEARCH FOR ONOMATOPŒIAS.

'Alphana vient d'equus sans doute,
Mais il faut admettre aussi
Qu'en venant delà jusqu'ici
Il a bien changé sur la route!'

THE last objection we have found urged against the Onomatopoetic theory is—

5. The difficulty and illusoriness of the search.

If the search were 'lawless,' if it were 'detrimental to all scientific etymology,' the objection that it was also one in which we are peculiarly liable to be misled by the imagination might hold. But be it remembered that up to a certain point, and that point very far back in the history of the word, the search of the Sanskritist, and the search of those who hold the Imitative theory, would be *identical*. Without pledging ourselves to the *invariable* applicability of Grimm's law, we should guide our enquiry by certain recognised rules of phonetic change, except in cases where there was good reason to admit that such rules are superseded by other more general and more potent influences. The only difference would be that we should carry our research rather farther back, and should hold in our hand a clue both simple and natural, which we believe to be sufficient to suggest many discoveries and explain many anomalies. Considering the *extreme* uncertainty of many etymologies confidently proposed by Sanskrit scholars, and the great improbability of the conclusions to which they often point, the importance of some broad fundamental principle to guide the researches of etymology can hardly be overrated.

That there *is* an uncritical as well as a critical school of Etymology we do not of course deny; but we do deny that an acceptance of the Imitative theory at once stamps a man as belonging to the *uncritical* school. There is nothing whatever in the theory which supersedes the necessity of 'acting in subordination to the well-discovered principles and rules of phonology, so as not to swerve a foot's breadth from them unless plain actual exceptions shall justify it.' Etymologists of *every* school ought cordially to reecho the wise and weighty words of Diez:[1]—'How little often can etymology accomplish! how doubtful are its results! The highest point reached by the etymologist is the consciousness of having acted scientifically. For the attainment of absolute certainty he has no security. Some insignificant new thing may hurl down from him under his feet a result previously gained with great labour. This will happen to him in every extended investigation; it is included among the daily experiences of the etymologist, from which even the most keen-eyed are not free. Therefore modesty! even when every fact seems to support our theories.' For a long time to come a large number of proposed derivations can only be regarded as plausible and tentative.

---

[1] I quote the translation from Dwight's *Mod. Philology*, i. 238.

'I cannot help observing,' says Professor Pott in a private letter, which I am sure that he will forgive me for quoting, 'that the giving chase to onomatopoetical terms seems to me to be somewhat unfruitful, because of the numerous illusions to which such a study would be necessarily exposed.' Now caution is of course necessary; but we do not think that, in modern times at any rate, the charge of mere reckless guessing and fancying can be brought with more justice against philologists of this school than against those of any other school which may choose to monopolise the title of 'Scientific.' After the philological labours of men like Bopp, and Grimm, and Pott, and Diez, and Curtius, and Max Müller, and of English scholars like Professor Key, the main laws of Etymology are too generally understood to render tolerable any defiance of them. Doubtless the ancient grammarians [1] furnish us with many amusing vagaries, and it would not be difficult to select scores of them from the 'Etymologicum Magnum;' but this was but natural, in days before Etymology existed, or could have existed, as a Science, nor is it in the least chargeable on their vague recognition of the onomatopoetic principle, but resulted from their unavoidable ignorance of every language except their own. This is quite enough to account for what De Quincey[2] calls, 'the unspeakable spirit of absurdity which came over both Greeks and Romans the moment they meddled with etymology.' But since philology *has* been a Science, can it be proved that onomatopœia has been a greater source of error than any other principle? Cannot etymological extravagance be illustrated *at*

---

[1] See Lersch, *Sprachphil. d. Alten*, iii. 82.
[2] Works, viii. p. viii. (Black's ed.)

least as abundantly from the pages of Bopp and other eminent Sanskritists as from any who hold the views here supported? If a philologist like Benfey[1] could derive ὑάκινθος from ὑ = 'to bring forth,' and ἄνθος 'a blossom,' and if a scholar so eminent as the late Dr. Donaldson could connect *dulcis* 'sweet' with δόλιχος 'long,' because fruit lengthens as it ripens,—surely the scientific etymologists ought to see how liable they are to error, and ought to take care how they throw a slur upon the labours of those who after all only carry their views one step farther back. If I select no more instances to enforce the obvious advice that 'those who live in glass houses should not throw stones,' it is because such a task, when one is engaged in trying to establish a reasonable theory, and not in exposing the errors of others, is both ungracious and irksome.

But fortunately Professor Müller offers us some illustrations of his assertion that if we look for the interjectional or imitative element in roots we become lawless and fanciful. Let us examine these, and see if there be any occasion to admit that they are erroneous and illusory. We do not think there is.

In both of his volumes (i. 354, ii. 92) he selects the etymologies proposed for the words *foul, filth, fiend,* &c. These words Mr. Wedgwood (*Etymological Dictionary,* i. p. xiii.) had derived, through various stages, from an

---

[1] See Benfey, *Wurzel-lex.* i. 413. His error is exploded by Donaldson, *Cratylus,* p. 653. His derivation of *dulcis* I only learn by the report of a listener to one of his Cambridge lectures. Obviously *dulcis* is onomatopoetic in origin, no less than γλυκύς with which it is connected; both belong to the universal root *lk,* an imitation of *licking* the lips, &c. *Origin of Lang.* p. 84. For a very amusing exposition of several dogmatic vagaries in which learned philologists have indulged, see Professor Hewitt Key's pamphlet *Quæritur,* &c.

ultimately interjectional root, the instinctive expression of disgust, foh! fie! faugh! This, argues Professor Müller in both his volumes, is impossible, and to accept it would be to undo the patient labour of years, and to throw back etymology into a condition of chaotic anarchy. 'For *fiend* is the present participle of the Gothic *fijan* to hate; and as a Gothic aspirate always corresponds to a tenuis in Sanskrit, the same root in Sanskrit would at once lose its expressive power. It exists in fact in Sanskrit as *pîy* to hate, to destroy.' He adds in his Second Series of Lectures, 'Besides *pîy* to hate, there is another root in Sanskrit, *pûy* to decay. From it we have the Latin *pus, puteo, putridus*; Greek *pyōn* and *pȳthō*; Lithuanian *pulei* matter; and *in strict accordance with Grimm's law,* Gothic *fuls*, English *foul*.'

Now surely the answer to these reiterated objections is absolute and triumphant. 'He does not observe,' says Mr. Wedgwood, 'that the sound of breathing, and the interjection of disgust, are represented as often by the combination *pu* as by *fu*.' This single short sentence is sufficient not only to crumble to the dust Professor Müller's objection, but even to turn all his examples into so many additional illustrations of the interjectional element of language, from which it is quite clear that *pîy* to hate, and *pûy* to decay are as much derived as are the Teutonic forms of similar words beginning with *f* or *ff*. For, in point of fact, *p* and *f* are frequently united in the same instinctive vocal-gesture of disgust, especially when it assumes its strongest form as in the Latin word pfui! That this is really the primitive element of these words we may conjecture as securely as that there was once a form κμέλας[1] when we compare the two forms μέλας and κελαινός. But what force is there then in this instance,—selected and repeated by Professor Müller himself, and therefore one to which he evidently attaches great importance? In what way does it tend to refute the Interjectional theory? So far from overthrowing that theory, it tends directly to its support!

Another instance which he gives of the supposed illusoriness of onomatopœia is the word 'squirrel' (i. 350). But although every one who has ever heard squirrels rustling amid the whispering leaves of a grove, must feel a certain harmonious appropriateness in the sound, yet who has ever dreamed of urging it as an instance of *original* imitation? Certainly the 'some people' to whom he refers for the opinion must have been tiros of the most ignorant description, seeing that *sciurus* the shadow-tail is a word known to all schoolboys, even if they are not aware that our English word, like so many animal names in the Romance languages, comes from the diminutive sciuriolus (as *abeille* from *apicula, grenouille* from *ranuncula*, &c.). That squirrel *might*, however, have been very naturally expressed by an imitative sound is clear from the Persian *warwarah*, the Latin *viverra*, the modern Greek βερβεριτζα.

A third instance is *katze*, cat. In my 'Origin of Language' I quoted it from Mr. Wedgwood as a probable onomatopœia, adding, 'It must however be

---

[1] See Buttmann, *Lexil.* s. v. κελαινός. The form κμέλεθρον for μέλαθρον in the *Etym. Magn.* is an additional proof. Similarly the existence of σύν and cum would at once lead us to infer a form ξύν even if it were not found.

admitted that there is no sibilant in kater.' This fact Mr. Müller adduces (i. 351) to explode the notion of its onomatopœian origin, and says that though the Sanskrit *mârjâra* sounds like purring, it really means the animal that cleans itself. Of 'cat' I have already spoken, and will only add that if *katze* and *mârjâra* be not of imitative origin yet they are words which an imperious instinct—an instinct of which the workings are powerfully apparent in language—has at any rate forced into an imitative form; and if this unconscious instinct can work so powerfully in finished languages, we are the more necessitated to believe in its primary influence.

The only other case urged to show 'how apt we are to deceive ourselves when we once adopt this system of onomatopœia' is the word thunder, which likewise figures in both series of the *Lectures on Language* (i. 350, ii. 93). Now, although no philologist would *select* the particular words *tonitru, donner, tonnerre*, to illustrate the system of onomatopœia, because of their frequently asserted origin from the root *tan*, to stretch, —for which reason I formally excluded the word both on a previous page, and in a previous[1] work,—yet it is not a word on which we need object to accept the challenge of an opponent; and that for the two following reasons:

(1) It is known, and admitted, that if a list of names for the thunder[2] be collected from languages in every region of the globe, the imitative principle is, in the immensely preponderant number of instances, distinctly

---

[1] *Origin of Lang.* p. 82.
[2] See the treatises of Grimm and Pott previously referred to, and add Adelung, *Mithridat.* i. xiv.; Renan, *De l' Orig. du Lang.* p. 139.

perceptible. This therefore proves that the most natural and simple mode of nomenclature for the phenomenon would be that of onomatopœia; and this again defends us from the charge of *fancifulness* when we assert that the form assumed by the word thunder (whatever its origin) is the result of the onomatopoetic instinct,—which is no other than an imperious sense of the *necessity* that in certain instances there should be a perceptible analogy between sound and sense.

But (2), even if we waive all discussion of the *certainty* of the etymology of *tonitru* from *tan*,—what is *tan* itself? Mr. Wedgwood would class it with such words as to *din*, to *dun*, and other words expressive of continuous sound. Professor Müller replies that there are certain *laws* which change *tan* into *than*, and quite a different root *dhvan* into *dun*, and that these two roots preserve their individuality, and are and have been separate from the commencement. He says, indeed, 'There may be, for all we know, some distant relationship between the two roots *tan* and *dhvan*, and that relationship *may have its origin in onomatopœia*.' We believe that the history and meaning of many words derived from these two roots show this to be the case, and if so *our point is proved*. At present, however, we are only concerned with the root *tan* to stretch.

'From [1] this root we have in Greek *tonos*, our *tone*, tone being produced by the stretching and vibrating of cords.' It expresses 'that tension of the air which gives rise to sound.' Now we ask is it even *conceivable* that those fathers of our race who framed the Aryan language should have been so perversely eccentric, as, out of

[1] *Lectures*, i. 356, ii. 92.

the *thousand*[1] possible relations which might have been selected as a characteristic, to choose the notion of *stretching* as a natural, obvious, or intelligible one, wherewith to express the thunder? Supposing, as we must do, that external objects and simple phenomena must have been among the earliest things to receive names, is it conceivable that a word for *stretching* should have been chosen as peculiarly applicable to the most terrible phenomenon of storms? Is it conceivable that at a period so very early in human history they should have noticed that 'tension of the air which gives rise to sound,' (?) and that too when they must have had at hand a host of roots expressive of sound, any one of which would have suited better the object to be named? And if on the other hand they only selected the root *tan* because it was a root which they already possessed, and because it was well adapted to express the sound produced by *the vibration of cords*, why then, *tan* being an onomatopœia (cf. the very obvious cognate words *twang*, τήυελλα, &c., words which spontaneously present themselves as imitative of the sound produced by tremulous strings), *tonitru*, *tonnerre*, &c., are not only imitatively *moulded*, but are after all of an *origin* demonstrably onomatopœian even accepting all the premisses of our opponents. How then do they show the illusory nature of our search?

But here surely the *unsuitableness* of the particular onomatopœia ought at once to convince our common sense that our history of the word is incorrect. Could any human being have ever dreamed of per-

---

[1] *Origin of Lang.* l. c.

ceiving any *analogy* between *thunder* and *harpstrings*? We may indeed imagine how

> Wind that grand old harper smote
> His thunder-harp of pines;

and we can understand such a metaphor as

> Now strike the golden lyre again,
> A louder yet, and yet a louder strain!
> Break his bands of sleep asunder
> And rouse him like a rattling peal of thunder.

We can, I say, understand this because 'thunder' becomes very rapidly, as language advances, a word for *any loud noise,* and indeed a mere epithet or intensive prefix as when we hear in low comedies of a person being a 'thundering brick!' But all these expressions belong to the mechanical or artificial stage of language, and it is, we repeat, inconceivable that the reason why the Sanskrit *tanyu,* thunder, should have been derived from *tan* to stretch, was because some old Aryan on hearing *thunder* was reminded of the resonance of tense strings. If indeed he were reminded of any instrument at all, it would have been a wind instrument, as Homer was when he wrote

> ἀμφὶ δ' ἐσάλπιγξεν μέγας οὐρανός,
> The vast heaven *trumpeted* around;

and as the Hebrews were when they confused the images of Sinaitic thunder with those of trumpets and archangelic voices (Ex. xix. 16, xx. 18, cf. 1 Thess. iv. 16, Rev. i. 10, &c.). But we may, I think, assume it as a certainty that 'thunder' was a phenomenon which received its name long before any musical instrument, either wind or string, was known.

The only way out of these difficulties and contradictions appears to be as follows. *If* it be accepted as certain that tonitru, &c., come ultimately from *tan*, and that the primitive conception of the root *tan* was that of 'stretching,' we must assume that some word like τόνος or *tone*, for the voice, was derived from or connected with it, not because the ancient Aryans knew anything about the *chordæ vocales*, but from the more general notion of stretching the throat in speaking and singing. The steps in the word's history will then be as follows: 1. *Tan* is an onomatopœia to express the sound made when a tightened string is twanged, and

In its clear vibration sings
Like to the swallow's voice.[1]

2. This onomatopœia was transferred to the human voice, because the throat, during loud utterance, is obviously in a tense state. 3. The word 'voice' was naturally transferred to thunder, just as it was in Hebrew where the word קוֹל Kōhl means *both voice and thunder*—the voice of the Lord (Ps. xxix., Ex. ix. 23, &c.) How natural is this analogy may be easily shown. In the book of Job we read of 'the thunder of the captains.' In the narrative of the Evangelists, when a voice came to our Lord from heaven, 'The people that stood by and heard it said that it *thundered*; others said, An angel *spake to him*.'[2] In modern literature the metaphor of thunder as applied to eloquence or poetry is one alike of the commonest and the most natural.

We are quite ready and indeed are very glad to admit, if need be, that 'the very same root *tan*, to stretch,

[1] ἡ δ' ὑπὸ καλὸν ἄεισε χελιδόνι εἰκέλη αὐδήν. Hom. *Od.* xxi.
[2] John xii. 29.

yields some derivatives which are anything but rough and noisy,' such as tender, thin, &c., and we do not see at all that the relationship of these words would be hard to establish 'if the original conception of thunder' (i. e. of course the *word* thunder) 'had been its rumbling noise.' '*Thunder*,' as we have seen, unlike the words for the same thing in almost every other language, may be an onomatopœia not at *first* hand but at second hand, by one of those very processes of transference, analogy, and metaphor which we shall hope to illustrate in the next chapter; and, given the imitative basis, the fact that its linguistic superstructure should contain words so dissimilar in meaning from it as 'thin' and 'tender' is precisely what we should have expected, and precisely the fact which we shall subsequently urge as an additional proof that, given your seedlings of language in the form of a few imitative sounds, these sounds, when quickened by the intellect, possess a germinal force sufficient to make them bourgeon into the noblest tree which ever 'bore aloft on its immortal boughs the language and the literature of a mighty nation.'

CHAPTER XVII.

REFLEX IMITATIVE TENDENCY OF LANGUAGE.

'Se consideriamo il ragguardevol numero di onomatopee sparsi in ogni lingua, e sopra tutto in quello che serbano ancora intatte le impronte della primitiva loro formazione, appare manifesta la naturale tendenza dell' uomo a rappresentare gli oggetti per mezzo delle loro proprietà più distinte.'—BIONDELLI, *Studii Linguistici*, p. 114.

IF it be meant as a reproach to the assertors of the imitative origin of language that their etymologies are 'fanciful,' we have replied already that they are not one whit more so than those of the etymologists who arrogate to themselves the title of 'scientific.' But, in point of fact, the name 'fanciful' carries with it no stigma at all, as we hope to prove further in the next chapter. 'The very nature of association in the human mind is essentially fanciful;' and if a fancy, the most playful and bizarre, can be shown to have preponderated in the growth of abstractions, it might be expected to play its part in the origin of roots. But we really are not aware exactly at what point of the enquiry the fancifulness is supposed to begin. For

(i.) Professor Müller admits freely that 'an *arbitrary* imposition of articulate sounds to signify definite ideas, is an assumption unsupported by any evidence' (ii. 338); and

(ii.) That 'all roots, i. e. all the material elements of

language, are expressive of sensuous impressions, and sensuous impressions only.'

Here then again 'habemus confitentem.' For, if all roots were sensuous, and no root arbitrary, what follows? That every root must have been imposed, i. e. that every sound must have been chosen, for some *reason*. Now step by step we have shown that the easiest, and therefore the earliest, sounds must have corresponded to the earliest impressions; and there could have been no conceivable *reasons* for the earliest sounds except those which we have suggested. Are we then more 'fanciful' than those who accept the only possible alternatives, i. e. of considering that roots were 'inspired,' or of appealing to their supposed *occulta vis*? This much is certain:—Either the origin of Language was that which we have explained, and which even our opponents admit to be *possible*;—or the problem must be practically abandoned as inexplicable and insoluble, while at the same time it is treated of in a number of self-contradicting formulas.

The word '*sugar*,' as well as *squirrel*, is adduced as an instance of the deceptiveness of fancy. 'Who does not imagine that he hears something sweet in the French *sucre, sucré*? Yet sugar came from India, and it is there called *śarkhara*, which is anything but sweet-sounding.' True; but this remark has no connection whatever with the subject under our discussion. We do not even fancy that the word 'sugar' has any particular sweetness in its sound. The theory of an imitative origin of language is wholly unconnected with the mysticism of the Analogists, whose views we shall discuss hereafter, and who, when the Science of Language was unknown, and few men could speak any but their mother-tongue, may be excused for having held the erroneous notion of an inevitable, inherent, and intrinsic harmony between word and thing. The connection between sound and sense, as we have said already, was not *arbitrary*; but neither was it miraculous. It must always have arisen from some determinate *reason*; and the only conceivable reason that can be suggested is the Imitative and Interjectional origin of roots. We did not know that any one had ever adduced 'sugar' as an onomatopœia, though certainly it would be a natural error to connect it with the imitative roots *sugere, suck,* &c.

Let us consider some similar cases. St. Augustine,[1] after stating the Stoic belief in the onomatopoetic theory, continues, that, in the case of things without life, a certain analogy was allowed to come into play, so that the softness or harshness of words was allowed to carry with it an impression of the softness or harshness of things. 'The very words "*lenis*" and "*asper*,"' he says, 'have a leniency and asperity in their sound. *Voluptas* pleasure is a soft, *crux* cross is a harsh word. So that words suggest their own meaning. *Mel* "honey" is as sweet to the ear as honey is to the taste; *acre* "sour"[2] is bitter to both; "lana" wool and "vepres" a bramble are rough to the ear, as the things they mean are to the touch. The Stoics considered a concord between sound and sense to be the very cradle of language.'

Doubtless there is in this passage much confusion of

---

[1] *Dial. Princ.* c. 6. Quoted in that great storehouse of philological learning, Lersch, *Die Sprachphilosophie d. Alten*, iii. 47.

[2] Our 'eager' in its old sense, as 'eager milk,' the French 'aigre;' also sharp. 'It is a nipping and an *eager* air.' Shaksp. Cf. πικρός, which means both *pointed* and *bitter*.

thought. In his statement about the invention of words capable of reproducing a natural sound, the Bishop reports the Stoics correctly; but the vast portion of language not capable of resulting from direct and immediate imitation was formed, not by the very crude and often purely imaginary analogy to which he refers, but by processes of derivation and composition which we have partly observed already, and which we shall consider further in following chapters. Yet after these deductions have been made, there is in the passage which we have quoted a residuum of truth. There is unquestionably a certain meaning, appropriateness, and symbolic power in sound.[1] It is certain that, as a rule, and independently of all confusion between a word and the inevitable associations which it summons up, things beautiful, soft, and pleasing, are *generally* represented by soft and pleasing words,[2] while things which are mean and repulsive receive mean and repulsive titles. This, however, is often the result of long-continued association modifying the existing forms of language. It is only another exhibition of that instinct which demands in almost every language the observance of certain euphonic concords, and which fills with subtle specimens of paronomasia and alliteration every great work of poetry from the Psalms of David and the precepts of Meng Tseu down to the last volume of Tennyson's poems. The sense of hearing works in harmony with the other senses, and assimilates itself to the conditions and emotions of the mind to which it conveys its impressions; it demands, for instance, that

[1] Pott, *Etym. Forsch.* ii. 261. He gives many instances.
[2] See more on this subject with various instances in *Origin of Lang.* pp. 67–71.

pleasurable sensations should be described in pleasurable sounds, just as it demands that the cadences of poetry should be soft and smooth when they glide along the waves of beauty and happiness, but grating and rough when they deal with objects of wrath and terror. The Cyclopes of Virgil toil at the anvil,—

> Illi inter sese multâ vi brachia tollunt,'

and his giants heap the hills, one on the crest of the other—

> Ter sunt conati imponere Pelio Ossam,

in very different strains from those in which Camilla flies over the plain, or in which Ennius[1] makes his rapid cavalry rattle to the fight—

> It eques, et plausu cava concutit ungula terram.

And in Milton,

> On a sudden open fly
> *With impetuous recoil and jarring sound*
> *The infernal doors, and on their hinges grate*
> *Harsh thunder*, that the lowest bottom shook
> Of Erebus,[2]

in far different sounds from those in which

> Heaven open'd wide
> Her ever-during gates, harmonious sound,
> On golden hinges moving.[3]

There is then a sort of reflex action going on,—there is a circular motion in language, by which words start from an imitation, and then losing in the course of ages

---

[1] Ennius, *Ann.* xvii. ap. Macrob. *Sat.* vi. 1.
[2] *Par. Lost*, ii. 80.
[3] Ibid. vii. 204.

their imitative force are remoulded on the old natural principle by a certain imperious demand for an open congruity between sound and sense whenever it is at all possible or permissible. We have already seen this principle at work in the words *katze* and *thunder*; and to these we may add the Romance words for nightingale, Italian *rossignuolo*, Spanish *ruyseñor*, French *rossignol*, which are merely modifications of *lusciniola*, a diminutive from *luscus*, meaning the bird that

> Sings *darkling*, and in shadiest covert hid
> Tunes her nocturnal note,

and which yet are evidently meant to snatch an echo of onomatopoetic music. One might select many such instances, but every one can find them with ease. Who would not fancy that he heard something of the *kanonengebrüll* in the word cannon? Yet it merely comes from *canna*, a reed. *Clarion*, for all its sonorous fulness, is from *clarus*, and means the *clearly*-sounding instrument; *minstrel*, liquid and musical, is nothing but a corruption of the vulgar *ministerialis*; and *lute*, with all its vowel-sweetness, is nothing but the Arabic article *el* kneaded up into the substantive *ud*, as in alchemy or algebra, or, to take an instance from our own language, as the *n* of our indefinite article gets tacked on to *eft* in the word *newt*. Thus it is that language reverts to its primary instincts. Its earliest sounds were imitative, and after long deviations from their primitive source, after being subjected to a thousand varying influences, they yet tend to become imitative again. Carried far away from its primitive source, subjected to numberless modifications, its words still, if I may be forgiven the metaphor, are like those

Sinuous shells of pearly hue
Within, and they that lustre have imbibed
In the sun's palace-porch, where when unyoked
His chariot-wheel stands midway in the wave:
Shake one and it awakens; then apply
Its polished lips to your attentive ear,
And it remembers its august abodes,
And murmurs as the ocean murmurs there. [1]

---

[1] Landor. By a curious coincidence the same lines have been quoted to illustrate the same point by the 'Times' *since* these pages were written.

CHAPTER XVIII.

THE PART PLAYED BY THE IMAGINATION IN THE INVENTION OF LANGUAGE.

> 'What surmounts the reach
> Of human sense, I shall delineate so,
> By likening spiritual to corporal forms,
> As may express them best.' MILTON, *Par. Lost*, v. 37.

IN one of those pregnant concessions to the importance of the Imitative principle which make us sometimes hope that our eminent opponent is more than half convinced by the arguments adduced in its favour, after allowing that there is 'a large stock' of onomatopœias in every language, he says, ' And who would deny that some words originally expressive of sound only, might be transferred to other things which have some analogy with sound ?'

'But,' he continues (ii. 89), 'how are all things which do not appeal to the sense of hearing—how are the ideas of going, moving, standing, sinking, tasting, thinking, to be expressed?'

This is the last arrow, and meant apparently to be the most effective, which is shot Parthian-like into our forces. The point of it has already been turned aside by the considerations previously adduced. But in order to leave no argument unconsidered, I hope throughout this chapter to bring an abundance of instances which will be adequate to remove the suggested difficulty, or at any rate to show that it is neither fatal nor final.

Let us return for a moment to first principles.

I have said repeatedly that *no* school of etymologists pretends to explain the derivation of *all* words. The Imitative school indeed is the only one which offers *any* explanation of the ultimate origin of even a *large* number of words. We are not therefore in a *worse* position than any others, although we are convinced that the Science of Philology can go farther and attempt more than has yet been accomplished. Consequently it is no refutation of our principles to adduce any special group of words which we are unable to explain, any more than it would be a refutation of the arguments of Bopp, or Grimm, or Pott, to perform the easy task of assembling long lists of words in the Aryan languages of which they could give, and could pretend to give, no account whatever. Nevertheless, as we shall see, the linguistic processes which we shall illustrate in the next chapter are sufficient to account for the possible expression of *any* conceptions whatever; and with this we might perhaps rest content. Given the segment of a circle however small, and the whole circle can immediately be reproduced; given a distinct and decisive clue to the processes of language, and no serious difficulty remains in effecting its complete reconstruction. Of the group of words and conceptions which Professor Müller proposes as incapable of explanation on our principles, we shall have something to say before we enter on the more general enquiry. The riddle which he proposes is after all a riddle which is easily solved by the same clues which enable us to understand how modifications of the voice could effect the far more difficult result of expressing or describing the images which fall on the retina of the eye. Meanwhile, as an illustration is often more clear and convincing than many arguments, let me once more recur to the progress of writing to illustrate my position,—which it does in a very remarkable manner. I have already adduced the Hebrew alphabet to show the analogy between the imitative origin of writing and of speech; I now adduce the Chinese ideography to illustrate how elemental roots were extended into finished and all-expressive language.

The Chinese writing is ideographic, i. e. it has no alphabetic letters, but signs each of which stands for a conception. The most ancient Chinese characters (like our astronomical and chemical symbols) were *rude pictures of material objects,* just as we believe the earliest words to have been rude imitations of sounds chosen as the most obvious and self-explaining characteristics of such objects as admitted of such representations. These characters were about 200 in number, and are called Siang-hîng or Images, as—

Sun. Moon. Mountain. Tree. Dog. Fish.

We see that the picture was conventional or ideal rather than an actual copy. For instance, in the character for fish we see the scales and the tail conventionalised, or represented according to an accepted symbolism, as is the case with the roots and boughs of the tree; and as again, in language, mere imitations are ideally and articulately modified.

But soon arose the need for representing more complicated objects; and, for these, *new signs were not invented*, but the old ones were combined by the most ingenious combinations and the liveliest metaphors, just as imitative roots were transferred, agglutinated, compounded, or inflected, to express intellectual operations, and various conditions incapable of being externally perceived. Thus, for instance, to signify *light* we have the sun and moon; for *hermit* we have a man over a mountain; for *singing*, a mouth and a bird; for *wife*, a woman, a hand, and a broom; for *hearing*, an ear placed at a door; for *tears*, an eye and water, &c., as follows :—

Light.   Hermit.   Song.   Wife.   Listening.   Tears.

To express abstract ideas, or acts of the understanding, use is made of analogies and metaphors suggested by the simple characters; for instance, a *heart* represents the soul; a *house* stands for man; a *broom* for woman; a *hand* for artisan; three men, one behind the other, means 'to follow,' &c. The notions[1] of *roughness, rotundity, motion, rest*, were represented by a mountain, the sky, a river, the earth; the sun, moon, and

---

[1] So too with objects which would have been too difficult to represent in this manner, the mixed characters *hing-ching* are used, which are half representative and half syllabic. Thus the sign ⊕, 'place' (*li* in Chinese), joined to a fish, means the fish li or carp; and the word *pĕ*, white, is only pronounced in the character composed of a tree, ⽊⊖, *pĕ*, which means cypress.

stars stood for *smoothness, splendour,* anything artfully wrought or delicately worked; *extension, growth, increase,* were figured by clouds, the firmament, and vegetables; *motion, agility, slowness, idleness,* and *diligence,* by various insects, birds, fish, and quadrupeds. 'In this manner passions and sentiments were traced by the pencil, and ideas not subject to any sense were exhibited to the sight, until by degrees new combinations were invented, new expressions added; the characters dwindled imperceptibly from their primitive shape, and the Chinese language became not only clear and forcible, but rich and elegant in the highest degree.'[1] These characters are called *kia-tsieï,* or *borrowed.*

No more vivid notion than this could be given of the exactly analogous processes of language; but we have not yet done with our illustration.

For these characters, idealised as they are, do not in the more modern systems of writing, retain more than a dim and vague resemblance to the original picture, as follows:—

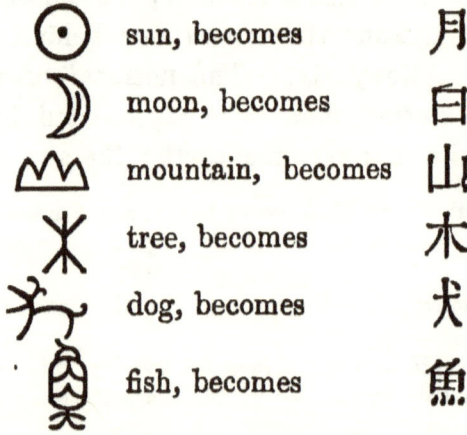

[1] Sir W. Jones, *Asiatic Researches,* ii. 195. He refers to the Chinese writer Li Yan Ping.

And to take one or two compound signs:—

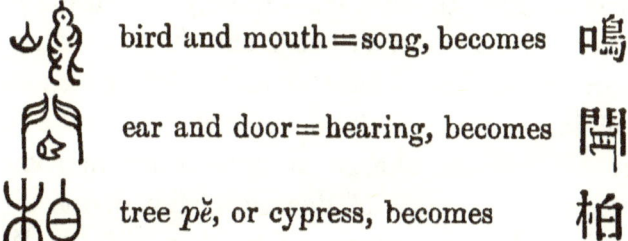

Now if all this were not a matter of historic certainty, only imagine how 'fanciful' a person would be called who should assert that the cursive sign stood for the object! How completely, for instance, in the above-written characters does the dog lose his head and legs! What a ghostly simulacrum is left him of his curly tail! The ear at the door looks more like three flags, and the moon assumes the resemblance of an eccentric ladder. Nevertheless, that eccentric ladder sprang by direct filiation from a very passable crescent moon, and the hatchet of the first compound sign was once a very sweet little mouth with a Cupid's bow for the upper lip! So much then for the reproach of 'fancifulness' in inquiries of this kind. For if written characters are liable to these Protean metamorphoses, how much rather should we expect them in the words spoken every day, and subject to all the changes likely to arise from their utterance millions of times by millions of mouths in millions of different vocal modifications?

But now suppose that the Siang-hîng or original image-characters had been lost, and some ingenious theorist, by the aid of an intelligent observation and analysis of the lî or modern system of writing, had conjectured its originally pictorial intention; and if he succeeded in *proving* that, say a thousand out of some

30,000 recognised signs had this origin, would he not be fairly entitled to conclude—there being in his procedure no intrinsic unlikelihood, but on the contrary an *à priori* probability—that the rest, which he was unable to explain, were similarly developed from rude imitations? Would the charge of uncertainty in some instances, or the charge of degrading the divine dignity of the invention, be a disproof of his position? Would it be fair to produce a group of indecomposable signs, and flout him with failure if he could give no account of them? Would it be philosophical to provide his critic with a nickname, and call his system the 'scrap-book' or the 'baby-scrawl' theory? Well then we say to each of our opponents, 'mutato nomine de te Fabula narratur!' The rule of Varro[1] is more equitable, viz., that he who has given many excellent derivations ought rather to be thanked for those than blamed for an occasional failure; particularly when he admits that for many words no etymology whatever can be offered.

And here we must again stop to object decidedly against the notion, common apparently to most philologers, that *verbal* roots, such as going, moving, tasting, &c., or as some prefer to call them, *predicative* roots, were the earliest. To us such a conception is logically inconceivable. The invention of a verb requires a greater effort of abstraction than that of a noun, for, obviously, we must have generalised from individual phenomena before we can express them verbally under the conditions of 'motion, action, or existence.' In

---

[1] 'Igitur de originibus verborum qui multa dixerit commode, potius boni consulendum, quam qui aliquid nequiverit reprehendendum; præsertim quum dicat etymologice non omnium verborum dici posse causam.' Varro, *De Ling. Lat.* vii. 4.

some places, indeed, Professor Müller[1] appears to hold the correct view, that at first 'roots' stood for any and every part of speech, just as the monosyllabic expressions of children do, and just as they do to this day in that language of arrested development, the Chinese. This is the view supported with such brilliant acumen, and illustrated with so much philological learning, by the late Mr. Garnett[2] in his *Essay on the Nature and Analysis of the Verb*. We believe with him that all language is reducible to roots which are either the basis of abstract nouns, or are pronouns denoting relations of place, which latter we believe to have arisen from interjectional elements. Now, 'a verb is not a simple, but, *ex necessario*, a complex term, and therefore no primary part of speech.'[3] From these views we cannot accept it as even *possible* that, 'from roots meaning to shine, to be bright, names were formed, for sun, moon, stars, the eyes of man, gold, silver, play, joy, happiness, love. With roots meaning to strike, it was possible to name an axe, the thunderbolt, a fist, a paralytic stroke, a striking remark, and a stroke of business.' It seems inconceivable that men should have needed, and, therefore, should have invented, a word meaning 'to shine' before they had any designation for the sun, or a verb meaning 'to strike' before they had the imitative sounds *tud, tup, tuph* (cf. our confessed onomatopœias *thud, tap, tat, rub a dub*, &c.),[4] which were amply

---

[1] *Lectures*, ii. 86. Bunsen, *Outlines*, ii. 130.
[2] *The Philol. Essays of the late Rev. Rich. Garnett*, edited by his Son, pp. 289-342. No more sound, or valuable, or interesting contribution to Philology has appeared for many years than this volume of Essays.
[3] Garnett, p. 290.
[4] So obvious is this imitation as to be found also in the Semitic languages. Cf. Hebr. תָּקַף, תַּף, &c.

sufficient for a host of derivatives in every language, as τύπτω, τύμπανον, drub, drum, thump, and so forth. We have already seen that the verb is represented by a combination of the noun in the history of Chinese ideography, and it seems to me impossible that it could have been otherwise in speech. In Chinese *ming* 明 'bright' is[1] from 月 *yih* the sun, and 日 *ngyněh* the moon; and 分 *fwun* 'to divide' is composed of 刀 *tao* a knife, and 八 *păh* eight. This is a conceivable process; the other would be, in the old sense of the word, preposterous. Nor is it a question as to what is merely *probable* in language; for we may regard it as established by the large inductive process of Mr. Garnett, and many others, that 'the radical terms employed to denote action, passion, or state, had originally rather the force of nouns than verbs,' and this especially in the Celtic, which, it need hardly be remarked, is one of the very oldest members of the Aryan family. If so, we must entirely give up the notion that the names of objects came from predicative or verbal roots. We hope, too, that the instance of the root *tup* and the origin assigned to it, will show our reason for not attaching any importance to the whole division of roots into primary and secondary, which is elaborated in Professor Müller's first series of lectures (p. 250).

It requires but the feeblest power of abstraction—a power possessed even by idiots—to use a name as the sign of a conception, e. g. to say 'sun;'—to say 'sheen,' as the description of a phenomenon common to all shining

---

[1] Marshman, *Chinese Gram.* p. 23.

objects, is a higher effort, and to say 'to shine' as expressive of the state or act is higher still. Now, familiar as such efforts may be to us, there is ample proof that they could not have been so to the inventors of language, because they are not so, even now, to some nations of mankind after all their long millenniums of existence. Instances of this fact have been repeatedly adduced. Even in the *Mithridates* [1] we find it noticed, that the Society Islanders have words for dog's tail, bird's tail, and sheep's tail, yet no word for tail; that the Mohicans have verbs for every kind of cutting, and yet no verb 'to cut,' and forms for 'I love him,' 'I love you,' &c., but no verb meaning 'I love.' The Choctaws [2] have names for every possible species of oak, but no word for the genus oak. The Australians [3] have no *generic* word for fish, bird, or tree; and the Eskimo, though he has verbs for seal-fishing, whale-fishing, and every other kind of fishing, has no verb meaning simply 'to fish.' 'Ces langues,' says Du Ponceau, in his admirable Essay, '*généralisent* rarement.' Thus, they have separate verbs for 'I wish to eat meat,' and 'I wish to eat soup,' but no verb for 'I wish;' [4] and separate words for a blow with a sharp, and a blow with a blunt instrument, but no abstract word for blow. Mr. Crawfurd [5] bears similar witness to the Malay languages. 'The Malay,' he says, '*is very deficient in abstract words*; and the usual train of ideas of the people who speak it

[1] Adelung, *Mithr.* iii. 325, 397. See, too, Pott, *Etym. Forsch.* ii. 167. Heyse, p. 132.
[2] Latham, *Races of Man*, p. 376.
[3] De Quatrefages, *Rev. des Deux Mondes*, Dec. 15, 1860. Maury, *La Terre et l'Homme*, p. 433.
[4] Du Ponceau, p. 120.
[5] Crawfurd. *Malay Grammar*, i. 68 seq.

does not lead them to make a frequent use even of the few they possess. They have copious words for colours, yet borrow the word colour, *warna*, from the Sanskrit. With this poverty of the abstract is united a redundancy of the concrete. No word for tree or herb, yet *urat*, fibre; *akar*, root; *pârdu*, tree-crown; *tangkai*, stalk; *battan*, stock; *tungal*, trunk; *däan* and *turuk*, twig; *tukut*, *tunas*, and *gagang*, shoot, &c.' He gives many similar instances, and an analogous one is to be found even in Anglo-Saxon, which had abundant words for all shades of blue, red, green, yellow, &c., but borrowed [1] from the Latin the abstract word 'colour;'— and abundant names for every form of crime, before it borrowed from Latin the abstract words 'crime' and 'transgression.' With instances like these before us— and they might be indefinitely multiplied—who shall believe that the sun, and moon, and earth, had not been named at all until they received names from roots meaning to shine, to measure, and to plough? or that cows and reptiles, and creeping plants, and flowing water, and clouds, made shift with being anonymous until after men possessed an indefinite number of verbs all meaning 'to go'?[2]

And now then, having cleared the way by these preliminary considerations, let us (though we might, as we have shown, fairly decline to accept any one particular test) very briefly consider whether there is no answer, on our principles, to the question, 'How are all things which do not appeal to the sense of hearing—how are the ideas of going, moving, standing, sinking, tasting, thinking to be expressed?' It would be tedious to go through

---

[1] Dr. D. Wilson, *Prehistoric Man*, i. 61.
[2] See Prof. Key, *ubi sup.*, 8–16.

them all; let us then take each alternate word. If the question can be answered for these, it can be as easily answered for the rest. Let it be observed that in attempting to answer it at all we are doing something *beside and beyond* what our opponents ever attempt to do; we are rising above 'that indolent philosophy which refers to a miracle whatever it is unable to explain.'

'Ideas[1] of going.' I am not aware that anybody has attempted to explain the origin of the Sanskrit verb '*ga*,' to go. Of other Sanskrit verbs with this meaning [2] there is at least a reasonable probability that 'pat' (also to fall) and *sr*, and *srp* (also to creep), *are* of imitative origin, as they are closely analogous to many formations of similar meaning which are confessedly so. Moreover, to confine ourselves to our own language alone, what shall we say of the words creep, crawl, dawdle, dance,[3] rush, hurry, patter, totter, stump, stamp, and many more, to say nothing of such as expressly imply noise combined with motion, as whizz, whirr, hurl, &c. ? Every one of these is an 'idea of going;' every one of these is—and the proof is easy—onomatopoetically expressed.

'Ideas of standing.'[4] It would have been difficult,

---

[1] I must remark, *en passant*, that I am not responsible for this use of the word 'ideas;' though, indeed, it is hopeless to redeem this noble word from the mass of confused usages into which it has fallen. Not one modern writer in twenty thousand uses it either carefully or accurately in its only true and proper meaning.

[2] As for the root 'i' 'go' in ἰέναι, &c., Plato says, τῷ δ' αὖ ἰῶτα πρὸς τὰ λεπτὰ πάντα, ἃ δὴ μάλιστα διὰ πάντων ἴοι ἄν. In other words *i* as the subtlest of the vowels, is chosen, by a sort of imitative analogy, to express notions of movement, penetration, &c. *Crat.* p. 426. I leave this as I find it.

[3] Cf. Hebr. רקד, *tanzen*, &c.

[4] Plato, whether in irony or earnest, derives στάσις from ἀ ἵεσις (not

perhaps, to choose any conceptions so apparently incapable of mimetic or interjectional expression as these; yet their origin can be explained. It has long been noticed that combinations of *s* and *t* have been chosen in many languages as expressions of stability, ἵστημι, *sto, setzen, sitzen, stemmen,* &c. There must have been some reason for this, and we believe it to be furnished by the simple instinctive *Lautgeberde* st! a sound peculiarly well adapted to demand attention (compare whist! usht! &c.), and therefore well adapted to express stopping and standing as the immediate results of an awakened attention. Even Heyse was struck with the fact that the *Lautgeberde* offers a close analogy to the imperative sentence, and that st! was equivalent to the command sta![1] stop!

'Ideas of tasting.' An unfortunate selection to prove the difficulty of extending imitative words, because we believe that the word *taste* itself, together with nearly all its synonyms and words which express similar meanings, are very easy onomatopœias. Taste, for instance (Ital. *tastare,* Germ. *tasten,* &c.), is from *taxitare,* a frequentative of *taxare,* a verb defined by Aulus Gellius to mean 'pressius crebriusque tangere.' Now tax is an open and unconcealed imitation, as '*Tax, tax* tergo meo erit,' in Plautus.[2] And as for the difficulty or impossibility of similarly expressing other ideas of tasting, what does Professor Müller say to the words לקק; Arabic, *lalūka;* Sanskrit *lih, lak;* λείχω, lingo, ligurio? or the words

---

going) with an euphonic epenthesis st! (ἡ δὲ στάσις ἀπόφασις τοῦ ἰέναι βούλεται εἶναι, διὰ δὲ τὸν καλλωπισμὸν στάσις ὠνόμασται. *Cratylus,* p. 426).

[1] *System,* p. 73.
[2] *Pers.* ii. 3, 12.

trinken, drink, quaff, *saufen, souper*, sup, soup, quaff? or to *sugere, succus, saugen*, suck? or to *schmecken* and smack? or to gurgle, gulp, gobble, guzzle, &c.? or to hundreds more whose origin may be less transparent, but is hardly less certain? Are these 'ideas of tasting' or are they not? are they onomatopœias or not? The answer to either question can hardly be doubtful.

I think, therefore, that on this point also the challenge has been most fairly accepted, and fairly met; for it would be no less easy to go through the 'ideas of moving, sinking, and thinking.' And here for the present I may leave the controversy.

CHAPTER XIX.

METAPHOR.

Περὶ τῶν ἀδήλων ἀπὸ τῶν φαινομένων χρὴ σημειοῦσθαι. Καὶ γὰρ καὶ ἐπίνοιαι πᾶσαι ἀπὸ τῶν αἰσθήσεων γεγόνασι κατά τε περίπτωσιν καὶ ἀναλογίαν καὶ ὁμοιότητα καὶ σύνθεσιν συμβαλλομένου τι καὶ λογισμοῦ.
Epic. ap. Diog. Laert. x. 32.

BARON BUNSEN, in one of those eloquent and magnificent bursts of dogmatism which are to be found in his noble book, *The Philosophy of Universal History,* after describing the Imitative theory in a manner which at any rate does not apply to any of its present holders, and which is based on complete misapprehension of their views, says that such a theory is not only disproved by all history and diametrically opposed by facts (!), but is '*a most absurd supposition in itself, as most objects have no sound whatever.*'[1]

If the former pages of this volume have not satisfied the reader as to the utter groundlessness of the first assertions, it is hardly worth while to argue further; and I trust that he will have already seen enough to show that the last assertion is none the less erroneous for sounding at first mention plausible. If not, the following chapter will show that as an objection to our theory it has *no weight whatever.* Indeed, as we have several

---

[1] Bunsen, ii. 131.

times observed, it is not true, to begin with, that 'most objects have no sound whatever.' Even the mass of objects in the dumb and inanimate world are so constituted that the sound produced by them is generally the best and truest indication of their character and properties. The clang of various metals, from the deep reverberations of iron to the tremulous shiver of thin steel, and the sharp tinkling of brass and tin—the whisper and splash of cohesionless liquids—the crackle, and blare, and roar of flame—the ringing resonance of stone and marble—the creaking of green boughs—the ripping of dead wood—the clink of glass—the dull thud of soft and yielding bodies—the discontinuous rattle of hard, dry substances—the flap or rustle of woven fabrics in the wind—every one of these sounds, and of thousands more, betrays instantaneously to the ear the nature of every substance, and is recognisable even from a distance and in the dark. And every one of these sounds is capable of articulate representation. It is not too much to say that there is hardly an inanimate substance in the creation which does not in some way or other connect itself with sound—that does not in some way or other recall an acoustic image of itself.

We have observed the influence exercised over language by the emotions (*interjections*), by the will (*Lautgeberden*), and the deep-lying instinct of imitation (onomatopœia); it remains to see how the materials thus provided were moulded and multiplied by the imagination and the fancy.

At first sight there might have appeared to be a difficulty absolutely insuperable in making audible sounds the exponents of impressions which come to us through the gateways of four most different senses—in translating for the ear the perceptions which we form through the medium of touch, and taste, and smell, and sight; in giving expression—by means of the undulations of air sent pulsing upon the tympanum by vibrations of the vocal chords, and motions of the lips and tongue—to all that pleases or disgusts in contacts, and savours, and odours, and in the infinite many-coloured world of visual images. Yet over this seemingly fathomless abyss of separation, Nature flings in one wide arch, and without an effort, her marvellous aerial bridge!

The difficulty is at once enormously reduced by observing that nothing corresponding to the impressions of the senses has any objective or actual existence. There is no such thing in the abstract as a smell, a taste, or a colour. There is nothing in any way analogous to these words beyond the boundary-line of our own individualities. Infinitely small particles floating invisibly in the air rest on the fibro-mucous membrane which lines the nasal cavity, and by mechanical or chemical combinations affect the olfactory filaments, and we say that there is a smell; movements of air undulating on the tympanum are conveyed to the auditory nerve, and modified by the exquisite and dimly-understood mechanism of the cochlea, otolithes, and semicircular passages, and we say there is a sound; rays of light falling on the cornea, and variously refracted by the crystalline and vitreous humours, produce an inverted image of objects upon the network of optic nerves, and we say that we see; the delicate surface of the skin, conveying the impression of resistance under various forms, leads us to say of an object when we touch it that it is hard, or round, or square; and other impressions are conveyed by the tongue or palate which we say are sweet or acid. But what are the objective realities corresponding to the words 'a smell,' 'a colour,' 'a sound,' 'roundness,' 'sweetness?' There *are* no such objective realities, they are pure nonentities. The words are absolutely meaningless, except so far as they express the modifications, however produced, of one and the same sentient subject. Even substance is but a purely hypothetical postulated residuum after the abstraction of all observable qualities. Nothing has any existence for us except as a *synthesis* of attributes, and even these attributes are not inherent in matter, but are merely affections of our personality which we project into the external world, and endow with a purely imaginary objectivity; they are but shadows of the inward microcosm flung by the light of our own life upon the external universe, and invested by imagination with an independent reality.

When therefore we express by words the impressions of every sense, we are not translating from a number of languages which have no analogy with each other, but we are merely expressing a single subject—namely, ourselves. We are dealing, not with external realities, but with subjective sensations. The impressions, however various may be the sources whence they are derived, all act upon a *sensorium commune*;[1] however diverse may be our sensations, they are all of them nothing more than material changes in one common brain. In point of fact, we have not five senses, but only one

[1] 'Wie hängt Gesicht und Gehör, Farbe und Wort, Duft und Ton zusammen? .... Wir sind ein denkendes *sensorium commune* nur von verschiedenen Seiten berührt—Da liegt die Erklärung.' Herder, s. 94. By the name *sensorium commune*, however, I do not mean merely the brain, but the brain, the nerves, the organs of sense, &c. See Bain, *The Senses and Intellect*, p. 61.

sense, the sense of feeling. There may be no connection between a sound and a colour; but since both the sound and the colour are but states produced in a thinking subject, the brain which is affected by the sound can *use* sound as a means of expressing the effect of the colour also. A smell, the striking of a clock, muscular resistance, and the form of a triangle, are separated from each other by an abyss of difference; there is nothing in common even between different sensations received by the same organ—as white and black. Language expresses nothing but the *relations* of things, and as these are *purely subjective*, the mind which creates these supposed relations is also capable of expressing them.

Hence, by an apparently instinctive process—a process, at any rate, not derived either from logical inference or physical research—we find throughout all language an interchange between, rather than a confusion of, the words which properly belong to different senses. This is especially the case in the terms expressive of light and sound. We find nothing to alter in such verses as 'All the people *saw* the thunderings and lightnings, and the *noise* of the trumpet' (Ez. xx. 18), or 'I turned to *see* the *voice* which spake with me' (Rev. i. 12). In Æschylus, 'The voice [1] and the clash are seen (*Prom. Vinct.* 21, 22); in Sophocles the pæan flashes (*Œd. Tyr.* 187), and the echo gleams back from the distant rock (*Œd. Col.* 137): by the voice the blind beholds, the ears of the deaf are sightless.'

All the effects produced by the senses are indeed but different threads which Nature has woven into one web;

---

[1] Boyes, *Illustrations to Æschylus*, &c., p. lii.

but between light and sound, the two most infinite in their revelations of the outer world, there seems to be a distinct and peculiar connection. 'They are,' says Lamennais,[1] merely 'two different organs of the same faculty, two different manifestations of the *same* sense.' Hence, the Greek Apollo is the god both of melody and of brightness.

The imaginative power to perceive these analogies works instinctively and without reflection; the mere copy or imitation of a sound is, by a new step in the progress of language—which is due to the imagination —elevated into a symbol for things which it cannot directly imitate, and finally, this symbol is promoted by the understanding into a general sign; but each step is taken naturally and unconsciously. Nothing is more common in ordinary language than to hear people adopt these self-explaining and vivid analogies.[2] We speak indifferently of a clear tone or a clear light; and the word '*tone*' itself is applied to a picture no less than to a harmony. No one is struck with a sense of incongruity when we speak of a *gamut of colours*, or a *chromatic sequence* in a piece of music. Sophocles speaks of a man as '*blind* both in *ears* and eyes.'[3] Who does not see the beauty of this sentence in a modern writer? 'And as the chorus swelled and swelled till the air seemed made of sound, *little flames*, vibrating too, as if the sound had caught fire, burst out between the turrets of the palace and the girdling towers. That

---

[1] *Esquisse d'une Philosophie*, in E. Arnould's *Ess. d'Hist. Lit.* 168.

[2] I gave some striking instances from the poets in the *Origin of Lang.* p. 126. In French there are several which are hardly admissible in English, as 'sombres gémissements,' 'lueurs éclatantes,' &c.

[3] τυφλὸς τά τ' ὦτα τόν τε νοῦν τά τ' ὄμματ' εἶ. *Œd. Tyr.* 371.

sudden clang, that leaping light, fell on Romola like sharp wounds.'[1] 'Is not the delight of the quavering upon a stop of music,' says Lord Bacon, 'the same with the playing of light upon the water [2]—

> Splendet tremulo sub lumine pontus?

Are not the organs of the senses of one kind with the organs of reflection—the eye with a glass, the ear with a cave or strait determined and bounded? *Neither are these only similitudes, as men of narrow observation may conceive them to be,* but the same footsteps of nature, treading or printing upon several subjects or matters.'[3] Hence it is that, by a purely unconscious sense of analogy, we find repetitions of light expressed by precisely the same kind of reduplication as repetitions of sound; so that purpura and marmor indicate waves of light no less naturally than murmuro and susurro indicate waves of sound.[4] Quick motions, also producing a sort of flash in the air, are represented by imitative reduplications, as *papilio,* the butterfly, which in Basque is chickitola, and in Botocudo is kiaku-keck-keck.

---

[1] *Romola,* ii. 85. There is a direct etymological connection between *fragor* and *bright*; between φάος, 'light,' and φημί, 'I say.' Vide Heyse, s. 115. A writer whom I have previously quoted says, 'We can readily imagine the imitative *tinkle* passing into the French étincelle and the English *twinkle*—the sharp delicate impression on the ear recalling that upon the eye.' *Macmillan's Mag.*

[2] Compare 'It is like listening to the mysterious music in the conch sea-shell; it is like watching the fleeting rays of light which shoot up to heaven as we are looking at the sunset.' Robertson, *Addresses,* p. 227. Every one knows how Sanderson, born blind, compared '*red*' to a trumpet-note; the reverse story of Massieu, the deaf-mute, comparing a trumpet-note to the same colour, is not so generally known.

[3] *Adv. of Learning,* bk. i.

[4] Dwight, *Mod. Philology,* 2nd Series, p. 210.

Nor is this interchange of the terms proper to different senses at all confined to the eye and the ear. 'Ye have made our *odour* to be abhorred in the *eyes* of Pharaoh,' we find in Ex. v. 21; and 'truly the *light* is *sweet*,' in Eccl. xii. 7. Dr. Kalisch correctly observes that what such expressions lose in logical accuracy they gain in richness and force; and hence we find them frequently in the poets, as in Æschylus, κτύπον δέδορκα, 'I see a sound,' and in Lucretius, 'loca *vidi* reddere *voces*.' Crashaw talks of 'the murmur of a *sparkling noise*;' Akenside of '*tasting* the *fragrance* of a rose;' Byron of '*inhaling* an *ambrosial aspect.*' The adjectives *soft, sharp, hard, mild, rough, smooth*, are used indifferently of sounds, of lights, of touch, of taste;[1] the adjective *nice*, which belongs properly to the region of taste alone, is on the lips of some people an epithet of universal meaning; and other adjectives, not properly belonging to the domain of any sense, are transferred indiscriminately to each sense, so that, for instance, we are not surprised to hear of a rich colour,[2] a rich tone, or rich viands; of delicate tints, delicate odours, or delicate textures. To such an extent is this carried that we hardly notice it in ordinary conversation, nor are we struck by anything metaphorical in the turn of expression when we hear a person speaking colloquially of a glorious day or a glorious concert; of bitter

---

[1] The whole subject is admirably treated by Wilhelm von Humboldt, *Ueber die Verschiedenheit d. menschl. Sprachbaues*, s. 78, fg. But it is not easy to establish any clear distinction between words used symbolically (καθ' ὁμοιότητα) and analogically (κατὰ ἀναλογίαν). See Lersch, iii. 53; Heyse, p. 95. One or two of the instances given above are quoted by Mr. Boyes, in his *Illustrations to Æschylus and Sophocles*.

[2] In Chinese the word for a *gem* is also applied to a dainty.

cold, bitter experience, or a bitter taste; of a sweet smell, a sweet voice, a sweet taste, a sweet look, or a sweet feeling.

We see then that there is no difficulty in expressing anything with which all the senses are conversant in terms derived from the instinctive or imitated sounds furnished to us by one of them; and thus we are at once supplied with a nomenclature sufficiently ample for all the phenomena of the material universe. At every step in this part of the progress of language, the imagination is dominant. From this source is derived the whole system of genders for inanimate things, which was perhaps inevitable at that early childish stage of the human intelligence, when the actively-working soul attributed to everything around it some portion of its own life, but which has been wisely discarded by our own language as a useless encumbrance. To the quick fancy of the child of nature it seems impossible to regard anything as absolutely without life. The Indian thinks that the shade even of his arrow will accompany him to the regions of the blest. Hence, well-nigh everything is spoken of as masculine or feminine. How completely fanciful were the analogies which in each case suggested the gender is seen from the different genders attributed in different languages to the same thing, and cannot be more clearly illustrated than by the fact that the sun, which in nearly every other language is masculine, becomes feminine in German (*die Sonne*); and the moon, which so many nations worshipped as a goddess, is, in German, made masculine (*der Mond*).

By a similar play of fancy, the names for various parts of the body are catachrestically applied to things without life.[1] We talk of the *leg* of a stool; of the *foot, crest, spur,* or *shoulder* of a mountain; of the *teeth* of a saw or a comb; of the *neck* of a bottle; the *tongue* of a balance or a shoe, the *eye* of a needle, the *head* of a cabbage, the *arm* of a chair, the *breast* of a wave, the *bosom* of a rose. Even an island is an oe or 'eye;' an isthmus is a neck; a harbour, a jaw;[2] a central place, a navel;[3] a crag is a tooth; a river-bank, a lip; and a promontory, a ness, naze, or nose. Plants are named from animals or the limbs of animals, as fox-tail, mouse-ear, goat's-beard, cock's-comb, hare's-foot, crane-bill, lark-spur. Even dead instruments or parts of them are called by the names of animals, as a monkey, a battering-ram, a pig of lead,[4] chevaux de frise, a frog; *cochlea,* a screw; *testudo,* a penthouse of shields; *lupus,* a bit; ἐχῖνος, a pitcher; κόραξ, a grappling-iron; ὄνος, a windlass. Ships and ploughs, both as wholes and in their parts, are spoken of as living things.[5] Attributes and functions of animate beings are transferred to the inanimate, as *living* water, the *living* rock, *quick*-silver, lively colours, couleur morte, bleu mourant, a living coal, dying embers; a comparison *stumbles;* an alley is *blind;* the ground *thirsts,* and *drinks in* the dew. By a reverse process, the life of vegetables is symbolically

[1] Heyse, p. 99.
[2] Σαλμυδησία γνάθος, Æsch. *Prom. V.* 571. Both Job and Sophocles talk of 'the eyelids of the morn,' Job iii. 9; and in Ps. cx. 3, we even have 'the womb of the morning.'
[3] Judg. ix. 37; Ezek. xxxviii. 12; Ps. lxxiv. 12; Soph. *Œ. T.*; Eur. *Med.*; Plin. iii. 12. It is hardly worth while to heap up references for the other instances; for 'tooth,' see 1 Sam. xiv. 4; Job xxxix. 28. For lip, Gen. xxii. 17, &c. *Heb.*
[4] Which the Greeks called a *dolphin* of lead. Thuc. vii. 41.
[5] Heyse quotes Grimm, *Gesch. d. deutsch. Sprache,* p. 56 ff.; Pott, *Metaphern vom Leben,* in Aufrecht und Kuhn's *Zeitschr.* ii. 2.

applied to the life of man; we talk of the scion of a noble *stock*; the *fruit* of good works; 'a rod of the *stem* of Jesse ;' a *seed* of thought; the *propagation* of the Gospel; a *green* memory and a *green* old age. We may notice, in passing, how powerfully the poetic instinct reproduces these tendencies of early language. What Mr. Ruskin has called 'the pathetic fallacy,' is the indomitable desire to see in Nature, or at least to attribute to her, a sympathy in our joys and sorrows, our hopes and fears. Hence, to the imaginations of the Psalmist and Prophet, 'the hills clap their hands, the valleys stand so thick with corn that they laugh and sing;' 'the morning stars shout for joy;' 'the mountains[1] skip like rams, and the little hills like young sheep;' the fir-trees howl, for the cedar is fallen; the raging waves of the sea foam out their own shame; the heavens declare the glory of God, and the firmament showeth his handywork; the sun is as a bridegroom going out of his chamber, and rejoiceth as a giant to run his course. In modern poets the same fancy recurs with constant intensity, so that there is hardly a single aspect of nature which has not been made to express or to interpret the thoughts and passions of mankind, and hardly a single modern poem which does not illustrate this imaginative power.

To the same source is due the universal prevalence of personification (or, as it is technically called, Prosopopœia) in ancient times. To many ancient nations

[1] It is curious to find the very same expressions in Chinese. 'Chu-king ait, Montes et colles pro gaudio tripudiant, volucres et bestiæ lætitiâ exultant et saltant ad citharæ sonum.' P. Premare, *Notitia Linguæ Sinicæ*, p. 243. I am aware, however, that Premare's theories may have led him to heighten the similarity. See Stanislas Julien, *Lao Tscu Tao-te-Ting*, pref.

the earth itself was a living creature, the stars were divine animals, and the very rainbow lived and drank the dew. No wonder that their

> Fancy fetched
> E'en from the blazing chariot of the Sun
> A beardless youth, who touched a golden lute,
> And filled the illumined groves with ravishment.

No wonder that, in their belief, an Oread danced on every hill, a Naiad lurked in every fountain, a Hamadryad lived or languished in every tree, and troops of Napæads and young Fauns or gamesome Satyrs sported among the forest glades, while

> On the level brine
> Sleek Panope and all her sisters played.

Mythology no less than language springs in great measure from these plays of a self-deceiving fancy. The primal men thought thus because they could not otherwise express their feelings, and they spoke thus because this inability to express themselves otherwise in turn reacted on their thoughts. Nor is Mythology unknown even in these days. We have long personified under the name of Nature the sum-total of God's laws as observed in the physical world; and now the notion of Nature as a distinct, living, independent entity seems to be ineradicable alike from our literature and our systems of Philosophy.

In the same manner human *relationships* are constantly attributed by analogy to external things. In Æschylus the Salmydessian harbour is a *stepmother* of ships; flame-smoke is the *sister* of fire; dust the *brother* of wind; and plunderings are the blood-relations of runnings to and fro. In Pindar, Autumn is the tender *mother* of the Vine stalk; and in Hipponax, the fig-tree is a sister of the vine. In the Semitic languages this figure occurs with astonishing frequency; e.g. in Hebrew and Arabic, sparks are the sons of fire, an arrow the son of a bow, a disease the firstborn of death; a sound from heaven is the daughter of a voice;[1] a brave man is a son of valour; an infant is the son of a year; a confirmed boy is a son of the law; a condemned criminal is a son of death; a bad woman is a daughter of worthlessness; lions are sons of haughtiness; a lynx is the son of howling; a vulture is the daughter of a wing.[2] The figure is more rare in modern poetry, yet Peele calls lightning 'the faire spouse of thunder,' and Tennyson says—

> Earn well the thrifty months, nor wed
> Raw Haste, *half-sister* to Delay.

But it is time to pass to still more important applications of the imaginative principle. It is not difficult to see how by its obvious aid man might, by the methods we have been observing, frame a nomenclature for all that he could see, or hear, or taste, or smell, or touch. But how was he to name the abstract, the ideal, the spiritual, the mental, the imponderable, the unseen? how to name the intuitions of the reason, the conclusions of the understanding, the thoughts of the mind, the yearnings of the spirit, the emotions and passions of the soul,—nay how was he even to find names for the reason, the understanding, the spirit, the mind, the soul themselves?

Could he have invented new terms? would any mystic

---

[1] Compare Milton,—
> 'Left that command
> Sole daughter of his voice.'

[2] For a large number of similar expressions in Arabic, especially in the names of birds and animals, see Bochart, *Hieroz.* vol. ii. p. 230.

'roots' have appeared by some inexplicable parthenogenesis in his intelligence? Whatever *might* have happened, this *did* not happen. Even if it had been possible to him, the instinctive dislike to needless neologisms, observable in every stage of the history of language, would have probably checked the development of such a power. At any rate the permutations and combinations of the few roots already supplied by onomatopœia and interjections, were found amply sufficient for the new purpose for which they were required; and this application of existing sounds was at once easier and more agreeable than a fresh exercise of the power of Invention. We see from hundreds of instances that even the misappropriation of an old term is greatly preferred to the elaboration of a new one. The Greek, whose commonest relish was boiled fish ὄψον (from ἕψω I boil), used this same word even when his relish happened to be garlic or cress; and he preferred to say a horse-comber of camels (ἱππόκομος καμήλων) to saying a camel-comber; and a hecatomb of twelve oxen (from ἕκατον = 100) rather than invent an accurate name. The Romans with their military proclivities called *any* interspace an *intervallum*, which properly meant a space between the stakes of a palisade. 'The silver pyxis' is quite a proper expression, though *pyxis* properly means a *box* made of *box*-wood. Homer does not hesitate to say ἰκτιδέη κυνέη, or helmet of weasel-skin, though *literally* the expression meant 'a weasel-skin dogskin,' just as 'ærea galea' would mean etymologically 'a brazen catskin.' In Exod. xxxviii. 8 we read of 'looking-*glasses* of brass' where the misapplication is as perfectly correct as the phrase 'a white blackbird,' because the word 'looking-brass' would be intolerably novel. Mr. Tennyson shocks no one by the line 'Whose blazing *wyvern weathercocked* [1] the spire.' The French talk of 'un cheval ferré d'argent' rather than compose a proper term for shoeing a horse with silver. A new name is *never* resorted [2] to unless it is absolutely essential and indispensable.

But quite independently of the necessity for finding articulate *sounds* to describe the phenomena of the mind—to express the strange unseen world of the Ego no less clearly than that of the Non-ego—there was another reason why all that was subjective should have been named by means of mere modifications of roots already acquired. For this shadowy unseen subjective world was *incapable of being known at all* except by analogy of those things of which we acquired a knowledge through the action of the senses. The mind, like the eye, becomes conscious of itself only by reflection from other things. We have seen already that men always explain and name the hitherto unknown by adopting the name of that known thing which most nearly resembles it; and that they seem incapable of understanding new phenomena except by the aid of such analogies as are supplied them by phenomena with which they are already familiar.[3] This may be an intellectual weakness, but it is one which recurs with the regularity of a law; and in the nomenclature of mental and spiritual entities it was inevitable, because those invisible things were only revealed and rendered cog-

[1] Unless it be by the verb! Imagine its being conjugated thus: I weathercock, thou weathercockest, he, she, weathercocks, &c.!

[2] Savage languages *specialise* everything because they have so few abstract terms; but it is a law of progressing language, to get rid of all exuberance, and to content itself with the fewest words possible.

[3] Charma, p. 258.

nisable by the things that are seen. 'It is a false assertion,' said Bacon[1] long ago, 'that the senses of man are a measure of all things; because on the contrary, all perceptions, of the senses no less than of the mind, are from the analogy of man, not from the analogy of the Universe. And the human intellect is presented like an unequal mirror to the rays of external things; it mingles its own nature with the nature of things, which it distorts and confuses.' And this remark is the same as that of Proclus, being in fact a mere truism— τὸ γίγνωσκον κατὰ τὴν ἑαυτοῦ γιγνώσκει φύσιν—'that which knows, knows in accordance with its own nature.'

Let us then see a few of the analogies which suggested a terminology for the world of mind.

It is strange to observe with what unanimity the names for the *soul* of man have been borrowed from the most obvious of invisible agencies,—the wind 'which bloweth where it listeth,' or possibly rather from the *breath* of life.[2] Thus in Hebrew, alike נֶפֶשׁ *nephesh*, the animal life (Job xii. 10), רוּחַ *ruach*, the human principle of life, and נְשָׁמָה *neshâmâh*, life considered as an inspiration of the Almighty,[3] all have the meaning of breath or wind; and therefore resemble the Greek words πνοή, πνεῦμα, and ψυχή, of which the latter is derived from ψύχω, I blow. The Latin words *animus*

---

[1] *Novum Organum*, i. 1, *aph.* 41; comp. Boethius, *De Consol. Phil.* 'Omne quod recipitur recipitur ad modum recipientis.'

[2] Just as 'blood' is often used for life, Lev. xvii. 2. See Gesenius, *Thesaurus*, ii. 901.

[3] Of these words *neshamah* is never, and *ruach* rarely (Eccl. iii. 21), applied to animals. In Gen. ii. 7, 'a living soul' should be rather 'a living animal,' or 'creature.' The Hindoos distinguish between *Brahmâtmah* and *jivâtmah*, 'the breath of God' and 'the breath of Life.'— Vide Bohlen, *Genes. ad l.*

and *anima*, the German *Geist*, and the English *ghost*, have the same origin. If we take other words of similar meaning, we shall still find them to have been derived from the analogy offered to the rapidity of thought by swift physical motion. Thus our 'soul,' the German '*Seele*,' is probably from the same root as the word Sea [1] and the Greek σείω; and the Greek θυμός comes from the root θύω, ἀπὸ τῆς θύσεως καὶ ζέσεως τῆς ψυχῆς.[2] Again, the word *reason*, ratio, oratio, the German *Rede*, &c., come from the Latin *reor*, which is in all probability connected with the Greek ῥέω, I flow; an etymology which, if correct, is curiously analogous to the derivation of 'soul' from the same root as the word 'sea.' If we enquire how men found a word for an act which most men consider so purely immaterial as that of *thinking*, we get to this result;—that, since thought is inconceivable and impossible without *signs* of some description, and since words are the most universal of signs, it has been assumed that there is an indissoluble unity between thought and speech. Hence in Hebrew אָמַר and דָּבָר mean first to speak and then to think, while שִׂיחַ and הָגָה pass through the meanings of (first) to think, and then to speak, sigh,[3] and murmur. Other words to express the same thing are derived from the notions of cutting (dividing, dissevering), seeing, and acting (compare *thing* and think, res and reor). The Greek φράζειν is to speak, φράζεσθαι, to say to oneself, i.e. to think, which, according to Forster, the South Sea Islanders express by 'speaking in the stomach.' In Latin, however, external

---

[1] See Heyse, p. 97.
[2] Plato, *Crat.* p. 419 c.
[3] The similarity of the Hebrew שִׂיחַ, and our sigh, is a noticeable instance of resemblance due to onomatopœia.

accidents of thought are selected to represent thought, as *considerare*, (perhaps) to fix the eyes on the stars, like our expression 'star gazing;' *deliberare*, to weigh in the balance, like the French *penser*, and our 'to weigh a matter;' *cogitare*, to act with the mind; and, among others *reor*, which Horne Tooke renders *I am thing-ed*,[1] (!) and which, if the Romans ever attached such an astonishing notion to it, would well deserve the title which Quinctilian[2] gives it of a 'verbum horridum.'

Again, the soul with its faculties, emotions, and desires is shadowed forth in language by the various parts of the body in which they were once supposed to be localised, or by which they are capable of being externally indicated.[3] Thus in Hebrew the heart, the *liver*, and the kidneys are used for the mind, and understanding; 'the bowels' means mercy, like the Greek σπλάγχνα; 'the flesh' means lust; the loins, strength; the *nose* is used for anger, so that 'long of nose' means patient, and 'short of nose' irritable; a 'man of lips' is a babbler (Job xi. 2); the *neck* is the symbol of obstinacy; the head of superiority; *thirst* or *paleness* the picturesque representatives of fear. In Greek the diaphragm (φρήν, *renes*, reins) is used for the understanding; the liver for feeling; the breast for courage, the nostrils for contempt (cf. μυκτῆρες, &c.); the stomach and the bile for anger. Similarly in Latin, the nostrils are used for taste and refinement; the nose for satire;[4] the eyebrow for sorrow or disdain; the stomach for anger; the

---

[1] *Diversions of Purley*, ii. 5.

[2] Quintilian, *Instt.* viii. 3.

[3] See numberless passages in Glass. *Philolog. Sacra*, p. 866 sqq.

[4] Homo obesae, or emunctae naris in Horace, &c. In Turkestan, 'to be long-nosed' means to be proud. See Vámbéry's *Travels*.

throat for gluttony. The Lithuanians use the same word for soul, heart, and stomach; and the same is probably true of many nations. Many of these metaphors have been transferred to English, and we also use the blood for passion (hot, or young blood), the phlegm for dulness, the spleen for envy; we say that a person has *sanguine* hopes; we talk of a melancholy man, which means properly a man whose bile is black; a man has a nervous style, or is nervous in the hour of trial; and we say of a bitter-minded critic that he has too much gall. The words 'body' or 'head' are common in all languages to express personality. The North American Indians constantly use 'body' in speaking of themselves, just as the Greeks used δέμας and κάρα; 'c'est un plaisant corps' is a common expression in French; and in English, 'head' has even passed into compounds such as boy-hood, widowhood, and 'so much a-head.'

We are again reminded of the analogy between speech and writing. Tzetzes has preserved the following valuable fragment of Chœremon on Hieroglyphics.[1] 'For joy,' he says, 'they paint a woman playing on a drum; for misfortune, an eye weeping; for non-possession, two empty hands outstretched; for rising, a snake coming out of a hole; for setting, the same going in; for return to life, a frog; for the soul, a hawk, and the same for the sun, and for God; . . . for a king, a bee;—for the earth, a bull;—a boy signifies increase;—an old man, decay; a bow, sharp force; and there are a thousand other such.' We know, from modern researches,[2] that a cynocephalus stood for anger, a hand with a pair of oars

---

[1] Quoted in Sharpe's *Egypt. Hieroglyphics.*
[2] *Encycl. Britan.*, art. *Hieroglyphic.*

for a workman, a crux ansata and serpent for immortal, and so on in an endless series of metaphorical pictures.

It is a proof of the extent of metaphor that almost every *colour* recalls at once its emblematic meaning.[1] Black is indissolubly connected with notions of death, mourning, villany, and misfortune; white with innocence, candour, and festivity; rose-colour with beauty and freshness; purple with magnificence, luxury, and pride; red and scarlet and crimson with shame, and sin, and crime; yellow with old age, decay, and jealousy; green with springtime, vigour, and youth.

It might have been supposed that if there were any one domain of language, however restricted, from which Metaphor no less than Onomatopœia must necessarily be excluded, it would be the names of numbers. Yet what do we find on examination? Rapidly as they come to be regarded as abstractions, the signs of the *most* abstract conceptions, yet they like all other abstractions were once living metaphors, images borrowed from natural phenomena. Thus *five* (the same word precisely as cinq, cinque, quinque, πέντε, the Gothic *fimf*, the German *funf*, &c.) is derived from the Sanskrit *pâni*, a hand; just as in Celebes, and among various Indian tribes, the words for 'hand' and 'five,' or sometimes the words for 'hand' and 'two,' are identical. In Chinese *ny* and *ceul*, 'two,' also mean 'ears.' The Abiponian word for four is *gejenknatè*, which means the foot of an ostrich, from its four toes.[2] The name *mille*, a thousand, is in all probability connected with *milium*,[3] millet

---

[1] See Pott, *Etym. Forsch.* ii. 263 fg., where many illustrations are given.
[2] Pott, *Zählmethode*, p. 4; Pictet, *Les Orig. Ind.* ii. 578.
[3] This is at least as probable as the derivation from μύριοι. Dr. Donaldson, *Varron*. p. 263, connects it with *miles*, ὀμ-ιλία. Festus

grass, from the same root as mola, mill, &c., which are of onomatopoetic origin. It is therefore a metaphor of the liveliest description. The Greek χίλιοι is derived by some etymologists from χῖλος a heap of fodder,¹ χέω I pour, &c. Myriad is derived from the imitative root *mur*, which we find in murmur, the Greek μύρω, I pour, &c. The syllable *tama*, which in Galla forms the compounds of ten, is derived by Professor Pott from *tahamet*, hair, and Gilj² informs us that the Orinoko Indians touch their hair to indicate a large number, just as the Abipons heap up handfuls of grass, or handfuls of sand. The Mexicans used the word *tzontli*, 'hair,' for 400, and their hieroglyphic for 200 is half a feather. Their word for 8,000, *xiquipilli*, means 'sack,' because they had sacks which would exactly contain that number of cacao grains. In Chinese the word *tome*, which means 1,000, is borrowed from a root meaning 'mist,' and therefore resembles the Latin phrase 'Nubes peditum,' and a 'cloud of witnesses.' In Sanskrit the word *jaladhi*, 'ocean,' is used for 100 crores of lacs of rupees. The morbid imagination of the Hindoos made them familiar with excessive numbers, and though they formed some compound up to a million (pra-yu-ta), with the syllable *yu* to add, yet for numbers like 10 billions they were obliged to resort to symbols such as *padma* or *abja*, 'lotus,' from the extreme fecundity of this plant,

states that *milium* comes from *mille*, but obviously the reverse of this is the fact. L. Benloew, *ubi infra*, p. 68.

¹ Donaldson, *Varron. ib.* It is connected with a Sanskrit root, *Hila*, seed.

² 'Si toccano i lor capelli in alto di stupore.' Gilj, ii. 332, quoted by L. Benloew, *Recherches sur l'Origine des Noms de Nombre*, p. 64. Many of the particulars about numbers here mentioned are borrowed from Pott's *Zählmethode*, p. 120, &c.

of which the fruit produces millions of grains. In Egyptian a lotus-leaf attached to its stem was the sign for 1,000.[1] The Greek ψῆφος, the Latin *calculus* both recall the day when numeration was impossible without the aid of pebbles. If we examine the Semitic numerals we find a repetition of the same facts.[2] For instance the Hebrew *eleph* meaning 1,000, is properly a herd of oxen, and possibly there may be an allusion to this meaning in the punning speech of Samson after his victory at Ramath-lehi; *meâh* 100 is not improbably derived from *mo* water; *shibnâh* 7 is considered by Dr. Mommsen to mean 'a finger' from a root 'to point,' because after counting five on his left hand, and beginning the number six with the thumb of the *right* hand, the forefinger or indicator would be seventh in order;[3] *shenayîm* 'two' was doubtless suggested, like the name and form of the letter *shin* itself, from *shén* 'a tooth, either from the bicuspid teeth or the double row in the mouth which may also account for the invariable dual form of the word for teeth in Hebrew. Strange as this may sound it admits of many parallels. In Thibet and Java 'two' is expressed by *paksha*[4] a wing, or by other

---

[1] I must again refer to the able and interesting pamphlet of M. L. Benloew, who has however borrowed most of his facts from Prof. Pott.

[2] We may here observe that whatever may be the apparent resemblance of the Sanskrit *éka* 'one' to the Hebrew *echâd*, and the Sanskrit *shash* 'six' to the Hebrew *shesh*, it is nearly certain (in spite of Dr. Donaldson's authority in *Maskil le Sopher*, p. 42 sqq.; *New Cratylus*, pp. 187, 194 sqq.) that the resemblance is *merely* apparent, and purely accidental. It is not indeed *impossible* that the Aryans borrowed from the Semites the *single* number *saptan* seven (Hebr. שִׁבְעָה) from its mystery and importance in the Semitic system. The reader may see the question clearly discussed in M. Benloew's pamphlet, p. 95, &c.

[3] Hofer's *Zeitschr.* i. 262; quoted by Dr. Donaldson, *Maskil le Sopher*, p. 42. [4] Pott, l.c.

members which are double as *báhu* arm, *vétra* eye, &c. Among the Samoieds between the Yenisei and the Lena, the Sioux Indians, &c., two is expressed by 'hand' for the same reason. The history of the Hebrew word *gnashtei* 'eleven' is very curious; from *gnáshath* to labour comes *gnashtoth* a thought, and thence comes, according to Simonis, the word for *eleven*, meaning ten counted on the fingers and one in thought.[1] In English the word *score* is from the root *Sciran* to shear, because 'our unlearned ancestors to avoid the embarrassment of large numbers, when they had made twice ten notches, cut off the piece or *Talley* (Taglié) containing them; and afterwards counted the scores or pieces cut off.'[2] If then in a region so unpromising as that of numbers we find it so easy to trace the influence of onomatopœia and metaphor where need we despair? May we not infer the origin of words in cases which are doubtful, from their origin in cases which are proved? May we not say with De Maistre, ' Ce qu'on sait dans ce genre prouve beaucoup, à cause de l'induction qui en résulte, pour les autres cas: ce qu'on ignore, au contraire, ne prouve rien excepté l'ignorance de celui qui cherche.'

[1] Gesenius, *Thes.* s. v. [2] *Diversions of Purley*, ii. 4.

CHAPTER XX.

METAPHOR *continued.*—METAPHOR IN VARIOUS LANGUAGES.

> 'Among these, fancy next
> Her office holds, of all external things
> Which the five watchful senses represent,
> She forms imaginations, aery shapes,
> Which reason joining, or disjoining, frames
> All what we affirm or what deny, and call
> Our knowledge and opinion.'
> MILTON, *Par. Lost*, v. 105.

THE pictorial Metaphors with which all languages abound become obscured in course of time under the wearing and modifying processes of literary cultivation, into 'a mass of arbitrary, opaque, uninteresting conventionalisms.' But the more ancient, and the more uncivilised a language is, the fewer are its abstractions, and the more numerous are its undisguised metaphors. These metaphors, no less than those of every poet, are due to the spontaneous and unconscious[1] play of the fancy and the imagination. An abridged personification, says J. P. Richter,[2] is the natural and necessary language of savage life. In modern languages it is by no means always possible to trace the sensuous image underlying

---

[1] Heyse, p. 100. Steinthal, *Urspr. d. Sprache*, p. 27.
[2] J. Paul Richter, *Aesthetik*, § 56.

every word which implies conceptions incapable of any but a symbolical expression. But in such a language as Arabic we may still see what the condition of every language *must* once have been. There the dominion of fancy and poetry is still obvious, and every word is a picture of which the colours are still bright and clear; with us the power of abstraction is riper, and the sensuous element has left nothing more than the *traces* of its former prevalence.

In fact a style abounding in metaphors is now generally accepted as a proof of weakness, since for an advanced stage of thought it is necessary as far as possible to attach to each word one clear meaning, as little mingled as possible with mere external analogies. Bergmann tells us that the turns of phraseology which the Kalmucks most admire in their own language 'are precisely those which a more advanced civilisation, and a corresponding development of taste, would reject as spurious.' Similarly, 'the Koran is held by the devout Mahommedan to be the most admirable model of composition; but exactly those ornaments of diction and imagery, which he regards as the jewels of the whole, are most entirely in the childish taste of imperfect civilisation.' The gorgeous luxury of Oriental prose would with us be thought extravagant even in the most elaborate poetry, and we have long got beyond the stage which makes it almost impossible for an Oriental even to find a title for a book without calling it a mirror, a flower, or a pearl.

A glance at the metaphors of some Semitic, Aryan, and Allophylian nations will perhaps illustrate and relieve our subject.

In Hebrew the paucity of words necessitates the constant use of metaphor. 'The Hebrew has scarcely any individuated words. Ask a Hebrew scholar if he has any word for a *ball* (as a tennis ball, pila lusoria); he says, "O yes." What is it then? Why he gives you the word for *globe*. Ask for *orb*, for *sphere*, &c. Still you have the same answer. The individual circumstantiations are swallowed up in the general outline.'[1] This latter instance is rather *catachresis* than metaphor; i.e. it is rather the application of the *same* word to different things, than the direct suggestion of a comparison. But we can best see the rapid working of metaphor in the extraordinary diversities of meaning of which the same Hebrew word[2] is capable. Take for instance the word תּוֹר (Tōr), which means a turtle-dove, an ox, 'a string of pearls,' a turn, and a manner? Or again take the word גּוּר (*goor*); in its meaning of 'a lion's whelp' we see the imitative principle again at work; but how comes the *verb*, *goor*, to acquire the meanings to sojourn, to assemble, to be afraid, to reverence, to worship? Or take the word עָרַב *gnârabh*, which in its various conjugations means to mix, to exchange, to stand in the place of, to pledge, to interfere, to be familiar; and also to disappear, to set, and to do a thing in the evening; besides all this, with various vowel modifications the same three letters mean 'to be sweet,' a fly, or beetle, an Arabian, a stranger, the weft of cloth, the evening, a willow, and a raven. Assuming that all these significations are ultimately deducible

---

[1] De Quincey *on Language*, Works, viii. 81. To this is due the extreme uncertainty of rendering many Hebrew words.
[2] 'Non est mirum doctissimos etiam Judæorum hodie nihil certi de rerum nominibus, ut animalium, plantarum, metallorum, vestium, instrumentorum, docere posse.' Gesner, *Hist. Quadrup.*

from one and the same root, we see at once the extent to which metaphor must have been at work. In most instances the steps of the transition have vanished. In Hebrew the same word means *fatness* and *ashes*;[1] perhaps this may be because the ancients used ashes for manure; but who shall tell us with any certainty why לְבַב means 'to become wise,' and לְבֵּב to make cakes?

Again, all Hebrew *literature* abounds in metaphor. Glassius in his laborious *Philologia Sacra* (pp. 807–912) has collected innumerable examples of metaphor drawn from the sun, and moon, and stars; from the times of the day and night; from fire, air, and water; from the body, the life, the senses, and the actions of men; and in short from almost every observable phenomenon of nature and of life. To take one set of phenomena alone, the mere names of the vine, the olive, the cedar, the lion, the wolf, the serpent, the fox, the horse, the heifer, the goat, the sheep will call up at once in the memory of the Biblical student the bold metaphors with which they are associated. Christ is 'the true vine,' 'the branch,' 'the Lion of the tribe of Judah,' and 'the Lamb that was slain;' Herod is 'that fox;' Esau is 'a wild ass of a man;'[2] 'without are dogs,' and the Gentiles are 'dogs;' Satan is 'a serpent,' and 'a roaring lion;' the Cretans are 'evil beasts.'

With the use of metaphor in Aryan languages we are familiar, and therefore choosing the Greek tragedians as our storehouse of illustrations, we may from

---

[1] Plin. xvii. 9. Gesen. *Thes.* s. v. יָשֵׁן

[2] Compare the Sanskrit *nara-sinha* man-lion, and 'two lion-like men of Moab.' 2 Sam. xxiii. 20.

their pages glean the further fact that in the metaphors of a language we may always learn the habits, the amusements, and the tastes of a nation. For no metaphors are so common among these Athenians as the very ones which we should *expect* to be most frequently before their minds, namely those derived from hunting, and from rowing. Θηρᾶν 'to hunt' comes to be a mere ornate word for 'to pursue.' Thus Xerxes desires 'to hunt Athens' (*Pers.* 229); an ambitious man 'hunts for the tyranny' (*Œd. Tyr.* 540); 'it is not right to hunt impossibilities' (*Ant.* 92); 'they will have come to hunt after marriages which cannot be hunted' (*Prom. Vinct.* 860). Nautical metaphors are still more frequent. As for ἐρέσσειν 'to row' we have it in all kinds of conjunctions; we hear of 'rowing a plan' (*Ant.* 159); to row with another is to aid him (*Aj.* 1307); the two Sons of Atreus row threatenings (*Id.* 246); 'row round your heads the tabouring of your hands' (*Sept. c. Theb.* 836). A fair wind from a person's eyes wafts away a lukewarm friend (*Trach.* 812); we even are told of 'the harbour of a cry,' 'the prow of the heart,' and 'the rudders of horses.' The Greeks are generally supposed to have had little or no sympathy with external nature, yet the euphemistic pleasure which they display in the incessant use of the word 'blossom' (ἄνθος), no less than their fondness for garlands, shows that they were far from being dead to impressions of natural beauty. 'Disease *blooms* forth upon the flesh. The nightingale is shrouded in a *bloomy bower of woes.* The hoariness of old age is a white *blossoming.*[1] The misfortunes of a noble family

---

[1] Cf. Eccl. xii. 5.

are made to burst forth *into bloom.* The haughty speech is the *efflorescence* of the lips. Groans are the *flowers* plucked from the tree of anguish, and the chanters of the funeral dirge shower these upon the bier; so that not only the custom but the very language of the Greeks, veiled as it were the deformity of death, and scattered the corpse with flowers.'[1]

Before leaving the subject of Aryan metaphors we may further observe that the metaphors of a writer, no less than those of a nation, always carry upon them the strong mark of his own individuality,—as for instance the constantly recurring 'bow' and 'wings' in the *Divina Commedia* of Dante; and that the metaphors most frequently adopted at any particular epoch stamp with terrible energy the characteristics of the age. Take for instance the commencement of the *Christiade* by F. Hojeda:—

> Canto al Hijo de Dios, humano y muerto
> Con dolores y afrentas por el hombre:
> Musa divina, en su costado abierto
> Baña mi lengua y muevela en su nombre,—

'I sing the Son of God, who was man and died for man amid anguish and insults; divine Muse, *steep my tongue in his open side,* and make it move in his name.' Well may M. Arnould,[2] from whom I quote the lines, ask whether any one but a Spanish monk in the time of Philip the Second could ever have written them!

If we now turn to the metaphors in use among

---

[1] Boyes, p. liv. Mr. Boyes has so amply and so happily illustrated this subject of the metaphors in Greek tragedy, that in this paragraph I found all that I wanted done to my hand.

[2] *Ess. de Théorie et d'Hist. Lit.* p. 203.

savage races we shall find them still more distinct and picturesque. Take for instance a few specimens of *Kafir* metaphors.¹ *Ingcala* 'flying ant' means 'great dexterity;' *inja* 'dog' means a dependant; *quanka* 'to be snapped asunder' means 'to be quite dead;' *zikhla* 'to eat oneself' means 'to be proud,' and therefore is an exact parallel to Mr. Tennyson's expression,—

Upon himself, himself did feed.

'He is a wolf' means 'he is greedy;' 'he is an ox' means 'he is strong.'²

Some of the *Malay* metaphors are very lively. Thus *mabuk-ombak* 'sea-sick' means properly 'wave-drunk;' *mata-ari* 'the sun' is literally 'the eye of day;' *mata-kaki* 'the ankle' is 'the eye of the foot;' *mata-ayar* 'a spring' is 'the eye of water' (compare the Hebrew עין). The expression for an 'affront' is '*charcoal on the face*;' a key is the 'child of a lock;' a knee-pan is the '*cocoanut of the knee*;' malice is 'rust of the heart;' sincerity 'a white heart,' like the Latin 'candidum ingenium;' impudent is 'face of board.'³

Scarcely less ingenious are the metaphors in *Chinese*. 'Capricious' is expressed by 'three mornings, four evenings;' cunning or persuasive speech by 'convenient hind-teeth, ready front-teeth;' 'disagreement' by 'you East, I West;' attention by 'fine-heart.' *Neng* 'a bear' means 'powerful;' '*hao* 'a boar' is 'a brave man;' *non* 'the roar of water among stones' is 'anger.'⁴

---

¹ Appleyard's *Kafir Grammar*, p. 71. Some of these are quoted by Prof. M. Müller, in his Second Series of Lectures. I had however made a note of these long before I saw them there.
² Appleyard, p. 128.
³ Crawfurd's *Malay Gram. and Dict.* i. 62.
⁴ Premare, *Not. Ling. Sin.* p. 242.

We encounter once more in Chinese the phenomenon which we have observed in Hebrew, in the number of different meanings possessed by the same root; a phenomenon not solely but *mainly* explicable by the influence of metaphor. For instance, *chou* means a book, a tree, great heats, Aurora, and the loss of a wager;[1] *Oû* means 'me,' and also an orator, nothing, a bat, and a kind of tree;[2] Yû means 'me,' and also to agree, to rejoice, a kind of measure, stupid, a black ox, &c.; Yù 'thou' means also milk, tender, to eat, honey-cake; Y 'he' or 'she' is also to laugh in spite of oneself, to sigh, a new-born infant, respect, a stout dog, &c.; Tchy the sign of the genitive means also it, him, branches, to sustain, yellow fruit, a dead tree, and a labourer![3]

We must here digress for a moment to remove a misconception. It has been the fashion to compare these homonyms with others which have not the remotest connection with them. Thus we have seen (in the note) that the sound 'cent' has six different meanings in French, but these words had *no* original connection with each other, since *cent* comes from centum, *sans* from sine, *sang* from sanguis, *sent* from sentit, *sens* from sensus, *sont* from sunt, and *s'en* from se inde.[4] Thus *aune* means an alder-tree and an ell,

---

[1] The missionary Bourgeois, in his *Lettres édifiantes*, bitterly complains of the consequent difficulty which he experienced in learning Chinese.

[2] It might be supposed that such a multiplicity of homonyms would introduce endless confusion into a language. Practically, however, such is not the case; e.g. in French the words cent, sang, s'en, sans, sent, sont, sens, widely different as is their meaning, are never confused. It is the same in English with heir, ere, e'er, air, and Ayr, &c.

[3] Benloew, *De quelques Caractères du Lang. Prim.* p. 41.

[4] Heyse, 210, 220. Similarly we have *vers* 'towards,' from *versus*;

but in the former meaning it comes from *alnus*, in the latter from *ulna*; Hail! as a salutation in English is the German *heil*, but as congealed water-drops it is the German Hagel; pêcher 'a peach' is Malus *Persica*, pêcher 'to fish' is from *piscari*, and pêcher 'to sin' from *peccare*; *tour* 'a tower' is from turris, and when it means 'a turn' i. e. a walk, it is from a late vulgar sense of tornare; *louer* 'to praise' is from *laudare*, louer 'to let' from *locare*. These instances are only false analogies of those which we have been considering. They are accidental, being due merely to the phonetic corruption or disorganisation of a language in its advance; whereas those in Hebrew, Chinese, or Coptic are truly primordial and arose from that indetermination which characterises every primitive language,—an indetermination which it is the object of every cultivated language to mould into gradual precision.

There are certain dialects or languages spoken by whole classes of men in all countries, yet unowned by any nation. Such are the Italian *gergo, furbesco*; the Spanish *germania*; the Portuguese *Calāō*; the German *rothwelsch* (red Italian?); the Dutch *bargoens* or *dieventael*; the English *cant, slang, thieves' Latin, pedlar's French, St. Giles's Greek, flash-tongue, gibberish*, &c.; the French *narquois* or *Argot*. This language of crime and misery—'this pustulous vocabulary of which each word seems an unclean ring of a monster of mud and darkness,' is formed—(and the

---

vers 'a verse,' from *versus*; *verre* 'glass,' from *vitrum*; *ver* 'a worm,' from *vermis*; *vère* 'truly' (in old French), from *veré*. In fact, so numerous are these *homonyms*, that in 1807 a *Dictionnaire des Homonymes* was published in Paris by M. de la Madelaine. Charma, p. 272. An interesting list of English homonyms may be found in Dwight's *Mod. Philolog.* ii. 311.

same remark applies partially to the harmless *lingua franca* of the Mediterranean, the *Ligoa geral* of South America, the Chinese pigeon-English, the Haytian French, the jargons of the Bastaards of Africa, the Canadian half-breeds, and the English, French, and Chinooks in Columbia)[1]—by the adoption of foreign words, by the absolute suppression of grammar, by grotesque tropes, wild catachresis, and allegoric metonymy. The study of these corrupt dialects is a most fruitful field for the philologist, and suggests many of the primitive expedients and tendencies of language. But Metaphor is the widest and most important basis of them all, and it is adopted conventionally for the express purpose of disguise and concealment. The words chosen are all from the vernacular, but the senses are entirely different, and are all allegorical. Borrow points this out in his book on the Gipsies, and M. Michel,[2] who has thought the Argot worthy of a serious historian, and who is the greatest authority on the subject, says, 'La métaphore et l'allégorie semblent former en effet *l'élément principal* de ce langage. . . . Un fait qui ne saurait manquer de frapper un esprit philosophique à l'aspect de ce dialecte, *c'est que partout l'argot est basé sur le même principe, c'est-à-dire sur la métaphore*; et à cet égard toutes les branches de

---

[1] See specimens in Latham, *Var. of Man*, p. 320; Appleyard, *Kafir Gram.* p. 10; Nodier, *Notions de Linguistique*; Hutchinson, *Ten Years among the Ethiopians*, pp. 21–32, &c.

[2] *Etudes de Philologie Comparée sur l'Argot*, par F. Michel; Paris, 1856. Victor Hugo dwells on it in *Les Misérables, Le Dernier Jour d'un Condamné*, and *Notre Dame de Paris*; and it is also touched on in Vidocq, Eugène Sue, &c. There are several English slang dictionaries, &c., beginning as far back as the year 1560; and also in other languages, as *Studii sulle Lingue Furbesche*, Milan, 1846.

ce jargon se ressemblent.'[1] Again, M. Victor Hugo, whose splendidly powerful chapters on this subject in *Les Misérables* are well worth the study of the Philologer, says, 'Slang is nothing but a vestibule, in which language having some wicked action to commit, disguises itself. It puts on these *masks of words, these rags of metaphors*. In this way it becomes horrible and can scarcely be recognised. The metaphors say everything and conceal everything. The devil becomes "the baker." "Les sorgueurs sont sollicer les guils à la lune," "the prowlers are going to steal horses at night." This passes before the mind like a group of spectres, and we know not what we see.'

Metaphor then is universal, and the Imagination plays a prominent part in every form of human language. It is in their earliest dawn (as we have seen already) that languages are most metaphorical. As civilisation advances, the fancy, to which the origin of the word was due, is forgotten altogether, or remains a dead letter to the popular consciousness even when the etymology of the word is known.[2] The intermediate factor vanishes, and the word appears as the immediate expression of the representation in its totality. To take one or two instances out of thousands: the word 'caprice' is in very common use, and is a word to which a most definite meaning is attached; yet out of the myriads who use it correctly how many are distinctly aware that it is a metaphor derived from the swift, short

---

[1] Michel, *ubi supra*, pp. i., xxiv. The singular points of resemblance in the Argots of different nations are pointed out by Biondelli, *Studii Linguistici*, in a very interesting paper, *Origine, Diffusione, ed Importanza delle Lingue Furbesche*, pp. 107–120.

[2] Heyse, 164.

leaps of the wild goat on the hills[1] (*capra*, compare αἴξ from ἀΐσσω), just as the Italian *nuce* comes from *nucia* a goat, and *ticchio* a freak from *ziki* a kid, and the French *verve* from vervex a bell-wether? Or again how often do people when they 'make a stipulation' recall the fact that the origin of the expression is a custom, dead for centuries, of giving a straw in sign of a completed bargain? or when they talk of money remember that the word is derived from the accident that gold and silver were coined by the Romans[2] in the temple of Juno Moneta? We speak of muskets without being aware that the word is ultimately derived from the onomatopœia *musso* I buzz, whence come *musca* a fly, *muscatus* speckled, *muscheta* a sparrow-hawk, and hence a musket;[3] we talk of varnish without recalling the golden tresses of Berenice;[4] of intoxication with no reference to the poison with which arrows were once smeared; of a dunce without any intentional insult to the memory of Duns Scotus; of a poltroon with no allusion to being maimed in the thumb; of a saunterer

---

[1] See Diez, s. v. *Capriccio*; Scheler, s. v. Mr. Wedgwood, with less probability, connects the word with the roots *riccio*, *ericius* (a hedgehog), *hérisser*, φρίσσειν. *Etym. Dict.* s. v.

[2] Probably the Romans thought just as little of the interesting historic fact fossilised in the word *pecunia*; and the Greeks of that involved in the derivation of ὄβολος, which shows that money was first used in ingots (βέλος).

[3] This derivation seems at least as probable as the one suggested by Mr. Wedgwood. The Italians called their muskets, &c., by the names of hawks, falconetto, sagro, &c.; compare the French sacre, couleuvrine, &c. The Italian *terzuolo*, a pistol, properly means a male hawk, perhaps from the fancy that the third bird in a nest was a male, or because the male was one third smaller than the female.

[4] This word, however, is disputed. It may come from the city Berenice, where amber-coloured nitre was found, or from *vitrinus* glassy. See Diez, s. v. *Vernice*, ed. Donkin.

with no reference to the Holy Land; and not to multiply instances which any one can find in hundreds for himself, we go on ending our year with the months of *September, October, November,* and *December,* without once troubling ourselves with the consideration that the months are really the 9th, 10th, 11th, and 12th, and that our nomenclature merely continues to embalm an error of Romulus nearly three thousand years ago.

This complete evanescence of the original meaning of words and phrases gives rise to that *confusion* of metaphors which is so common in every literature. There is perhaps in careful writers too pedantic a scruple against ever mingling two conceptions originally distinct. We are not of course advocating such reckless intermixtures as Lord Castlereagh's 'My Lords, the main *feature* on which this *question* hinges,' or as that by the poetic young tradesman, quoted by Coleridge, who said that sorrows

> Round my heart's leg tie their galling chain.

But when Milton wrote in one of his finest sonnets

> I bate no jot
> Of heart or hope but still bear up, and steer
> *Uphillward,*

we cannot but regret that the mere confusion of metaphor involved in the words 'steer uphillward'[1] would have made him alter that fine expression into the much

---

[1] Comp. *Sams. Agonistes*:
'I hear
The tread of many feet *steering* this way.'
Probably the metaphor is a reminiscence of Euripides, *Iph. Taur.* 266:
ἄκροισι δακτύλοισι πορθμεύων ἴχνος.
The word πορθμεύω might have been added to the naval metaphors before alluded to, for Euripides employs it constantly.

tamer phrase 'Right onward.' Who is annoyed by the confusion involved in Mark vii. 21, 22, *Out of the heart* proceed evil thoughts, &c., '*an evil eye*;' or in 1 Tim. vi. 19, 'Laying up *in store* a good *foundation*' (ἀποθησαυρίζοντες); or in 2 Cor. v. 2, 'to be *clothed* upon with our *house*;' or in 2 Tim. ii. 26, 'that they may recover themselves (lit. *grow sober*, ἀνανήψωσι) from the *snare* of the devil?'[1] The greatest poets have not been the most careful to avoid these incongruities. Æschylus talks of '*a beacon-light* being a lucky *throw of the dice*'[2] for a sentinel. Horace says

> Urit enim fulgore suo, qui *prægravat* artes
> Infra se positas.

And Shakspeare, to say nothing of his 'taking up arms against a sea of troubles,'[3] shows in every play his lordly disregard of mere pedantic conventionalities in the way of accuracy. This passage, 'extrait d'une pièce intitulée La Tempête,' particularly offends the critical sense of M. Varinot, the author of the *Dictionnaire des Métaphores*.[4]

> The charm dissolves apace,
> And as the morning *steals* upon the night
> *Melting* the darkness, so their rising senses
> Begin to *chase* the *ignorant fumes* that *mantle*
> Their clearer reason.

What English reader with ordinary breadth of understanding, found anything to jar upon his mind in this

---

[1] Glass. *Phil. Sacr.* p. 919.

[2] τρὶς ἐξ βαλούσης τῆσδ' ἐμοὶ φρυκτωρίας. *Agam.* 33.

[3] 'No image of the sea is suggested; and arms, incongruous in relation to the literal sea, is not so in relation to a multitude; besides that the image *arms* itself evanesces for the same reason into *resistance*.' De Quincey, *Works*, vii. 121 (Black's ed.).

[4] *Paris*, 1819.

passage? Yet listen to the groan of the French critic!
'Il y a là tant de choses mal-assorties, que l'esprit ne
peut rien voir avec clarté. Le matin qui se *glisse* fur-
tivement sur l'obscurité, et qui en même temps la *fond,*
les esprits des hommes qui *chassent des fumées,* des
fumées *ignorantes,* et des *fumées* qui *voilent.* Un
poète peint un *ange* (!!) qui franchit les airs, et le
représente au même moment comme étant à cheval, et
comme *faisant voile* sur le *sein* de l'air. Il est impossible que l'imagination se forme un tableau net d'objets
aussi confus.' Poor outraged historian of French metaphors! and what a drunken savage Shakspeare must
have been!

Many have bewailed the necessity of metaphor as the
source of constant error, and the strongest proof of the
weakness of our intellectual faculties. 'Verborum trans-
latio,' says Cicero, 'constituta est inopiæ causâ.'[1] Undoubtedly it is so; but with such faculties as we *have,*
metaphor, and the necessity for the metaphoric element
in language, becomes fruitful of blessings.[2] It becomes
a means whereby we observe and compare the analogous
phenomena of the physical and intellectual world. It
adds something of the grace, and charm, and mystery
of nature to the thoughts of man. It is the very essence
of our most poetical conceptions, and the best mode of
shadowing forth our profoundest intuitions. 'Thought,'
says the eloquent and ingenious Du Ponceau, 'is vast as
the air; it embraces far more than languages can express; or rather, languages *express* nothing. They only
make thought flash in electric sparks from the speaker

---

[1] Cic. *De Oratore,* iii. 39. Cf. Seneca, *De Beneficiis,* ii. 34, &c.

[2] See this subject more fully discussed in the *Origin of Language,*
p. 136 sqq.

to the hearer. A single word creates a crowd of conceptions, which the intellect combines and marshals with lightning-like rapidity.'[1]

It is idle therefore to complain that metaphor supposes a certain indigence, and that if the intellect were endowed with the power of directly and immediately seizing any phenomenon, and of providing an independent expression for every modification of our minds, it would be unnecessary to drag ourselves from one analogous idea to another.[2] Obviously we must take the mind as we find it; and since it has *not* been endowed with the power of direct intuition into the nature of things it cannot dispense with tropes and allegories; which so far from hindering and obscuring our power of insight, are, on the contrary, its mightiest assistants.[3] In the true and etymological sense of the word, they *illustrate*, i.e. they pour a flood of light upon our thoughts. And, reversing the metaphor, we may say with equal truth, that they are the gracious clouds, through whose vail it is alone possible for us to gaze upon the too-dazzling sun.

A Language without figures and metaphors would of necessity be a language without poetry. We have already shown the truth of this assertion[4] by comparing the language of *Science* with the language of common life. It will be interesting to illustrate it further by taking the instance of any 'philosophical language'

---

[1] Ét. du Ponceau, *Syst. Gram. des Langues de l'Amérique*, p. 32.

[2] Charma, p. 100.

[3] See Arist. *Rhet.* III. i. 2. In fact they perform in language something of the same function as the symbolic actions of orators or poets. They make our thoughts more clear, graphic, vivid.

[4] *Origin of Lang.* p. 134 sqq.

framed in strict accordance with these supposed principles of perfection.

'Une langue philosophique!' says Du Ponceau, 'bon Dieu, qu'est-ce qu'une langue philosophique? . . . une langue philosophique! et pourquoi non un monde, une création tout entière de la main et de la façon des philosophes?' There have however been several attempts at languages framed on these accurate principles, intended by their inventors to serve as an unerring medium of communication among all nations.[1] The seventeenth century seems to have been particularly fertile in them. A German prince offered a reward of 300 crowns for the best universal language, and Becker wrote in consequence his *Notitia Linguarum universalis*. The prince repaid him by compliments, and asked him to dinner, 'which was more,' says Du Ponceau, 'than the thing was worth.' It was published in 1661 at Frankfort, and is now very rare. In the same year was published Dalgarno's *Ars Signorum, vulgo Character universalis*. Lond. 1661.[2] It is founded on the assumption that there has been a complete and certain distribution of all things and ideas. A few years after (in 1668) appeared the celebrated *Essay towards a Philosophical Language* of Bishop Wilkins, occupying an enormous folio volume. Its ingenuity was undoubted, and 'uni-

---

[1] M. Charma, pp. 290-300, gives a long list of writers who have touched on this subject, as Herm. Hugo, Bacon, Des Cartes, Dalgarno, Wilkins, Becker, Kircher, Jo. Voss, Leibnitz, De Brosses, Changeux, De Maimieux, Destrutt de Tracy, Laromiguière, Grosselin, &c. See especially Degerando, *Des Signes et de l'Art de penser*, iv. 10. Some of these systems were founded on a self-explaining pasigraphy, in which e. g. necessity was expressed by a chain, duration by a clock, equality by two parallel lines, a method by a geometrical instrument, &c.

[2] See Hallam, *Lit. of Europe*, iii. 362.

formity, the perfection of small geniuses, was observable throughout it.' The substantives were a series of antitheses. Thus *da* meant God, *ida* devil; *dad* heaven, *odad* hell; *dab* soul, *adab* body; *pida* presence, *pidas* absence; *tadu* power, *tadus* imbecility. The numbers were fashioned on similar principles,—*pobal* 10, *pobar* 100, *pobam* 1,000. It would be impossible to imagine any spoken language so inconceivably dry, and dreary, and bald, and dead as this. 'I do not know,' observes Du Ponceau,[1] 'whether any one ever studied, learnt, or cultivated this language. It is only found in some libraries, a sad monument of the aberrations of the human intellect.' Without absolutely endorsing so severe a remark, we may certainly agree with Hallam that 'it is very fortunate that neither of these ingenious but presumptuous attempts to fasten down the progressive powers of the human mind by the cramps of association had the least success.'

The metaphors without which no language worthy of the name can even exist are a proof of the *human*

---

[1] He mentions also the Spécieuse-Générale, a philosophic language by which Leibnitz designed to reduce to a sort of calculus the expression of all truths. It appears from a work of Raspe (*Hist. Linguæ Characteristicæ*) to have represented every idea by numbers, and was supposed capable both of eliminating all errors, and leading to new discoveries. 'It only wanted a grammar and dictionary to make it complete!' Another was invented by a M. Faignet, and England was imposed upon by a pretended language of the Island of Formosa, invented by a French deserter, who ludicrously called himself Psalmanasar! See Du Ponceau, pp. 26–31. Probably hundreds of such attempts have been still born. Quite recently I have seen one by M. Letellier, *Etablissement immédiat de la Langue Universelle*, 1862. There must be singular fascination in a problem which has interested so many great minds. Among others Mr. Babbage was once attracted by it. *Passages from the Life of a ilosopher*, p 25.

invention of language, because they are confessedly formed on indirect and imperfect analogies, and are sources of constant[1] ambiguity and error. But for this very reason they are best suited to our limited human condition. Who would insult the stars because at night he can no longer see the sun? We live but in the twilight and the moonlight, and the very dimness of our vision saves us perhaps from a thousand dangers. The old *bon mot*, found in so many different forms,[2] 'that the true use of speech is not so much to express our thoughts as to conceal them,' false as it is in one sense, is capable, in another sense, of an innocent application. At no period of history was it more evident than now, that the passions of men would be far more furious and uncontrollable than they are, if it were not possible to maintain a truce by the common acceptance of words and formulas which are fairly and honestly capable of expressing widely different forms of belief. The gracious shadows, the beneficent imperfections of language, save us from being scorched up by a fulness of truth for which we are yet but ill-adapted. Unhappy would be the nation which should have a perfect language. It would be a field of battle continually bathed in blood; language would then be the mirror of our thoughts, and would reveal with intolerable clearness all our passions, and all our susceptibilities.[3]

---

[1] See Mill's *Logic*, i. 48.

[2] Goldsmith's *Citizen of the World*. The saying is usually but erroneously attributed to Talleyrand; it occurs also in one of Voltaire's dialogues, and in a couplet of Young's. See *Pearls and Mock Pearls of History*.

[3] Du Ponceau, p. 225. This is one of the many striking thoughts with which his singularly able Essay abounds.

We have spent some time over the consideration of metaphors, but perhaps not too long, when we consider that by their means a breath of air may be said to become the picture and exponent alike of the seen and of the unseen Universe.

CHAPTER XXI.

OTHER LINGUISTIC PROCESSES.

'Ο λόγος διάφωνος καὶ ὁ νοῦς ποικίλως τρέπεται.
PYRRHO in Diog. Laert. ix. xi. 95.

It may be well, before we proceed farther, to sum up briefly the main results which the previous pages have been intended to develop, to illustrate, or to prove.

Language then was not a direct Revelation of the Almighty; nor was it an inevitable result of our physical organisation; nor was it a purely mechanical invention, accepted by general agreement, in consequence of a felt necessity:—but the *capacity* for Language was a part of our human constitution, and in the development of this capacity, the Senses, the Memory, the Understanding, the Emotion, the Will, and the Imagination all played their part. The great secret— the Divine Idea of Language became intuitively evident to man from the working of his Intellect upon two strictly analogous facts. He found that the effect of powerful passion was to force from him involuntary spontaneous sounds, which, when repeated, recalled the passions by which they had been originally stimulated, and not only recalled them by virtue of the Law of Association to him who had originally felt them, but also conveyed and expressed them to others who were similarly affected by similar causes. But besides this, as may still be observed in children, the delicate sensibility of the nervous system in the still fresh and unworn human organism gave rise to a spontaneous echo of external sounds, an echo which partly repeated and imitated the sounds themselves, and partly modified them in accordance with the ideal impression which they reproduced. Originally this repercussion of the sounds which had thrilled the auditory nerve was not due primarily to an instinct of conscious imitation, but to a far subtler law of physical sympathy with the outer world; but as it conveyed a pleasurable sense of power it would at once be adopted as a voluntary exercise apart from any necessity. In this instance also it would be instantly discovered that the imitative sounds, however modified by organic or subjective influences, inevitably recalled, by the same law of association, the external phenomena with which they were connected. In both cases it would be instantly discovered that sounds were capable of becoming signs not of sounds only but of things. Here then were the elements of language; here lay hidden the germs of that infinite discovery which made man worthy of his destined immortality; here, ready provided by the working of divine laws, were the materials by which he was enabled to express his own sensations, and to recall the most striking aspects and influences of the world in which he lived.

The nascent intelligence, sharpened by the wants of life, at once saw the importance of this marvellous faculty, and began with unerring and unconscious instinct to work upon it. Man soon found that it was not necessary to rest content with crude interjections and vowel sounds, to express his own feelings, or rough reproductions to recall the living creatures and numberless influences of the outer world. The interjections and imitations were more and more modified, till they barely retained the faintest echo of their sensuous origin. They were soon accepted as purely ideal signs, and their history and derivation was in the course of ages as completely forgotten or obscured as if they had been meaningless tokens arbitrarily adopted and absolutely devoid of any historical connection with the meanings for which they stood.

The intimate relation,—perhaps we may say the ultimate identity,—of the effects produced by different senses, would at once suggest the possibility of observing analogies so far as to translate into sounds addressed to the ear alone, the impressions produced by every other sense; and it would be an easy transition to adopt the same principle in shadowing forth by self-suggesting symbols those spiritual and intellectual phenomena which were none the less really felt from their being intangible and unseen. The power of Imagination, however simply and almost unconsciously exercised, was fully adequate to the task thus imposed upon it. In fact it is very probable that long periods would elapse before it was c..lled upon in any large measure to claim its dominion over the higher realms of speech. The rich religious, spiritual, metaphysical, and moral vocabulary of the most civilised Aryan nations must not be taken as any measure of the wants of primeval language. If to this day the Chinese can only express the notions of 'virtue' or 'happiness' by crude analyses four-words-long;—if many savage nations are destitute of words for the conceptions of the very commonest and most ordinary virtues;—if, even in languages of considerable cultivation, it is a matter of no slight difficulty to find a proper term for the Divine Being;—nay, more, if a language so powerful and noble, so greatly enriched from a thousand different sources as the English, had until two centuries back no word for 'selfishness,' the most prevalent of all human vices,—is it likely that Language would be overburdened at its commencement with the demands likely to be made upon its capacity for metaphorical expression?

The word 'selfish' to which I have just alluded was due to an accidental flash of individual genius, and this has probably been the source of many words most valuable and astonishing in their picturesque or imaginative power. Many a poet who never sang,—many an unknown demigod whose discoveries have never been recorded, has thus contributed his forgotten share to the sum of human wisdom and knowledge. There must have been hundreds of tentative words, maintaining side by side a precarious life in the struggle for existence, before the vitality of those that deserved permanence could be fully tested. . We have seen already that every sound produces an impression which admits of *manifold* forms of vocal expression; and it is still more true that all those phenomena which were incapable of *direct* vocal representation, admitted of many different names because they might be regarded in a thousand different aspects, and furnished a thousand different characteristics. Many of these characteristics must have been simultaneously seized upon as marks of the conception before any one of them was finally chosen. Never perhaps was there a higher scope for heaven-born genius than that which was offered to men before the plasticity of language had been moulded by writing and literature into rigid, determinate, and intractable forms.

As an instance of the different points of view from which the same thing could be regarded let us take the word 'left.' In the Polynesian languages it means '*South*,' because the Islanders turn to the *west* to find the cardinal points; yet in Latin 'læva' is used for the *East*, and in Greek ἀριστέρα is used for the *West*, because in taking omens the Greek augur turned to the North, and the Roman to the South; and in the Semitic languages again, from the custom of turning to the East for devotion, 'left' means *North*. Hence 'left' has been used among different nations *for every one of the four points of the compass*.[1]

It is however still more strange to find the *same* root not only used for *different* notions, but actually applied to things which are *essentially contradictory*. Thus in Chinese *louan* means both 'to make a disturbance,' and 'to govern well;' *ton* is both 'to poison' and 'to nourish;' *kon* is both a worm-eaten vessel, and 'to mend a vessel;' *tsing* 'pure,' 'clean,' is used for 'a sink.'[2] In Hebrew[3] ברא means both 'he created' and 'he destroyed;' ברך means both he 'blessed' and 'cursed;' הלל means both 'to shine' (Job xxix. 3)

---

[1] See Garnett's *Essays*, p. 287. Hundreds of instances might be given where the shades of meaning acquired by the same word in different languages have been widely different from each other. Thus the root *wilwan* 'to plunder' furnishes both the Latin *Vulpes*, and the German *Wolf*. The German *Stuhl* means a stool; the Russian *stol* a table. The German *Zaun* means 'a hedge,' and is the same word as our 'town,' &c. Benloew, *Sur les Noms de Nombre*, p. 85.

[2] Premare, *Not. Ling. Sin.* p. 242.

[3] Glass. *Philol. Sacr.* p. 746. Gesenius, *Thesaur.* s. v. נבר.

and to be inglorious (Ps. lxxv. 5); חסד is used for both reproach and kindness; כסל both for infidelity and for constancy; קדש is applied both to the holiest and the most contaminated things; תאב implies both longing and abhorrence. The Hebrew root אבה to be willing means in Arabic to be unwilling; one word in Arabic means both to be kindled and to be extinguished, and the same root is used for to be righteous and to be unjust. In Sanskrit *bhîruka* means both timid and formidable. We find similar contradictoriness in the applications of the Greek[1] roots which occur in ἄγος, χρεία, ἅπτω, &c., the Latin words *carus, sacer*, &c., the English *fast, dear*, &c. Thus too in Greek the prefix ἀ is sometimes negative, sometimes copulative or perhaps intensive; and in German the inseparable prepositions *ent-* and *ver-* sometimes express negation and sometimes not. The explanation of the phenomenon is to be found in the Law of Association of Ideas, and the harmony of the apparent discord is generally discoverable in the history of the word itself. In some cases the word or root which has acquired opposite senses was really a μέση λέξις like the Hebrew *Barak* involving the notion of a solemn address to God, and therefore equally applicable to blessing and cursing; or the Latin 'sacer' which means set apart or tabooed, and therefore is equally applicable to things sacred and things accursed.

But in other cases of contradictory roots the explanation lies in the fact that Association works often by contrasts, and a thing recalls its opposite, and therefore at once suggests that use should be made of the same *name*. For 'the number of things[2] known to us, and

---

[1] See Dr. Donaldson, *New Cratyl.* p. 80. [2] Mill's *Logic*, i. 231.

of which we desire to speak, multiply faster than the names for them. Except on subjects for which there has been constructed a scientific terminology, with which unscientific persons do not meddle, *great difficulty is generally found in bringing a new name into use*; and independently of that difficulty it is natural to prefer giving to a new object a name which at least expresses its resemblance [or contrast] to something already known, since by predicating of it a name entirely new, we convey no information. . . . The more rapid growth of ideas than of names thus creates a perpetual necessity for making the same names serve, even if imperfectly, on a greater number of occasions.' In this principle we find the explanation of the contradictory application of roots; it becomes easy to understand why in Hebrew (in which language the most striking instances of the fact are supplied) חָטָא means 'to sin,' and חִטֵּא 'to expiate sin;' שָׁרֵשׁ 'to root up,' and שׁוֹרֵשׁ 'to take root.'

The ancient philosophers and grammarians singularly mistook this principle of nomenclature, which they called κατ' ἐναντίωσιν or the naming by opposites. Nothing can be more confused than their method of treating it, and this perhaps arises from their utter and necessary ignorance of the Science of Etymology. Observing that in some rare and extreme cases Euphemism,[1] the use of pleasing and well-omened words, passed into Antiphrasis, the denomination of things positively harmful by beneficent names (as in 'the gentle ones' for the Furies, and 'the better' or 'the well-named' for the

---

[1] Probably, however, neither Manes nor Parcæ, though so often adduced, are instances of Euphemism. Of this subject we shall treat further on.

left hand), they carried the same principle into ordinary words, and were content to derive *lucus* 'a grove' *a non lucendo*, from its excluding the light;[1] *cœlum* 'the heaven' from *celatum* 'concealed,' because it was open; *bellum* 'war' from bellum beautiful, 'quod sit minime bellum;' *aridum* 'dry' from ἀρδεύειν 'to water,' because it had ceased to be watered,[2] &c.! These absurdities are pardonable enough in Varro, Donatus, or Charisius, but it is strange that they should have been repeated for so many centuries. It is quite true that Irony, preventing any possibility of error by a change of tone, often contemptuously pronounces the opposite of what it intends, as when Micaiah the son of Imlah says to Ahab, 'Go up to Ramoth-Gilead and prosper, for the Lord shall deliver it into the hand of the king,' or as when the indignant Ida exclaims—

> You have done well,
> And like a prince and like a gentleman.

And sometimes the feeblest and most meaningless kind of Irony confines itself to a single word, as when a dwarf is nicknamed Atlas, or a very ugly woman is called Venus. But it may safely be asserted that no such preposterous and pointless process as this could ever have been deliberately adopted as a method of providing words. *Many* instances can be adduced in which the relation of contrast has led to the adoption of the same root to express, under slight modifications, opposite conceptions; but this differs entirely from the

---

[1] *Lucus* is another form of *locus*, and originally means *a clearance in a grove*, which explains its connection with lux. The derivations of *cœlum* and *bellum* are obvious.

[2] Lersch, *Sprachphil.* iii. 133. Lobeck has written one of his exhaustive papers *De Antiphrasi et Euphemismo*.

ancient notion of Antiphrasis, or a deliberate calling of things after properties which they do *not* possess,—an erroneous notion which may be finally banished from the list of linguistic processes.

Proclus, in his commentary on Plato's *Cratylus*,[1] gives a *catalogue raisonné* of some fifteen methods for forming words, as for instance—1. by imitation (κατὰ μίμησιν), as to *hiss* (σίζω); 2. by reference to something else, or analogy; 3. by catachresis, the recognised misapplication of a word, as when we say that a sound is sweet; 4. pseudonymously, i.e. with a disregard of the etymological meaning, as when we talk of a *silver box*, or a *brass* looking-*glass*; 5. with a reference to history, as ὀβολός an obol, from βέλος an ingot; 6. by an extension of meaning (ἐπιδιατετακότα), as ζωγράφος, properly a painter of *animals*, to a painter of any other objects; 7. hyperbolically, as when we talk of a man's *having no heart*; 8. euphemistically, as when we call the Furies 'gentle ones;' 9. analogically, as when we talk of the *head* of a mountain, or the *leg* of a table; 10. from resemblance, as when we say that a man's frame of mind was crude and bitter; 11. by slight modification of existing words; 12. elliptically, as τράπεζα for τετράπεζα; 13. from discoverers, as when we call wine 'Bacchus;' 14. from things invented, as when we call Vulcan 'fire;' 15. by excess (καθ' ὑπεροχήν), as when we call a cask 'a tile' (κέραμος), and a physician 'a chirurgeon' (χειρουργός); and to these he might have added many others,—for instance, by synecdoche, as when we speak of 'a thousand *head* of cattle.'

There is very little value in this enumeration of Pro-

---

[1] P. 44. Quoted by Lersch, iii. 94.

clus's, for a cursory examination [1] shows that all the processes which he has separated, naturally fall under the three heads of—1. Imitation, 2. Metaphor, and 3. Antiphrasis,—with the exception of one or two (e.g. 11. by modification, and 12. by ellipse) which belong to formal etymology, and need no explanation, or further remark. His allusion, however, to the *Historical* origin of words (under which head fall 13. and 14. in the above list) is new and important, and on it is based the whole of that beautiful and valuable Science which has received of late the title of Linguistic Palæontology.

[1] Lersch, iii. 95.

CHAPTER XXII.

THE NATURE OF WORDS.

Λόγος βάθυς καὶ ἀπόρρητος ὁ περὶ φύσεως ὀνομάτων.
ORIG. *c. Cels.* i. 24.

WE have now advanced sufficiently far in our enquiry to be able to estimate more accurately the nature and import of Words.

It was the endeavour to arrive at some secure conclusion upon this subject which led to the constant and eager controversies on the origin of Language which occupied some of the clearest intellects among the Greeks and Romans. In the hands of the Grammarians the question degenerated from the high philosophical import which it had in the minds of the ancient Philosophers; but in one form or other, with numberless modifications, it was a problem which occupied a thousand years of thought and argument. It is the one thread, which under various colours, runs through the whole history of Greek philology[1] from its dawn in the loftiest regions of metaphysical speculation to its decline into a dry and dusty register of grammatical forms and dialectic varieties.

The nomenclature of the controversy, and with it the views of the combatants, shifted continually from age to

[1] Lersch, *Die Sprachphil. d. Alten*, s. 2.

age; but amidst a crowd of differing terms the main fundamental question always was this, Did words originate by Nature (φύσις) or by Convention (θέσις, συνθηκή)? Was their form and significance determined by some inward necessity, or by mere arbitrary caprice? Have words any abstract propriety and fitness (ὀρθότης), or are they merely invented anyhow and at haphazard? Is there in words any intrinsic 'force and meaning, or are they mere accidental labels stuck upon things which we wish to mention? Is there any connection between names and things, or are names mere artificial counters used to assist our mental calculations?

Those who decided in favour of the first of these hypotheses—those who held that names existed by nature, and had a necessary and mystic connection with the things they signified—were called Analogists:— those who regarded words as mere conventional signs of our conceptions were called Anomalists.

It was to be expected that the discussion of a subject which the Ancients had no means of deciding, and the use of watchwords and party cries[1] capable of such widely different acceptations as Φύσις and Νόμος, would lead to infinite confusions of thought, and would render it difficult in many cases to decide to which school any particular thinker really belonged. Moreover, our materials for forming an opinion of what was really held by the great thinkers in the Golden Age of Greek Philosophy, are often to be derived from prolix commentators and puzzle-headed scholiasts. Heraclitus and Democritus were at opposite poles, yet if Democritus

---

[1] 'So wirken Schlagwörter allemal um so weiter, je weniger sie verstanden werden; und die Parteien zerfallen sobald sie sich ihr Schlagwort klar machen wollen!' Steinthal, *Grammatik*, p. vii.

called words 'sounding images' (ἀγάλματα φωνήεντα) he used a phrase which Heraclitus himself might readily have adopted. Pythagoras is distinctly classed by Proclus among the Analogists, and by Ammonius no less clearly among the Anomalists. Epicurus, and his glorious exponent Lucretius, attack Pythagoras[1] for believing in a Namegiver, and attribute language to the instincts of nature sharpened by the spur of necessity; yet nothing can be more clear than that their views were utterly at variance with the mystical conceptions of many other eminent Analogists. In Plato's great dialogue, the *Cratylus*, where this subject is treated, the difficulty of arriving at any clear conception of the view propounded is so great, that no two commentators have ever been found to agree in the exact interpretation of it. Instead therefore of entering into this war of words, and labyrinth of indistinct conceptions, it will be sufficient to contrast the assertions of one or two of the chief supporters of both schools, and see how far they contain any germ of truth; for the problem, baldly stated, 'Is Language due to Nature or to Convention?' is very nearly meaningless, and has no value as an intelligible formula. For convention requires discussion, agreement, concert; and as these are impossible *without* Language, we are at once involved in a vicious circle.[2] The controversy had its root (as we see very distinctly from the *Cratylus*) in the opposition between the Ionic and Eleatic Schools of

---

[1] On this subject see Lersch, i. p. 25; Steinthal, *Geschichte der Sprachwissenschaft*, pp. 150-176. Lersch's book derives immense value from its rich collection of quotations from all the ancient philosophers and grammarians; but it is eminently bewildering, and deficient in clearness and critical power. See Steinthal, *Gesch.* p. 74.

[2] See Herbart, *Psychol.* § 130, quoted by Steinthal, *Grammatik*, p. 315.

Physiology,[1] of which the former maintained the perpetual flux (πάντα ῥεῖ), and the latter the stability and reality of all things. In its ultimate consequences and developments it involves many of the most important questions in Theology, in Philosophy, and even in Science. But we need go no farther than the *Cratylus* to learn that there is in Language *both* a natural and a conventional element, and that (if we *must* use abstractions) both the human understanding, and that mysterious entity 'the nature of things,' contributed their respective quotas to the Laws and Forms of speech.

Heraclitus, the very prince of all ancient philosophers, may be regarded as the father and founder of the Analogists. He held (if we may accept the flickering lamp of Ammonius as adequate to illuminate his proverbial darkness[2]), that Names were the immediate product of a Natural power which assigned to each thing its proper designation as a necessary element of that thing's existence,—the relation between the two being similar to that which exists between a sensation and the object which causes it.[3] Names, he thought, were like the *natural*, not like the artificial images of visible things, i.e. they resembled the shadows cast by solid objects, or the reflections in mirrors and on the surface of still water. 'Those who use the true word do really and

---

[1] Lersch, i. 10.

[2] Ὁ Σκοτεινός was his name even among the ancients; yet the fragments of him which have come down to us are luminous, nay radiant, with thought and meaning. His alleged obscurity, like that of Bishop Butler, must simply have arisen from the novelty and profundity of his speculations, not from any defects of expression or any intellectual vagueness.

[3] Such, we suppose, must be the meaning of the sentence, ὥσπερ αἴσθησιν ἄλλην ἐπὶ ἄλλοις τῶν αἰσθητῶν ὁρῶμεν τεταγμένην. Ammonius, *ad* Arist. *de Interpr.* p. 24, in Lersch, i. 12.

truly *name* the object, while those who do not, merely make an unintelligent noise. Hence the philosopher's object is to discover the *true names* which nature has assigned to things, just as it is the part of a keen observer to distinguish accurately the appearances of objects.'[1] Nothing then can be clearer than that Heraclitus here enunciates the most absolute views of the Analogist school,—that Words are the immediate copies of Things, produced by Nature herself, not due to any subjective influence of human caprice, but corresponding to Realities by an objective necessity. On this subject we shall have more to say hereafter. The Analogism of Epicurus was of a very different character; he too held that Words were a natural product, but by 'Nature' he only meant a physical organic necessity,— which is a very low and onesided view of Language, even when invested with poetic colours in the orgiastic and splendid verse of Lucretius, or arrayed in some shadow of scientific authority in more modern writers.[2]

Democritus, that Fichte of the ancients, held an opinion the direct reverse of that propounded by Heraclitus. He referred everything to opinion, and custom; —with him even the experience of the Senses[3] was but a reflex of established prejudices, and Speech the mere result of arbitrary human agreement! Nay, he not only asserted this, but he tried, according to Proclus,[4] to prove it by four philological arguments; viz. 1. By the existence of Homonyms, or identical words for different

---

[1] Ammonius, l. c.
[2] E. g. in Becker's *Organism. der Sprache.*
[3] νόμῳ γλυκύ, νόμῳ πικρόν, νόμῳ θερμόν, νόμῳ ψυχρόν, νόμῳ χροιη. Democr. *de Anim.* Vide Lersch, i. 13.
[4] Proclus, *Schol. in Plat. Cratylus*, p. 6. Id.

objects, as, for instance, κλείς to mean both a key and a collarbone; 2. By Polyonymy, or the existence of different synonyms for the same object, as ἄνθρωπος, μέροψ, and βροτός, for 'man;' 3. By the possibility of changing a proper name; for if names corresponded to some inward characteristic, we could not change a man's name [1] from Aristocles to Plato, or from Tyrannion to Theophrastus; 4. By the accidental absence of some words formed analogously to others; e.g. we have φρονεῖν from φρόνησις, but no similar verb from δικαιοσύνη. Few Heracliteans, we suppose, would be appalled by the production of such raw arguments as these, even when they received a practical illustration from the Megarian Diodorus, who called one of his slaves 'But in truth' (ἀλλὰ μήν), and another by some other conjunction, to show that in Language Use is the only important principle, and that no word has any other meaning than the one which you may choose to attach to it! Still, the Analogists had equally little in the way of argument to produce on their own side. Heraclitus held that the Study of Words was a direct road to the discovery of abstract truth,[2] but there is little enough of truth, abstract or otherwise, in the Etymologies which occupied the attention of his followers; and as for the attempts of the grammarian Nigidius[3] to support them by arguing that when we say the word *Vos* we indicate by the movement and protrusion of the

---

[1] Hermogenes in Plato's *Cratylus* illustrates this by the constant changing of *slaves*' names. *Cratyl.* p. 384.

[2] 'Εξαιρετόν φασι τοῦ 'Ηρακλειτείου διδασκαλείου τὴν διὰ τῶν ὀνομάτων ἐπὶ τὴν τῶν ὄντων γνῶσιν ὁδόν. Proclus *in Parmenid.* i. 12. 'Qui imagines rerum in verbis sic ut in cerâ expressas putarent.' Lobeck, *Aglaopham.* ii. 871.

[3] Quoted by Aul. Gellius. x. 4.

lips the persons to whom we are speaking, whereas when we say *Nos* we draw in the breath and the lips,—the less we say about them the better! They belong to an infinitely worse form of hypothesis than that already quoted from St. Augustine; they are far more futile than the attempts which have amused so many writers, from Plato down to Dr. Wienbarg and Mr. D'Arcy Thompson, to discover the distinct psychology and physiognomy of particular alphabetic letters.[1]

But the Analogists were less guided by definite arguments than by deep mysterious convictions. They appealed to the names of the gods, as being peculiar and appropriate, because they were felt to be too sacred to admit of being changed.[2] They called attention to the effects of blessing and cursing, which, they argued, could not be mere arbitrary words, because they often worked their own achievement, and possessed an inherent power,[3] which proves that Speech binds together God and Man, Heaven and earth, words and things in a common band of thought.

The very universality of such views as these among nations in the most various stages of culture, and men of the most different capacities,—the fact that they have been held alike by Jews and Gentiles, by savages and philosophers, by the abjectly superstitious and the pro-

---

[1] Every one knows what Plato makes out of the letters R and L. *Cratylus*, p. 424 *seqq*. Moritz Drechsler occupied an entire book with the letter M (*Grundlegung zur wissenschaftlichen Konstruktion*, &c. Erlangen, 1830); and in Mr. D. Thompson's *Day-dreams of a Schoolmaster* we find traced the villanous lineaments and character of the letter K. Dr. Wienbarg in his curious little book, *Das Geheimniss des Wortes*, p. iv., says that he has listened diligently to 'the sylphlike waving and whispering of the letter-spirits.'

[2] Iambl. *de Mysteriis*, vii. 5. Lersch, i. 43.

[3] Ammonius. *Id. ib.*

foundly learned,—shows that they must rest upon some principle, or at any rate must deserve a careful examination. It must not be supposed that the enquiry has now become a mere meaningless anachronism. On the contrary, it lies at the root of many widely-reaching controversies. On it, for instance, ultimately turns the long dispute between the Realists and the Nominalists. St. Anselm declared that unless the abstract man were a reality, unless man, the idea which objectively corresponds to the word 'man,' had an actual independent existence,[1] the doctrine of the Incarnation could not be true. On the other hand, Fichte's singularly crude and unconditional acceptance of the theory which deprived names of all but a purely conventional value,[2] was a direct result of his subjective idealism. To this day the disputes which gather round the meanings of general terms both in Science and Theology are largely modified by the influence of some, often unconscious, theory respecting the nature of words.

It is then very important to try and illustrate what the most advanced Analogists held on this subject, and thereby to arrive at some point from which we can criticise their opinions.

The early Jews seem to have held the views of the Analogists in their extremest form. We do not indeed find the doctrine stated by them in so many words, the nearest approach to such a statement being a verse of questionable authenticity in the book of Ecclesiasticus (xvii. 5), 'in the sixth place he imparted them Understanding, and in the seventh Speech an interpreter of the cogitations thereof,' where Language is described as

---

[1] Hampden, *Bampton Lectures*, p. 478.
[2] *Von der Sprachfähigkeit*, Sämmtl. Werken, 8. Heyse, s. 57.

a divinely-created sense. But we find throughout the Bible so vast an importance attached to the mere physiological quality of certain sounds,—so solemn a method of inference from mere names and words,—as to leave no doubt respecting the views which suggested such a method of enquiry and illustration. No doubt the constant Paronomasiæ or plays on words which occur in the sacred writers may be due in part to the pleasure which all people, and the Orientals especially, seem to derive from the assonance of different parts of a sentence,[1]— a pleasure which, combined with the tendency to Pleonasms found in all early tongues, lies at the bottom of that whole system of Parallelism in which Hebrew poetry consists. But as similar alliterations and Paronomasiæ are most frequent at that *earliest* stage of language when the meaning of words is freshest, brightest, and least conventional, we must consider them as partly due to some vague belief in the inherent affinities of words. Thus in the very second verse of Genesis we

[1] The Arabic names Harut and Marut, Abel and Kabel (Cain and Abel), Dalut and G'ialut (David and Goliath); compare Kophy and Mophy in Herod. &c. In the Bible we have Huz and Buz, &c. A Hindoo constantly adds meaningless rhymes even to English words, and will talk of a button-bitten, kettley-bittley, &c. But a sort of παρήχησις is used, and used with admirable effect by the very best writers, as in the New Testament, πορνείᾳ πονηρίᾳ, φθόνοι φόνοι (Rom. i. 29, 31), ἀσυνέτως ἀσυνθέτως, κρίνεις κατακρίνεις, &c.; in the Prayer-book holy, wholly, giving and forgiving, changes and chances, &c. These assonances, which are common in Cicero and Sallust, are the *special* delight of St. Augustine. In poetry too they are frequent:—αἰσχύνομαι ἀλγύνομαι, Eur. Apprehends and comprehends, Shakesp. *Mids. Night's Dream.* Sorted and consorted, *Love's Lab. lost.* 'Sly slow hours,' *Rom. and Jul.* 'Is every breath, a death,' *All's well, &c.* 'Actions and exactions,' Daniel. '*Fear the fierceness* of the boy,' *Beaum. and Fletch.* 'Shrill, chill with flakes of foam,' &c. Tennyson. To enter fully into this subject would be to write a book on Rhyme, its origin, the source of its pleasurableness, &c.

find the words *Tohoo vabohoo* as a description of the primal chaos; and similar instances may be found in Job xxx. 19, Is. liv. 8, Ps. xviii. 8,[1] &c., degenerating in Judg. xv. 16, and in the apocryphal story of Susannah, into mere puns,[2] and rising in Is. v. 7 into very beautiful and pathetic force. Perhaps the best instance to prove that a distinct importance was attached to the mere sound is to be found in the vision of Jer. i. 11, 12, where the Lord says, 'Jeremiah, what seest thou? And I said, I see a rod of an *almond tree.* Then said the Lord unto me, Thou hast well seen: for I will *hasten* my word to perform it.' In this remarkable passage it is clear that the symbolic vision derives no small part of its force, if not its whole basis, from the similar sound and derivation of the two words *Shakeed* ' an almond tree ' and *Shâkad* ' to hasten.' Even this, strange as it may seem to us, is not a singular instance. In Amos (viii. 1, 2)— ' Amos, what seest thou? And I said, A basket of summer *fruit.* Then said the Lord unto me, The *end* is come upon my people,'—an important clue to the meaning lies in the similarity between *Kaytz* 'fruit,' and *Kêhtz* ' an end,' both which words have the imitative origin *Kâtsatz* to cut (cf. Ezek. vii. 6). Even in Dan. v. 28 there is evidently a play on Peres and the Hebrew Pârâs a Persian; and, to take an instance still more important, the title Nazarene, as given to our Lord, and referred to by St. Matthew as having fulfilled an ancient prophecy, seems to find its sole explanation in the similarity of the word Nazarene to *Netzer* 'a

---

[1] See Glass. *Philol. Sacr.* p. 951.

[2] In the story of Susannah the pun rests on the similarity of σχῖνος a mastick-tree, and σχίσαι to cleanse; πρῖνος a holm-oak, and πρίσαι to saw asunder; Luther admirably renders the pun by the words *Linden finden*, and *Eichen, zeichen.*

branch,' a title given to our Lord in Is. xi. 1. It seems nearly certain, if I may quote what I have said elsewhere,[1] that 'St. Matthew, well aware of the importance attached by Orientals generally, and the sacred writers in particular, to the mere quantity of certain sounds as connecting them with other sounds expressive of different conceptions, . . . may have been led to suppose that this passage in Isaiah bore out his general reference to the prophets, and indicated the fact which he narrates.' It is extremely probable that by bearing these views of language in mind we may throw great light on St. Paul's difficult expression, 'For this Agar is Mount Sinai in Arabia,'—since Agar means a rock, and was probably a local name for the Arabian mountain.

It is however in the method of treating proper names that the belief in their absolute significance is most clearly shown. The Jews seem to have held to the full that 'imago animi, vitæ, vultûs nomen est.' 'The name was, according to Hebrew and Eastern writers in general, an integral part of the object itself; it was not deemed indifferent; it was no conventional sign; it was an essential attribute.'[2] Hence we have *no less than fifty* etymologies in the Book of Genesis alone, and in almost every one of these instances the derivation connects the name, prophetically or otherwise, with some event in the person's life. It would however be an error to regard these as always meant for *mere* etymologies; indeed as such they are in many cases scientifically untenable. Even in Gen. ii. 23, *Isshah* 'woman' *cannot* be *derived*

---

[1] *Dictionary of the Bible*, s. v. *Riddle*, where numerous other instances are given, the number of which might easily be doubled.

[2] Kalisch, *Genesis*, p. 114. Hiller, *Onomasticon*, p. 950. Ewald, *Proph. d. alten Bundes*, i. 18.

from *Eesh*[1] 'man;' nor can Noah be derived from *Nâcham* 'to comfort' in Gen. v. 29; nor again, since Moses is an *Egyptian* name (Ex. ii. 10, cf. Gen. xli. 45), can it be possibly derived from the Hebrew *Mâshah* 'he saved.'[2] These instances, and they might be largely multiplied, show that in many cases the inferences drawn from names in the Bible are not intended as *etymologies*, but are adduced to illustrate the mystic relations of words, and to represent certain facts and influences in the lives of those who bore them. For to the Oriental every word appeared to have in itself a divine primeval character, and to retain some fragment of the creative breath.[3] It is well worth our enquiry whether there is not a still earlier instance of this view in the explanation of the name Adam? To suppose that it is derived from *Adamah* 'earth' is philologically difficult, if not impossible; and both words are probably connected with *adam* 'he was red,'[4]—red being the colour by which the Semitic race is depicted

---

[1] 'The similarity of the sound only could have been alluded to, and by no means the derivation of the word.' Mason and Bernard, *Hebr. Gram.* i. 122. See, however, on the other side, Ewald, *Hebr. Gram.* i. 318; Kalisch, *Genesis*, p. 116. Gesenius (*Thes.* i. 87) says that the derivation, 'quamvis non satis accurata, tamen scriptori sacro notatu digna videbatur.'

[2] Accordingly Josephus says, *Antt.* ii. 9, 6, τὸ γὰρ ὕδωρ μῶ οἱ Αἰγύπτιοι καλοῦσιν, ὐσῆς δὲ τοὺς ἐξ ὕδατος σωθέντας. On Noah, Mr. J. Perowne says, 'It is quite plain that the name "rest" and the verb "comfort" are of different roots; and we must not try to make a philologist of Lamech, and suppose that he was giving an accurate derivation of the name Noah. He merely plays upon the name after a fashion common enough in all ages and countries.' *Dict. of the Bible*, s. v.

[3] Wienbarg, *Das Geheimniss des Wortes*, p. viii.

[4] See Jos. *Antt.* i. 1, 2; Leuden, *Onomast.* s. v. *Adam*. The Indians have a tradition that man was made out of *red* clay; the Chinese say that it was yellow clay.

on the Egyptian monuments. We may then accept Gen. ii. 7 as one of those instances in which the name serves to remind the writer of some cognate or similar word,[1] which naturally suggested the same conclusion as that drawn by the Greeks from the similarity of λᾶας 'a stone,' and λαός 'people,'[2] and by the Romans from the resemblance of 'homo' and 'humus.' In this way at any rate we remove, for those who feel it, the difficulty (!) arising from the fact that the ultimate constituents of man's body are *not* dust and clay, but albumen, phosphate of lime, fat, hæmatin, and many chemical ingredients.

There are fifty of these allusive applications of names in the book of Genesis alone, and the instances of Isaac, Jacob, Seth, Esau, Edom, Judah, Gad, Dan, Peleg, Shem, Japheth, will at once occur to the reader's mind. In some instances, as those of Eve, Abel, Noah, Nabal, Solomon, the name was clearly supposed to have a prophetic character.[3] Even in the New Testament we find

---

[1] This mode of treating words is not uncommon; many etymologies of the ancients which sound so absurd to us were not always meant for 'etymologies' in the strict sense, but for allegorical interpretations, or sometimes even for a mere *memoria technica*:—as when the Roman Jurisconsults derive 'mutuus' '*quod ex meo tuum fiat*,' and *testamentum* from testatio mentis; or as when the Fathers connect 'Paschal' and πάσχειν, or the Pythagoreans forbade the use of peas and beans (λάθυροι, ἐρέβινθοι) because they were λήθης καὶ ἐρέβους παρώνυμα; or the Stoics derive θυμίαμα from θυμοῦ ἴαμα, and Solœcism from σόου λόγου ἀκισμόν, &c. Lobeck, *Aglaopham.* p. 869.

[2] There is possibly an allusion to this in Homer's play upon λαούς and λίθους. Comp. Pind. *O.* ix. 66.

[3] The ancients noticed the same fact in the name Hippolytus, &c.

'Protesilaë, tibi nomen sic fata dederunt,
Victima quod Trojæ prima futurus eras.
Idmona quod vatem, medicum quod Iapida dicunt,
Discendas artes nomina præveniunt.' Auson. *Ep.* xx.

our Lord himself in a solemn moment fixing on the mind of his greatest Apostle a new and solemn significance given to the name he bore. 'Thou art Peter, and on this rock will I build my Church.'[1] St. Paul also is probably playing upon a name when, in Phil. iv. 3, he affectionately addresses a friend as γνήσιε Σύζυγε, 'true yokefellow,'—since it is an ancient and very probable supposition that Syzygus or Yokefellow is there a proper name.

So deep was the sacredness attached to names that the great ebbs and flows in the tide of Jewish thought[2] may be traced by a diligent study of the names they adopted. Hence too their practice, under certain grave conditions, of changing men's names,—a practice which is strikingly illustrated in the histories of Abraham, Sarah, Jacob, Benjamin, Joshua, and Gideon. 'Call me not Naomi (pleasant), but Mara (bitter),' said the broken-hearted widow of Elimelech. In later times we find the name of Pashur indignantly changed by Jeremiah into Magor-missabib, i.e. 'terror on every side' (Jer. xx. 3 10), but no ingenuity has yet been able decisively to state why the name of Saul of Tarsus was, after his conversion, changed to Paul.

---

[1] 'Among the Hebrews even *anagrams* formed a part of the cabbalistic science, and afforded a clue to the discovery of those mysterious oracles which it was imagined the Almighty in his wisdom had connected with the giving of proper names.' Salverte, i. 12. One or two astonishing instances (Sheshach, &c.) from the two modes of interpretation called Athbash and Grammateia might be adduced. The belief in the significance of anagrams lasted till a very late period. The series of miracles connected with the 'garnet ears' of wheat were suggested from the fact that the letters of Pater Henricus Garnetius (hanged for complicity in the Gunpowder Plot, 1606) form the words 'pingêre cruentus aristâ.'

[2] See Ewald's article on Names in Kitto's *Cyclop.*

In one of the Chaldean oracles of Zoroaster we find the rule—

'Ονόματα βάρβαρα μή ποτ' ἀλλάξῃς,
εἰσὶ γὰρ ὀνόματα πάρ' ἑκάστοις θεόσδοτα
δύναμιν ἐν τελεταῖς ἄρρητον ἔχοντα.[1]

The Jews, however, did not share this reverence for barbarous or foreign names; on the contrary, their 'contumelia numinum'[2] was proverbial among the ancients and made them deeply unpopular. This was why they changed Bethel 'the house of God' into Bethaven 'the house of vanity;' Beelzebul 'Lord of heaven' into Beelzebub 'the Lord of filth;' Kir Heres 'the city of the Sun' into Kir Cheres 'the city of destruction;' Har Hamischah 'the mount of olives' into Har Hamaschith 'the mount of corruption;'[3] Jerubbaal and Meribbaal into Jerubbesheth and Mephibosheth, where *Baal* 'Lord' is altered into *Bosheth* 'shame.' This custom may very possibly have been confirmed in the Jews by a literal acceptation of Exod. xxiii. 13, 'Make *no mention* of the name of other gods, neither let it be heard out of thy mouth.' It was however equally common in the case of men; thus Achan was changed to Achor or 'trouble,' and the impostor Barchocebas 'the son of a star' was called Barchozibas 'the son of a lie.'[4]

Much of this notion respecting the intrinsic significance of names[5] rose from the belief that Language

---

[1] Cory, *Ancient Fragments*, p. 271.
[2] Plin. xiii. 9. Winer, *Bibl. Realwörterb.* s. v. *Gotteslasterung.*
[3] Selden, *de Diis Syr. Syntagm.* 2, p. 211. I am aware that nearly all these instances are strongly disputed.
[4] Salverte (*History of Names*, p. 12, ed. Mordacque) gives a Persian instance.
[5] Philo speaks of the *natural* power of words. See Bochart, *Hierozoi-*

was divinely inspired, and the result of Adam's incomparable wisdom. According to the Cabbalists Adam was taught by the Angel Raziel, and received a celestial alphabet; according to others his teacher was a certain Somboscer. Clemens Alexandrinus [1] distinctly attributes his power of naming the animals to a prophetic gift, and St. Chrysostom [2] took it as a proof of consummate intelligence. The phrase 'that was the name thereof' implied, says Eusebius, [3] that the name had an intrinsic and natural meaning. 'God called the light day, and the darkness he called night,' says Theophilus, [4] 'since man would not have been able to name these things, nor indeed anything else, if he had not received their designation from the God who created them.' The same views are still held by many, perhaps by the majority. 'Adam,' says South in his sermon on the State of Man before the Fall, 'came into the world a philosopher, which sufficiently appears *by his writing the nature of things upon their names*.' It is a curious and significant fact that we find the very same conception among the Chinese, who say that Fohi performed his duty of nomenclature so well 'that by naming the things their very nature was made known.' [5]

All that we have said about the Jews finds its parallel in the literature of the Greeks and Romans. All the Epic poets from Homer [6] downwards, all the Lyric poets beginning with Pindar, [7] all the tragedians—the pro-

---

con, vol. i. p. 58; Heidegger, *Hist. Patr.* p. 37, &c. Some of the views of the Rabbi and Fathers are quoted by Michaeler, *De Orig. Linguæ*, pp. 167–196.

[1] Clem. Alex. *Strom.* i. 335.   [2] Chrys. *Hom. XIV. in Gen.*
[3] Euseb. *Præp. Evang.* xi. 6.   [4] Theoph. *ad Autolyc.* ii. 18.
[5] Chou-king, *Dissert. Prélim.* p. 84.   [7] Pind. *Nem.* vii. 42.
[6] On the name Odysseus, *Od.* i. 20.

found and majestic Æschylus no less than the tender realistic Euripides,—nay even the orators,[1] who spoke for the people, resort to these plays on words, and especially on names, as a necessary ornament of their style. No doubt with some of them it became a mere trick of rhetoric,[2] a mere ἀστειότης capable of being reduced to definite rules; but with men like Homer, Pindar, and Æschylus it was regarded in a far different light. Throughout the whole of Grecian Antiquity reigned the popular belief that there existed a necessary mysterious connection between words and the objects signified by them, so that man unconsciously, as though under the guidance of a higher Power, expressed, in the words whereby he named things or persons, their innermost being and future destiny as though in a symbol incomprehensible even to himself.[3] If the commentators had understood this tendency they might have saved themselves their bursts of indignation against these '*putida et frigida etymologia, et tragicâ dignitate aliena.*'[4] We think the pun on a man's name the lowest kind of wit, but assuredly it was no intention to

---

[1] Chiefly however in jest, as Conon played on the name Thrasybulus; and Herodicus on the names Thrasymachus, and Polus, and Draco, saying that the laws of the latter were the laws of a Dragon. Herodotus (vi. 50) records the joke of Cleomenes on the name Krius (ram). Cicero is particularly full of these jokes, playing on the name Verres (boar-pig) with constant delight, as well as on the name Chrysogonus, &c. When Philippus, punning on the name Catulus, exclaimed ' Quid *latras*, Catule?' the happy answer was ' Furem video.' Quinct. vi. 3.

[2] See Arist. *Rhet.* ii. 23.

[3] Schwable in Steinthal, *Gesch. d. Sprach.* s. 17.

[4] Such a play on words seems to have acted like a red rag on commentators, from whom a curious florilegium might be gathered of vituperative phrases against this 'ludicra dicendi ratio,' 'illepida carminis forma,' 'argutiæ,' &c. Quinctilian leads the way with his 'frigidum sane.' *Instt. Or.* v. 10.

T

be witty which led Æschylus to spend twelve bitter lines of a splendid and passionate chorus in denouncing

> Sweet Helen
> *Hell in* her name, but heaven in her looks;[1]

nor did he imagine himself to be comic when he makes Cassandra in the mid screams of her heart-shaking prophetic frenzy play on the meanings of the names Apollo and Aguieus.[2] Nor again would Sophocles have admitted the charge of bad taste for beginning the tragic denunciation of Pyrrhus by Philoctetes with the terrible paronomasia,

> *Ὦ πῦρ σὺ καὶ πᾶν δεῖμα.*[3]

In all probability both he and his predecessor believed profoundly in the science of Onomantia. 'Modern translators have often tried to apologise for what might seem an unwarrantable play upon words, but no apology was needed in a city where to commemorate the self-sacrifice and courageous heroism of Leæna the inhabitants themselves had erected the bronze figure of a lioness.' Nor, it may be added, would such a method of treating names be considered unimportant among a nation whose chiefs were persuaded to a most important military enterprise by the accidental omen in the name

---

[1] Ἑλένη ἑλένας, ἕλανδρας ἑλέπτολις. Æsch. *Ag.* 689. See on this subject, Salverte, i. 37. The English lines are from Peele's *Edward I.*

[2] *Ag.* 1040, 1049. In Æschylus we also find these paronomasiæ on Epaphus (*Prom.* 875), on the river Hybristes (*Id.* 742), on Io (*Id.* 718), on Prometheus (*Id.* 86), &c. Sophocles has them on Ajax, Sidero, and Polynices; Euripides on Theoclymene, Theonoe, Thoas, Meleager, Aphrodite, &c.; Theocritus on Pentheus (xxvi. 26), &c.

[3] Any one who wishes to see the instances collected may consult Lersch, iii. 11–17; Sturz, *Opuscc.* p. 78, *De Nominibus Græcis*; Meineke, *ad Euphor.* p. 128; Elmsley, *Bacch.* 508; Creuzer, *de Arte Hist. Græc.* p. 52; Rost, *ad Phæn.* 639, &c.

of an envoy who was called 'Hegesistratus' or 'leader of an army.'[1]

The same feelings profoundly actuated the Romans. They would all have echoed the language of Ausonius (*Ep.* xx.):

> Nam divinare est nomen componere, quod sit
> Fortunæ, morum, vel necis indicium.

In their levies, Cicero informs us, they took care to enrol first such names as Victor, and Felix, and Faustus, and Secundus; and were anxious to head the roll of the census with a word of such happy augury as Salvius Valerius. Cæsar gave a command in Spain to an obscure Scipio simply for the sake of the omen which his name involved. Scipio upbraids his mutinous soldiers with having followed to the field an Atrius Umber a 'dux abominandi nominis' (Liv. xxviii. 28), being, as De Quincey calls him, a 'pleonasm of darkness.' The Emperor Severus consoled himself on the immoralities of his Empress Julia, because she bore the same name as the profligate daughter of Augustus. To come down to later times, Adrian VI. when he became Pope wished to retain his own name, but was prevented from doing so on being informed by his cardinals that all the Popes who had done so, had died in the first year of their reign.[2]

In almost every other national literature, and that not in consequence of a mere desire to imitate the ancients, but from an outgrowth of the same feelings which animated them, we find examples of the same

[1] See Herod. ix. 91. Grote, v. 259.
[2] Mervoyer, *Ét. sur l'Assoc. d'Idées*, p. 376. As bearing on the same subject I may refer to a paper of mine on *Curious Predictions* in 'the Museum.'

belief in the independent value of words and names. In Shakspeare the play upon names is often introduced in some of the most thrilling passages;—as in *Cymbeline* (v. 5):—

> Thou Leonatus art *the lion's whelp*
> The fit and apt construction of thy name;
> Being *Leo-natus* doth import so much;

and in *King John*, Constance even in the transport of her anguish exclaims (iii. 1):—

> O lawful let it be,
> That I have room with Rome to curse awhile;

and in *As You Like it* Claudio breaks forth with—

> O Hero, what a Hero hadst thou been
> If half thy outward graces had been placed
> About thy thoughts, and counsels of thy heart;

and once more in *Richard II.*, ii. 2, John of Gaunt replies to the King's address,—

> Old Gaunt indeed and gaunt in being old; . . .
> Gaunt am I for the grave, gaunt as a grave
> Whose hollow womb inherits nought but bones;

upon which the King asks in surprise,—

> Can sick men play so nicely with their names?

and Gaunt gives this very striking answer:—

> No! Misery makes sport to mock herself.[1]

Poets of undeniable taste have continued the process[2]

---

[1] 'God forgive me for making such bad puns,' writes Sir W. Napier in one of his indignant letters, 'but *a bitter feeling sometimes turns to humour to avoid cursing.*' *Life of Sir W. Napier*, ii. 241.

[2] All our earlier and Elizabethan writers supply similar instances. Thus in the comedy of *Patient Grissel* we have Furio thus addressed:

> 'When thou com'st to her rough and *furious*
> I pray thee on thy life be *like thy name*;'

and in Decker

> 'Thy name is *Angelo*
> And like that name thou art.'

down to the most recent times. Cowper says of the poet Bloomfield—

> While *fields* shall *bloom* thy name shall live;[1]

and even Wordsworth begins his touching lines to the memory of Charles Lamb with the allusion—

> From the most gentle creature born in fields
> Had been derived the name he bore,—a name
> Hallowed to meekness and to innocence.

The changes of name for purposes of scorn, compliment, or memorial are also common in all periods of history. The Athenians were christened by their enemies Gapenians (Κεχηναῖοι); Demosthenes sneers at Æschines for changing Tromes and Emprisa, his parents' names, into Atrometus and Glaucothea; Chrysippus received the contemptuous appellation Chesippus; Antiochus Epiphanes was changed by the angry Jews into Epimanes; Tiberius Claudius Nero from his drunkenness was nicknamed Biberius Caldius Mero; Ætius, not without a reference to his name, was called Ἄθεος,[2] and the Arians were nicknamed Ariomanites. Jerome changed the name of his adversary Vigilantius into Dormitantius; the original name of Servius II. was *Groin*, and this was the reason why he first of those who assumed the tiara changed his name; Louis XI. altered the name of his barber Olivier le Diable, first into Olivier le Mauvais, then to O. le Malin, and then into O. le Daim, and by a public decree forbade either of his former names to be mentioned;[3] Maria Theresa on the other hand called her minister Thunichtgut by

---

[1] He has a similar play on the name *Edgeworth*.
[2] Gieseler, *Church History*, i. 329, *Engl. tr.*
[3] P. Mervoyer, *Ét. sur l'Association d'Idées*, p. 377.

the much more promising title of Thugut. Salverte tells a story of a Delaware chief, who being accustomed only to names that had a *real* reference, asked the meaning of Colonel Sprout's name. 'The colonel was a man of remarkable size. The chief was told that the name meant "a shoot." "No," he said, "*he cannot be the shoot*, he is the tree itself."' He could not conceive the existence of a name which was not significant.

The universal prevalence of Euphemism as a principle of language is due to a belief in the mystic power of words to work their own fulfilment, as one of the laws of destiny.[1] It is hardly necessary to refer to the familiar instances of the Erinyes called Eumenides, or 'the gentle ones,' of Epidamnus changed into Dyrrhachium, Axeinos into Euxine, Maleventum into Beneventum, Egesta into Segesta, or Capo Tormentoso into Cape of Good Hope. 'These omens derived from names,' says De Quincey,[2] 'are common to the ancient and modern world. But perhaps they ought to be classed under a much larger head, viz. words, generally, no matter whether proper names or appellatives, viewed as operative powers and agencies, bearing, that is to say, a charmed power against some party concerned from the moment that they leave the lips.' After mentioning the utter avoidance of all direct mention of death, he continues, 'Good taste is not in itself sufficient to account for a scrupulousness so general and so austere. . . . This timidity arises from

---

[1] See Disraeli, *Curios. of Lit.* ii. 62. Mill's *Logic*, ii. 30. The mere euphonic changes of name are of course quite different; such as Diocles into Diocletian, De la Borgne to Strabo, Charpentier to Fabricius, Schwartzerd to Melanchthon, &c.

[2] De Quincey's *Modern Superstitions*, Works, iii. 303 (Black's ed.).

the old superstition still lingering amongst men. . . . No progressive knowledge will ever medicine that dread misgiving of a mysterious and pathless power given to words of a certain import, or uttered in certain situations, by a parent for instance to persecuting or insulting children;[1] by the victim of horrible oppression when labouring in final agonies; and by others, whether cursing or blessing, who stand central to great passions, to great blessings, or to great perplexities. And here, by way of parenthesis, I might stop to attempt an explanation of the force attached to that Scriptural expression "*Thou hast said it.*" It is an answer adopted by our Saviour, and the meaning seems radically to be this,[2]—the popular belief authorised the notion that simply to have uttered any great thesis, though unconsciously,—simply to have united verbally any two great ideas, though for a purpose the most different or even opposite, had the mysterious power of realising them in act. . . . An exclamation, though in the purest spirit of sport, addressed to a boy, "*You shall be our Imperator,*"[3] was many times supposed to be the forerunner and fatal mandate for the boy's elevation. Words that were blind, and words that were torn from frantic depths of anguish, oftentimes, it was thought, executed themselves. To connect, though but for denial or for mockery, the ideas of Jesus and the Messiah, furnished an augury of their eventual coinci-

---

[1] Jacob's deathbed prophecy, turning as it mainly does on the significance of names, will at once occur to the reader.

[2] By quoting this explanation for the sake of the thoughts which it involves, I do not mean to endorse its truth. That it does express the Jewish conception is illustrated by their belief in the famous *Bath Kol.*

[3] Such stories are told of Galba, and of our own Henry VII. among others.

dence. It was an *argumentum ad hominem*, and drawn from a popular faith.'[1]

Undoubtedly hundreds of instances might be adduced in which chance words *have* seemed to become living powers effectual for evil or for good. It is easy to explain this on the hypothesis of accidental coincidences; but the explanation has never carried conviction to the popular instinct, and there can be little doubt that this dark ominousness of words—their apparent power of meeting with malignant exterior influences, and cooperating with them for evil—has been one great ground for the views of the Analogists as to their inherent force. Again, there are words in all languages which *appear* to have been directly created, to have issued direct from the human mind. For, says M. Victor Hugo, 'it is the mystery of language to paint with words which have, we know not how or why, faces. This is the primitive foundation of every human language, or what might be called the granite. Slang swarms with words of this nature, words created all of one piece, it is impossible to say when or by whom, without etymologies, analogies, or derivatives—solitary, barbarous, and at times hideous words which have a singular power of expression, and are alive. The executioner, *le taule*; forest *le sabri*; fear *taf*; the devil *le rabouin*. . . . They form transparent masks, grotesque and terrible like a Cyclopean grimace.' Admiring the rare eloquence of this passage, we must reject its assertion that words are ever thus created. Their origin may be forgotten, but assuredly there was

---

[1] De Quincey quotes as another instance of stray words taking effect, and becoming fruitful of consequences, the answer of the impatient Pythia to Alexander the Great, ὦ παῖ ἀνίκατος εἶ.

always a definite and intelligible motive for the forms they assume. Nay even the instances which M. Victor Hugo selects are easily explicable. 'Taule' is derived from 'tollere,' the cry of 'tolle, tolle' being frequent in an old passion-play. *Sabri* is very possibly a mere metathesis for *arbres*. *Taf*[1] is a pure onomatopœia from a French proverb in which tif-taf is used like our own expression 'my heart went pit-a-pat.' Lastly *rabouin* is from the Spanish *rabo* 'a tail,' and means the personage with a tail; and M. Michel, from whose philological study of the Argot we borrow these derivations, thinks that the medieval belief that the Jews were born with tails rose from a consequent misinterpretation of the word Rabbi.

Another ground for accepting the mystic origin of language has been the extraordinary and inexplicable moral influence which words have exercised. The Athenians, by a tendency which they named Asteiotes or Hypocorisma, systematically substituted pleasant for unpleasant names, and gilded the most disagreeable subjects with tolerable and decorous designations.[2] The left hand being ill-omened they called 'the better' or 'well-named' hand; idiocy they called simplicity (cf. 'natural,' 'simpleton,' 'buon huomo'); 'taxes' were termed 'subscriptions' or 'contributions;' 'the prison' was 'the house;' the executioner 'a public servant;' a general abolition of debts was 'a disburdening ordinance.'[3] Now imagine the power and

[1] According to Michel, and Nodier, and Covarruvias, *taffetas* is also an onomatopœia from the noise made by the substance; and a passage in M. Vämbéry's *Travels* (p. 173) shows this derivation to be certain.

[2] τοὺς 'Αθηναίους λέγουσι τὰς τῶν πραγμάτων δυσχερείας ὀνόμασι χρηστοῖς καὶ φιλανθρώποις ἐπικαλύπτοντας ἀστείως ὑποκορίζεσθαι. Plutarch.

[3] See Stallbaum, *Plato, Rep.* p. 474 E. For the flattering hypocorisms

danger of this hypocoristic process in times when it was fashionable to fling a delicate covering over the naked hideousness of vice. Thucydides[1] in one of the most profound and memorable passages in his history tells us how the morals of the Greeks of his day were undermined, and how carefully they concealed the ruin of their character under the flowers of their speech. 'The customary meaning of words with reference to actions they changed,' he says, 'at their will and pleasure; for unreasoning rashness passed as "manliness" and "esprit de corps," and prudent caution for specious cowardice; sobermindedness was a mere "cloak for effeminacy," and general prudence was "inefficient inertness."'[2] 'Men are wont for the most part,' says Procopius, 'to be ashamed not of base deeds but of base names.' 'Venit ad me,' says Seneca,[3] 'pro amico blandus inimicus; vitia nobis sub virtutum nomine obrepunt; temeritas sub fortitudinis titulo latet; moderatio vocatur ignavia; pro cauto timidus accipitur.' We are familiar with the 'Steal? Foh! *convey* the wise it call'[4] of Shakspeare's rogue. The same hypocorisma runs through the whole vocabulary of the Argot. To take instances of such euphemism from Shakspeare alone, we find that 'Thieves' call

---

of lovers and parents see Plut. *de Leg. Poet.* p. 44; *De Adulat. et Amic. Discrimine,* 56 c; *De Auditione,* p. 44 F. (These are quoted at length in Stallbaum's *Plato, Legg.* ii. 5.) See too Lucret. iv. 1154; Hor. *Sat.* i. 3, 37-48, &c.

[1] Thuc. *Hist.* iii. 82.

[2] Compare a very similar passage in *Clarendon's Life,* ii. 39.

[3] Sen. *Ep.* xliv.; in *Ep.* cxiv. there are some striking remarks on this subject.

[4] Compare *K. Rich. II.* iv. 1:

'*Bolingbroke.* Convey him to the tower.

K. Rich. Oh! good! Convey? *Conveyors* are you all.'

The French *emporteur* has the same sense.

themselves 'St. Nicholas's clerks' (*Henry IV.* I. ii. 1), 'nut-hooks' (*Merry Wives*, i. 1), 'Michers' (*Henry IV.* I. ii. 4), 'Trojans' (*Love's Labour's lost*, v. 2),—anything in fact but *thieves*; just as to this day among the low and the vicious a lie is not a lie but 'a cram:' and to steal is not to steal but 'to bag' or 'to crib,' and this devil's vocabulary gives opprobrious names to virtues, as well as glossing names to every vice.[1] It is hardly possible to exaggerate the effects of such words, when we see throughout all history the influence of single expressions. Consider the effects produced on the Saxons by the word '*niedrig*,' on the French by the word '*gloire*;' on many nations by the simple onomatopœia 'barbarian;' on philosophy by the use of the word 'attraction;' on our Indian government by the misapplication of the term 'landed proprietor.'[2] All these are

[1] We must again refer to the chapter in *Les Misérables* by V. Hugo. 'One word,' he says, 'resembles a claw; another a lustreless and bleeding eye; and some phrases seem to snap like the pincers of a crab. All this lives with the hideous vitality of things which are organised in disorganisation. It is the ugly, odious, cunning, treacherous, venomous, blear-eyed, vile, profound, and fatal language of misery.... The words are deformed, wild, imprinted with a kind of fantastic bestiality. You fancy that you hear hydras conversing; in darkness it gnashes its teeth, and talks in whispers, supplementing the gloom by enigmas. It is a horrifying froglike language which goes, comes, hops, crawls, slavers, and moans monstrously in that common grey mist composed of crime, night, hunger, vice, falsehood, injustice, nudity, asphyxia, and winter which is the highnoon of the wretched....'

    'Mirlababi, surlababo
    Mirliton, ribonribette
    Surlababi, mirlababo
    Mirliton ribonribo.'

This is that shrill and leaping chorus of the galley-slaves 'which seems illumined by a phosphorescent gleam, and appears cast into the forest by a will-of-the-wisp playing the fife.' I abridge from the translation of *Les Misérables* by Sir F. Lascelles Wraxall.

[2] See *Origin of Lang.* p. 114.

instances of those 'rabble-charming words' which, as South says, 'have so much wild-fire wrapped up in them.' Consider again the marvellous correlation of Language and national morality;[1] the indefinable and indefinite unison of style and individual character. There is then 'a besotting intoxication which this verbal magic, if I may so call it, brings upon the mind of man. . . . Words are able to persuade men out of what they find and feel, to reverse the very impressions of sense, and to amuse men with fancies and paradoxes even in spite of nature and experience. . . . He who shall duly consider these matters will find that there is a certain bewitchery or fascination in words, which makes them operate *with a force beyond what we can naturally give account of.*'[2]

The facts which we have here passed in review must receive due attention from the philologist, whatever theory of language he may hold. It is not strange that when taken in conjunction with the subtle laws which influence what can only be called the germination of language, they inspired the ancient Analogists with a conviction respecting their own theories, which the jokes and sneers of the opposite school were quite unable to shake. But in spite of the apparent ominous force of language, in spite of its subtle sorcery, its hidden operative agencies, its imperceptible growth,[3]

---

[1] '*Genus dicendi imitatur publicos mores*; si disciplina civitatis laboravit et se in delicias dedit, argumentum est luxuriæ publicæ orationis lascivia: si modo non in uno aut in altero sint, sed approbata et recepta. *Non potest alius esse ingenio, alius animo color.*' Seneca, *Ep.* 114. See also Herder, *Geist der ebraischen Poesie*, i. 12. *Origin of Lang.* p. 145.

[2] South's *Sermons*.

[3] Prof. Max Müller (*Lectures*, i. 203) considers this expression 'incon-

its secret germinative power—in spite even of certain imponderable and inexplicable elements which remain after all that is discoverable in the history of language has been subtracted,—we have seen in the course of our previous enquiries, and shall see further in the next chapter, that the Analogists were wrong;—that language is no diviner than any other product of the human intelligence;—that it contains in itself the germs of no new truths;—that it has nothing whatever to tell us of the nature of things.

ceivable,' and as an instance in which 'poetical phraseology takes the place of sound and severe reasoning.' I can only reply that it is an obvious metaphor which approximately represents the facts and their unknown cause; and *it is one which he himself constantly employs.* See pp. 36, 40, 59, 66, 126, 130 of his *Lectures* (First edition). Indeed his terms are contradictory, for on p. 66 he says that his use of the word 'growth' means mere accretion, like that of the crust of the earth; yet on p. 49 'Language requires a *soil* on which to grow;' and again on p. 59 'Remove a language from its *native soil*, tear it away from the dialects which are its feeders, *and you at once arrest its natural growth.*' Moreover Bunsen, the last person whom he would wish to disparage, says even more strongly that language ' *has all the distinctive peculiarities of vegetable nature*, &c.' *Outlines,* ii. 135, and in i. 166 he talks of 'the analogy existing between the development of plants and words.' Schleicher says 'Die Sprachen *leben*, wie alle Naturorganismen; sie handeln nicht wie der Mensch, haben also keine Geschichte, woferne wir dieses Wort in seinem engeren und eigentlichen Sinne fassen.' *Comp. d. vergl. Gram.* p. 1.

CHAPTER XXIII.

THE NATURE OF WORDS—*continued.*

Words are the notes of thought, and nothing more;
Words are like seashells on the shore, they show
Where the mind ends, and not how far it has been.
                                    BAILEY'S *Festus.*

IT has been a favourite practice with writers on Language to illustrate the union of sound and sense in Words by the analogous union of Body and Soul in Man;[1] and the analogy is not unnatural, because Language owes its development both to physical and to intellectual laws. But we must not be misled by a mere figure of speech to the conclusion that the organic union of sound with sense is as inexplicable a mystery as the combination of soul and body into one living being. If the connection between them were purely arbitrary, if no account could be given of the conformity between the sign and the thing signified, we might accept the existence of language as an ultimate fact which no enquiry could penetrate or explain. But we have seen in the previous pages that there is no reason for assuming that the origin of Language has been veiled in this divine obscurity; so far from offering us an

---

[1] Becker, *Organism. d. Sprache,* § 1, 2, 4. Hermann, *Das Problem d. Sprache,* p. 1.

insoluble problem it is capable, as we have seen, of a perfectly simple, perfectly natural, and perfectly demonstrable solution. Sounds, the material of words, are furnished to us by the sense of hearing acted upon by the Voice,—the organs of the Voice being stimulated to energy by a reflex action resulting from nervous impressions, whether caused by external influences or by inward emotions. Direct imitation of sounds (onomatopœias), as well as instinctive utterances of feeling (interjections), are due to this close living sympathy between soul and body,—the instinct of imitation being probably, in its earliest stages, a purely nervous phenomenon and not a conscious act.

The material of speech having thus been supplied by the body, and by the senses, the Soul began to play its part. The Imagination, working by the Law of Association of Ideas, elevated the modified imitation or the instinctive cry into a *symbol* of the thing from which the sound emanated, or of the emotion by which the cry was caused.

Then, thirdly, the Understanding seized upon this symbolic mark as a *sign* of the object signified, a sign capable of being banished and recalled at pleasure, and capable further of being elevated above the mere individual representation into a pure concept of an entire genus or species.[1]

In every word then we can distinguish three factors: (i.) the sound, which is the incarnation of the thought; (ii.) the inner form of the word, or the special method of this incarnation; and (iii.) the meaning, i.e. the intui-

---

[1] See Heyse, pp. 95, 160. And for a still fuller treatment of the whole subject Steinthal, *Charakter. des hauptsächlichsten Sprachbauer*, 76–105. *Gramm. Log. und Psychol.* 235–320, *et passim.*

tions and concepts which the word expresses. In this respect a word resembles a work of art, which also contains three elements: e.g. the material of this statue is marble; the form of it is a virgin figure with sword and scales; and it *represents* Justice.[1]

Now the ancients very generally believed that words were images, copies, imitations, microcosms of the sensible world,[2]—and that they expressed the nature and essence of things; and similar expressions have been used down to the latest times;—this conception of them being, as we saw in the last chapter, common alike to the profoundest philosophers and the most untutored savage. Is there any gleam of truth in such a view?

Absolutely none, unless it may be supposed to lie in the *single* fancy that interjections being purely unconscious must, in the nature of things, have some mysterious unison with the feelings which they indicate;[3] and unless again it be imagined that there is some secret connection between the unknown essence of things and the manner in which they are capable of affecting the auditory nerve.

'Word' is etymologically connected, not with *werden*[4] to become, but with the roots *war, wahr,* ὀρ-άω, *verbum, ver-*um; and therefore involves the notion of something visible, or perceptible. To call a word a 'copy' of anything external is an expression almost

---

[1] Steinthal, *Urspr. d. Sprache*, p. 130.

[2] ἐοικέναι ταῖς εἰκόσι τῶν ὁρατῶν, Heracl.; ἀγάλματα φωνήεντα, Democr. They are also called δηλώματα, ἀπεικάσματα, μιμήματα, &c. Lersch, iii. 24, *et passim*.

[3] On this subject see Steinthal, *Grammatik*, p. 304. Wüllner, *Urspr. d. Sprache*, p. 3.

[4] Heyse, p. 115. For the derivation of Speech, v. ante. Language is from *Lingua*, which comes from the onomatopoetic root *lk*.

meaningless; for a word cannot in any sense be the exact equivalent either (i.) of a thing, or (ii.) of our notion of a thing.

(i.) Words can tell us nothing whatever about things.

For of things, of the external world, of matter, of the Non-Ego,[1] we know and can know nothing whatever; in other words, it is certain that the Non-Ego is not only unknown but incognisable. For even in receiving sensations the soul is active as well as passive;[2] unless it were so, it would no more perceive than a mirror perceives the objects reflected on its surface. It modifies every sensation which it receives,[3] and it creates by its own activity that synthesis of accidents which we call substance. It is true that in common language we talk of heat, colour, smell, &c., not only as sensations within us, but as qualities assumed to be inherent in things themselves. But this is a mere imbecility of language, since not only these secondary qualities but even the so-called primary qualities of figure, extension, solidity, &c., have long ago been proved by metaphysical enquiry to be mere modifications of our consciousness. Matter is not the *cause* of our cognitions, but only their *element* or *part.* 'Things and the senses can no more transmit cognitions to the mind, than a man can transmit to a beggar a guinea that he has not got.'[4] To say that our sensations teach us anything

---

[1] If any of my readers are wholly ignorant of philosophy and its terminology, they will find nothing to understand in the next two or three pages ; nevertheless they contain the reasonings and conclusions of some of the subtlest and profoundest thinkers who ever lived.

[2] Aristotle distinctly recognised this very important fact; οὔτε τῆς ψυχῆς ἴδιον τὸ αἰσθάνεσθαι οὔτε τοῦ σώματος. *De Somno,* i. 5.

[3] See Lewes, *Biogr. Hist. of Philosophy,* p. 579.

[4] Ferrier, *Inst. of Metaphysics,* p. 473, *et passim.*

whatever about things in themselves is nonsense. What can we know about salt, for instance, if its taste, whiteness, shape, &c., which form the abstract complex or collective impression of it, be merely accidents of our own consciousness, or forms of the apperception? Can an East wind be *like* the sensation of cold?[1] Can heat be *like* boiling water? Can pain be *like* the pricking of a pin? Can the nature of a poppy leaf be *like* drowsiness, or our sensation of the colour red? Can the bits of glass in a kaleidoscope be like the rose or star which we see in consequence of the arrangement of the mirrors placed inside the tube? The external world imparts as little of its own nature to the sentient subject as the finger of a performer to the strings on which he plays,—and the sensations which we receive *from* it as little resemble it as the music evoked from those strings resembles the epidermis by the contact of which they are evoked.[2] 'Just as the little green, red, or gold clouds which the eye, when blinded for any length of time by the sun, sees flitting before it, reveal only a certain internal disposition of the organ of sight; so also do the qualities in which the world mirrors itself before us, reveal only the internal natural constitution of our own intelligence.' Nay more, speaking logically, the external world is *posited* by the activity of the Ego; even the belief in its existence is the result of involuntary mental laws. The arguments of Fichte are logically unanswerable, that 'all that we could know of things without us, even their bare existence, is still *within* us, and is only a thought, a something thought

---

[1] Mill, *Logic*, i. 60; ii. 4. Victor Cousin, *Cours d'Hist. de la Phil. Mor.* 8me leçon.

[2] Chalybäus, *Hist. of Spec. Philos.*, Eng. Tr. p. 156.

of by ourselves;'—i.e. in Fichteán language 'the Ego posites the Non-Ego, and ascribes to it the activity, the causality which it is not conscious of exercising itself.' How then—even if we stop far short of this subjective Idealism—can words tell us anything whatever about the nature of things? Obviously they cannot. Experience is a mere 'tissue of relations.' The '*Ansich*' or intrinsic nature of things happily in no way concerns us, and whether it concerns us or not must for ever remain unknown.

(ii.) But perhaps Words, if they can tell us nothing about *things*, may yet tell us something about *notions*, i.e. about ourselves, and the modifications of our own consciousness?

Not in the least! The subject is and must ever remain for us as incognisable as the object, the Ego as the Non-Ego; and for the very same reasons. We only *know* the modifications, changes, accidents, sensations of the Ego, and we only assume an unknown something whose very existence *consists* in being thus affected. The Ego is nothing more than an assumed something stripped bare of everything whereby its existence is made conceivable,[1] and it is unknown alike to internal and to external experience. It is what remains of a bundle of faggots when every single faggot has been removed and excluded! 'It is the *thought* of an abstract something, invested by a paralogism of the reason

---

[1] Kant, *Krit. d. reinen Vernunft*, p. 431, quoted by Chalybäus, p. 39. 'That which we call "I" is the object of intellect alone. We are never objects of sense to ourselves.' Ferrier, *Inst. of Metaph.* p. 80. 'For my part, when I enter most intimately into what I call myself, I always stumble on some particular perception or other of heat, light, or shade, love or hatred, pain or pleasure. I never catch *myself* at any time without a perception.' David Hume, *Treatise of Human Nature*, i. 4, 6.

with imaginary attributes.' In the phrase of Fichte it is a self-intuition (*Sich-selbstanschauen*)—an internal reflection—'the subject before which its own image floats as object.' In the 'primitive dualism of consciousness,' the subject and object being inseparable, either of them apart from the other must be an unknown quantity; the separation of either is the annihilation of both.[1] 'The mental act in which self is known, implies, like every other mental act, a perceiving subject and a perceived object. If then the object perceived is *self*, what is the subject that perceives? or if it is the true self which thinks, what other self can it be that is thought of?'

If then we can know nothing about the Ego, and nothing about the Non-Ego, how can words reveal to us either the nature of things or our own essence? How can they be a $\mu\iota\mu\eta\sigma\iota\varsigma$ of either of two unknown quantities? And if it were conceivable that words *could* be, according to Becker, the exact organic equivalent of our notions, how would synonyms be possible? The existence of many different terms for the same conception is as valid against the theories of Becker as it was of old against those of Heraclitus.[2]

It is clear therefore that we cannot rest content with the modern definition that 'words are the names of things' any more than with the old one that they are the 'pictures of ideas.'[3] Nothing more accurate can be said of them than that they express the *relations*[4] of

---

[1] Herbert Spencer, *First Principles*, p. 65.
[2] Steinthal, *Gram.* p. 165.
[3] For some ancient and imperfect definitions of words see Voss. *de Arte Gram.* ii. 2, 9.
[4] Garnett, *Philol. Essays*, pp. 82, 282.

things; no better definition of them can be given than that of Hobbes that they are '*signs of our conceptions,*' 'serving the double purpose of a mark to recall to ourselves the likeness of a former thought, and a sign to make it known to others.'[1] It is obvious, says Hobbes, that they are not signs of the things themselves; for that the sound of the word *stone* should be the sign of a stone, cannot be understood in any sense but this, that he that hears it collects that he that pronounces it thinks of a stone.

And even as the signs of our conceptions, words are at the best but very imperfect, inadequate signs in themselves, touching the conception generally but at one single point like a sphere lying on a plane. Language, as we have said before, is but an asymptote[2] to thought. It does not express the objective and external, but the inward as affected by it; we speak rightly of 'expressing *ourselves*,' not of expressing the world. Words are but rude signs to represent approximately what *we think* about[3] the relations of things. We say *rude* signs, because no word is any way coordinate with the conception which it is taken to represent. Seizing on some characteristic mark of the conception it always expresses either too little or too much. It is sometimes distantly metaphorical, sometimes indefinitely assertive; sometimes too concrete, sometimes too abstract. In estimating *words* we must take them according to their etymological meaning,

---

[1] J. S. Mill, *Logic*, i. 23.
[2] *Orig. of Lang.* p. 117.
[3] *E. g.* when we say 'Sugar is sweet,' our consciousness can tell us nothing about the nature of sugar itself, but merely the relation which it holds to our organs of taste. Steinthal, *Gram.* p. 305.

and we shall then see how inadequate they are *in themselves* to involve the mass of facts which they connote,—as inadequate as is a thin and worthless bit of paper which yet may represent a thousand pounds. Take the name of an animal, and it may very likely express some trivial and not invariable fact about its tail, as in αἴλουρος, or a vague and shadowy echo of its cry, as in Ai-ai or cow. Take the Latin 'Homo;' etymologically it means a creature made of earth, and even this is but metaphorically true,—yet for what an infinite complex and aggregate of conceptions and relations does it stand! Take such words as Virtue or Tugend (from vir, and taugen), and what a world of explanation is requisite before the words can be shown to be even *possibly* coextensive with the concept![1] Or again out of numberless instances take a word expressive of the smallest possible modification of matter, —a word invented in the most expressive language in the world, and invented by no less eminent a philosopher than Democritus, and that too with great applause— the word *atom*, meaning that which cannot be cut. Yet simple as is the notion to be expressed, and great as were the resources at command, what a failure the mere *word* is! 'It expresses too much and too little, too much as being applicable to other things and consequently ambiguous; too little, because it does not

---

[1] The defectiveness of language is still more apparent when as in Chinese there is an attempt to reach, by *continuous analysis*, nearer and nearer to the expression of any conception; when, for instance, they express virtue by Tsun-hyan-tsye-i, i. e. fidelity-reverence-temperance-uprightness. The Sanskrit, as we have seen, has four names for elephant from different slight characteristics of the animal. 'Were it to express all these qualities by one word,' says Bopp, 'it would be obliged to join all these names together, and to add a number of others.'

express all the properties even of an atom.'[1] Its inadequacy cannot be more forcibly illustrated than by the fact that its precise Latin equivalent is by us confined to the single acceptation 'insect!' 'Thought is vast as the air; it embraces far more than languages can express, or rather languages express nothing;—they only make our thoughts leap out in electric sparks from the speaker to the listener. A single word suggests a crowd of ideas which the spirit combines and collects with the rapidity of lightning.'[2]

Words then must be dethroned from that exalted apotheosis which they received at the hands of the ancient Analogists. They are but the pyramidal point from which our conceptions broaden down.[3] The world of Ideas which seems in them to find its being, is created, not by *them* but by the Intelligence which uses them as the convenient notation by which its problems are worked out. They are the starting-point of our higher Intelligence, not by any means the goal at which it arrives. Their value and greatness consists in the fact that without that starting-point no great intellectual achievement would have been possible. Yet if words are but the starting-point of the *full-grown* Intelligence, they are nevertheless the goal of its earlier development. Although we believe that the Genesis of Words may be distinctly traced,—although we see in them nothing intrinsically mystical or essentially divine,—we are well aware how enormous is the importance of considering them carefully in the search

---

[1] Garnett, *Essays*, p. 88.
[2] Du Ponceau, p 32.
[3] '*Catervatim irruunt cogitationes nostræ.*' See Dante, *Inferno*, cant. xxiii. 10.

whether for moral, for scientific, for historical, or for religious truth. By earnestly studying them we are enabled historically to resuscitate the long-forgotten history of bygone millenniums, and to catch some glimpses into the past fortunes of nations whose very name and memory have been obliterated for ages[1] from every other record. Intellectually regarded, the study of them initiates us into the profoundest mysteries of the human understanding. It is the foundation of all metaphysics. For it is by words alone that we can discover 'the manner in which ideas, born of perceptions, present themselves all naked to the human intelligence, while it is still engaged in their discovery and still seeking to communicate them to others; we follow the labour which it undergoes to arrive at this result, and in the want of uniformity in that labour we see the influence of different intellects.'[2] Hence fresh languages wisely acquired may afford us a nearer approximation to many truths than would be otherwise attainable, by suggesting thoughts and conclusions which have evaporated from our native tongue.[3] For

---

[1] For instances see Weber, *Indische Skizzen*, 9. 'A dead language is full of all monumental remembrances of the people who spoke it. Their swords and their shields are in it; their faces are pictured on its walls; and their very voices ring still through its recesses.' Dwight, *Mod. Phil.* i. 341.

[2] Du Ponceau, p. 13.

[3] Leibnitz showed less than his usual acumen in the remark that 'si una lingua esset in mundo, accederet in effectu generi humano tertia pars vitæ, quippe quæ linguis impenditur.' *Opp.* iii. 297, *ed. Dutens.* If truth could be gained without an effort it would lose half its value, and these studies are the best discipline to prepare us for the search after truth. 'Studium linguarum,' says Valcknaer, 'in universis, in ipsis primordiis triste est et ingratum; sed primis difficultatibus labore improbo et ardore nobili perruptis, postea . . . cumulatissime beamur.' See Pott, *Die Ungleichheit*, &c., p. 169.

'language is the depositary of the accumulated body of experience, to which all former ages have contributed their part, and which is the inheritance of all yet to come.'[1] It is 'like amber circulating the electric spirit of truth, and preserving the relics of ancient wisdom.'[2] So important and indispensable is the right use of words to the progress of *Science* that some have gone so far as to call Science itself 'a well-constructed Language;' and, although this is an exaggeration, it is certain that in Scientific no less than in Religious history an ill-understood phrase, or an ambiguously-framed expression, has been sufficient to retard the progress, and kindle the passions, of men during centuries of warfare.[3]

Lastly who shall overstate the moral bearing and importance of words? They stereotype our desires, they mislead our consciences, they add intensity to our temptations, they determine our bias, they decide our destiny. Once spoken they are irrevocable, indelible for ever. 'Words, words, words, good and bad . . . millions in the hour, innumerable in the day, unimaginable in the year; what then in the life? what in the history of a nation? what in that of the world? And not one of them is ever forgotten. There is a book where they are all set down. What a history, it has been well said, is this earth's atmosphere, seeing that all words spoken from Adam's first till now, are still vibrating on its sensitive unresting medium!'

---

[1] Mill, *Logic*, ii. 225.

[2] Coleridge.

[3] How much were men's passions inflamed round the two words *Homoousion*, and *Homoiousion*, and how many became in consequence the 'martyrs of a diphthong!'

Be our scientific conclusions and our philological studies what they may, it is well for every man to consider solemnly such truths as these; it is above all a duty for one who writes a book, and that book a book on words. And therefore, gentle reader, I will add this word only about myself,—that before writing I have read diligently, and what I have written I have striven to write honestly, loving the truth and aiming at truth only, endeavouring not to forget even in the midst of controversy that 'it is by a man's words that he is justified and by a man's words that he is condemned.'

BOOKS CONSULTED.

It may be a convenience to students of this subject, if I add a list of those books which, among many others, I have expressly consulted in this work, and to which I have constantly referred. The extent to which I am indebted to the various authors will be indicated in the notes. I have never consciously omitted my fullest acknowledgments when I am indebted to others for any facts, thoughts, or expressions which I have adopted. There is no book in the following list which I have not myself read through, or frequently used; and I have omitted many to which more cursory reference was made.

GREEK.

PLATO, *Cratylus*. (Ed. BEKKER.)
ARISTOTLE, *Rhetoric and Poetics*.
All the most important fragments of the ancient poets, philosophers, and orators on this subject, and extracts from the most important grammarians, may be found collected in
L. LERSCH. *Die Sprachphilosophie der Alten*. Bonn, 1838–41.
A. GRÄFENHEIM, *Geschichte der Klassischen Philologie im Alterthum*. Bonn, 1846.

LATIN.

VARRO, *De Linguâ Latinâ*.
QUINCTILIAN, *Institutiones Oratoriæ*. (Ed. BURMANN.)
P. RUTILIUS LUPUS, *De Figuris*. (Ed. RUHNKEN.)
SANCTIUS, *Minerva*.
VOSSIUS, *De Arte Grammaticâ*.
LOBECK, *Aglaophamus*.
BOCHART, *Hierozoicon*.
GLASSIUS, *Philologia Sacra*.
MICHAELER, *De Origine Linguæ*.
PREMARE, *Notitia Linguæ Sinicæ*.

GERMAN.

GRIMM, *Ueber den Ursprung der Sprache.*
POTT, *Etymologische Forschungen.* Lemgo, 1833.
„ *Die Ungleichheit menschlicher Rassen.* Id. 1856.
„ *Anti-Kaulen.* Id. 1863.
„ *Doppelung.* Id. 1862.
STEINTHAL, *Der Ursprung der Sprache.* Berlin, 1858.
    „ *Grammatik, Logik, und Psychologie.* Id. 1855.
    „ *Charakteristik der hauptsächlichsten Sprachbaues.* Id. 1860.
    „ *Geschichte der Sprachwissenschaft.* Id. 1863.
    „ *Philologie, Geschichte und Psychologie.* Id. 1864.
AUG. SCHLEICHER, *Vergleichende Grammatik.* Weimar, 1861.
    „ *Die Darwinsche Theorie und die Sprachwissenschaft.* 1863.
HEYSE, *System der Sprachwissenschaft.* Berlin, 1856.
BOPP, *Comparative Grammar.* (Engl. Tr.)
M. DRECHSLER, *Grundlegung zur wissenschaftlichen Konstruction, &c.* Erlangen, 1830.
F. HITZIG, *Die Erfindung des Alphabetes.* Zürich, 1840.
HERDER, *Der Ursprung der Sprache.*
C. HERMANN, *Das Problem der Sprache.* Dresden, 1865.
C. VOIGTMAN, *Die Bau-wau Theorie, &c.* Leipzig, 1865.
F. WÜLLNER, *Ueber den Ursprung der Sprache.* Münster, 1838.
L. WIENBARG, *Das Geheimniss des Wortes.* Hamburg, 1852.
DIEZ, *Gramm. d. roman. Sprachen.* (Engl. Tr., CAYLEY, 1863.)
    „ *Etymologisches Wörterbuch.* (Engl. Tr., DONKIN, 1865.)

FRENCH.

E. ARNOULD, *Essai de Théorie et d'Hist. Littéraire.*
PICTET, *Les Origines Indo-européennes.* Paris, 1859.
EGGER, *Notions Élémentaires de Grammaire Comparée.* 5ᵐᵉ éd. Paris, 1857.
    „ *Apollonius Dyscole, Ess. sur l'Hist. des Formes Grammaticales.* Paris, 1854.
MAURY, *La Terre et l'Homme.*
RENAN, *Hist. des Langues Sémitiques.* Paris, 1858.
    „ *De l'Origine du Langage.* 2ᵐᵉ éd. Paris, 1858.
F. MICHEL, *Études sur l'Argot.* Paris, 1856.
CHARMA, *Essai sur le Langage.* Paris, 1846.
C. NODIER, *Notions de Linguistique.*
    „ *Dictionnaire des Onomatopées.* Paris, 1828.

VARINOT, *Dict. des Métaphores.* Paris, 1819.
SCHELER, *Dict. d'Étymologie Française.* Brussels, 1862.
NISARD, *Curiosités d'Étymologie Française.* Paris, 1863.
C. LENORMAN, *Comment. sur le Cratyle.* Athens, 1861.
SALVERTE, *Hist. of Names.* (Engl. Tr., MORDACQUE, London, 1864.)
ÉTIENNE DU PONCEAU, *Mém. sur le Système Grammatical des Langues Indiennes.* Paris, 1838.
L. BENLOEW, *Sur quelques Caractères des Langages Primitifs.* Paris, 1863.
L. BENLOEW, *Sur l'Origine des Noms de Nombre.* Giessen, 1861.
CHAVÉE, *Les Langues et les Races.* Paris, 1862.
LADEVI ROCHE, *De l'Origine du Langage.* Bordeaux, 1860.
F. BAUDRY, *De la Science du Langage et de son État Actuel.* Paris, 1864.
P. MERVOYER, *Études sur l'Association des Idées.* Paris, 1864.
MAINE DE BIRAN, *Origine du Langage : Œuvres Inédites,* iii. 229 sq.
Bulletins de la Société d'Anthropologie. Paris.
VENTURE DE PARADIS, *Gram. et Dict. abrégé de la Langue Berbère.* Paris, 1844.
LÉON PAGES, *Essai de Gram. Japonaise.*

ENGLISH.

BUNSEN, *Philosophy of Universal History.* London, 1854.
MAX MÜLLER, *Survey of Languages.* 2nd ed. London, 1855.
   „   *Lectures on the Science of Language.* (First Series.) London, 1861.
   „   *Lectures on the Science of Language.* (Second Series.) London, 1864.
GARNETT, *Philological Essays, edited by his Son.* London, 1859.
Dr. DONALDSON, *The New Cratylus.* 2nd ed. London, 1850.
   „   *Varronianus.* 2nd ed. London, 1852.
   „   *Maskil le Sopher.* London, 1848.
HENSLEIGH WEDGWOOD, *Etymological Dictionary,* i. ii. London, 1859.
Transactions of the Philological Society. London, 1844–1861.
LATHAM, *The English Language.* 4th ed. London, 1855.
  „ *Varieties of Man.*
DWIGHT, *Modern Philology.* First Series. New York, 1859.
  „   „   „   Second Series. „   1864.
BOYES, *Illustrations to the Greek Tragedians.*
HORNE TOOKE, *Diversions of Purley.* (Ed. TAYLOR.) London, 1860.
HARRIS, *Hermes.*
CROMBIE, *English Etymology and Syntax.* 8th ed. 1856.

LYELL, *Antiquity of Man.* London, 1863.
Dr. DAN. WILSON, *Prehistoric Man.* 1864.
Is. TAYLOR, *Words and Places.* London, 1864.
T. HEWITT KEY, *The Alphabet.*
　　　,,　　　*Quæritur: A Pamphlet.* London, 1864.
MARSH, *Manual of the English Language.* (Ed. SMITH.) London, 1862.
Sir G. C. LEWIS, *Essay on the Romance Languages.* 2nd ed. London, 1862.
EWALD, *Hebrew Grammar.* (Engl. Tr., NICHOLSON, 1836.)
CRAWFURD, *Malay Dictionary and Grammar.*
APPLEYARD, *Kafir Grammar.*
MARSHMAN, *Chinese Grammar.*
CALDWELL, *Grammar of the Dravidian Languages.*
THRELKELD, *Australian Grammar.* Sydney, 1834.
C. M. S., *New Zealand Grammar and Vocabulary.* London, 1820.
J. S. MILL, *System of Logic.* London, 1851.
G. H. LEWES, *Biographical History of Philosophy.* 2nd edition. London, 1862.
HERBERT SPENCER, *First Principles.* London, 1862.
CHALYBÄUS, *History of Speculative Philosophy.* (Translated by A. TULK.) London, 1854.
FERRIER, *Institutes of Metaphysics.* Edinburgh, 1854.
FLEMING, *Vocabulary of Philosophy.* London, 1857.

ITALIAN.

BIONDELLI, *Studii Linguistici.* Milan, 1856.

INDEX.

ABS

ABSTRACTION, rare in savage languages, 53, 199, 200, 219, *note*
Adam, his *onomothesia*, 10 *note*
— theories about, 47
— Cowper's lines on, *id*.
Ægles, story of, 102
Ælian, quoted, 74
Alphabet, origin of, 134
— Hebrew, 136
— Greek, *id*.
— analogy of its origin to that of language, 137, 192–196
Analogists and Anomalists, 22, 184, 257–263
— universality of Analogist views, 264 *foll*.
Analogy, the part it plays in language, 204
— the source of knowledge, 218
— of sound and sight, 81
Animals, the earliest objects to receive names, 16
Animal names, classes of, 23
— — generally onomatopoetic, 24
— — in Australian, 25
— — in New Zealand, *id*. *note*
— — in Algonquin, *id*.
— — in Chinese, 26
— — in Sanskrit, 26–28
— — in Hebrew, 29
— — in Egyptian, *id*.
— — in American languages, 30
— — in various Argots, 31, *note*
— — from observed qualities, 30
— — formed by misapplication, 31–34
Anomalists. *See* Analogists
Anthropomorphism, 8

CLA

Antiphrasis, 254
Argots, their philological importance, 35
— abound in onomatopœia, 36
— their character, 35
— various names for, 235
— deal in metaphor, 236
— Victor Hugo on, *id*., 283 *note*
Armenian merchants, 72
Art, a language addressed to the eye, 72
Artificial languages, 37
Atbash, 270 *note*
Augustine, quoted, 8, 185
Aulus Gellius, quoted, 102

BACON, quoted, 210, 219
Battus, story of, 102
Bekos, an onomatopœia for the bleat of goats, 14
Benfey, 174
Benloew, 225
Bow-wow theory, criticism of the term, 19

CANNON, 188
Cassiodorus, quoted, 75
Cat, 146, 176
Catachresis, 213
Childhood of mankind, 13
Chinese writing, 192–196, 198
— names for animals, 26
— metaphors, 216 *note*
— attempt at continuous analysis, 294
Clarion, 188
Claudius, his antisigma, 37

Colours, metaphors from, 223
Concepts, 66
Convention, 121
Cow, derived, 127, 142, 145 *note*
Crawfurd, quoted, 199
Cydippe, 114

DARWIN, his hypothesis, 49, 155 *note*
Deaf-mutes, their power of inventing signs, 16
— universally intelligible, 74
Democritus, 261
— his anomalist arguments, 262
De Quincy, quoted, 173, 178
Dog, 147
— barking not natural to, 148
— names for, onomatopoetic, 149
Donaldson, quoted, 174
Dove, 145
Duck, 144
Du Ponceau, 199

EAGER, 185
Epicurus, 109, 261
Etymology, 172
— its vagaries, 173
— Varro's rule, 196
— fictions of, 269 *note*
Euphemism, 278
Expression, by means of touch, 72
— by gestures, 73

FANCY, 183
— its influence on the development of language, 113
Frederic II., 13
Foul, &c., etymology of, 174

GARNETT, quoted, 54, 197
Garrick, story of, 77
Gender, due to fancy, 212
Genesis, account of origin of Language in, 17
Gesture, its power, 74
— its defects, 77
— its abuse, 78

Goatsucker, onomatopoetic names for, 142
Goose, 143
Gregory of Nyssa, quoted, 9

HEARING, 79
Hebrew, paucity and vagueness of its words, 228-230
Hen, 144
Heraclitus, 260
Herder, quoted, 11
Hieroglyphics, 135
— Chæremon on, 222
Hog, 146
Homonyms, 234, 262
Hypocorisma, 281
— its dangerous influence, 282

IDEAS, growth of, 7
— various, how expressed, 201
Ideography, Egyptian, 135
— Chinese, 192–195
Imagination, its influence on language, 114
— gender due to, 212
— leads to personification and mythology, 214 *foll.*
Imitation, instinct of, 72
— its importance, 109
— it is a kind of intellectual assimilation, 110
— reproduces impressions, 110
— may be phonetically coincident with words, 128
Interjections, their origin, 88
— two classes of, 89
— in different languages, 90
— not adverbs, 91
— Horne Tooke on, 92
— declinable in Basque, 93
— their linguistic rank vindicated, 94, 98
— the most immediate exponents of passion, 99
— their use in literature, *id.*
— their naturalness, 100
— their expressiveness, 101
— contain the idea of speech, 103

INT

Intuitions, 65
— correspond, in the parallel development of language, to roots, 119
Irony, 254

JAMES IV., 13
  Juventinus, Albus Ovidius, his Philomela, 128 *note*

KEY, Prof. T. Hewitt, quoted, 127 *note*, 174 *note*, 200 *note*

LACTANTIUS, quoted, 1
  Lamb, 143
Language, not revealed, 2–12
— its human origin asserted in the Bible, 8
— idea of, 19
— not a dead matter, *id.*
— stronger than Emperors, 37
— at a low ebb among some savage tribes, 43
— and among our own peasants, 59
— in what sense a discovery, 54
— reverts to its primary instincts, 58
— tactile, 72
— manual, 73
— its primitive freedom, 114
— its unerring instinctive power, 117
— becomes mechanical only by corruption, 138
— processes of, 255
— belief in its revelation, 272
— life of, 284 *note*
— not coextensive with thought, 294, 295
Languages, number of, 5
— of savage tribes, 50
— their supposed perfection tested, 52
— their cumbrous synonyms, 53
— their poverty of expression, 54
— Mr. Garnett on, 54
— Mr. Gallatin on, 55
— eked out by signs, 73
— rarely generalize, 199

MET

Languages, philosophical, 243
Lautgeberden, or vocal gestures, 18, 87
— may be represented by signs, 104
— rise above other interjections, 105
— are a stepping-stone to language, 105
— the origin of form-words, 124
Legends on the origin of language, 117
— Esthonian, 118
— Australian, 119
Leibnitz, quoted, 60, 296 *note*
Lersch, 259 *note*
Letters, their supposed symbolic power, 263
Lingua Franca, 125 *note*
Lute, 188
Luther, 8

MALAY, 199
  Man, once without language, 39
— on any theory, 41
— his primitive degradation, 42
— low races of, 43–45
— in a state of nature, 45
— in the image of God, 49 *note*
Metaphor, 204–246
— confusion of, 209 *note*, 218
— deliberate, 217
— founded on analogy, 218
— in numerals, 223–228
— necessary, 241
— and advantageous, 242-246
Metaphors, for the soul, &c., 219–222
— obscured by time, 227
— among the Kalmucks, 228
— in the Koran, *id.*
— in Hebrew, 230
— in Greek tragedy, 231
— characteristic of periods, 282
— in Kafir, 233
— in Malay, *id.*
— in Chinese, *id.*
— in various Argots, 236
— gradually evanesce, 238

Metaphors, confusion of, in Shakspeare, Milton, &c., 239-241
Minstrel, 188
Misapplication of words, 217
Müller, Prof. Max, apparent modification of his views on onomatopœia, 97
— vagueness, on the origin of roots, 107
— his objections to onomatopœia, &c., criticised, 130-202, *et passim*
Mythology, source of, 215

NAMES, their supposed mystic import, 269-271
— plays on, in the Bible, 270
— in the tragedians, 273-275
— among the Romans, 275
— in Shakspeare, &c., 276
— changed in scorn, 277
— — euphemistically, 278
Natural sounds, 17
Negro jargon, 126 *note*
Newt, 188
Nodier, Charles, his Dictionnaire des Onomatopées, 132
Nominalists, 4
Notions, 66

ONOMATOPŒIA defined, 122-126
— reverted to, when new words have to be coined, 30
— its instinctive use, 34
— progress of, 126
— used by the intellect to develope language, 127
— not an illusory principle, 171
— nor unscientific, *id.*, 173-177
— imperiously demanded by instinct, 178
— not fanciful, 183
— the only *possible* origin of language, 184
— in poetry, 186, 187
— reflex tendency to, 187, 188
— applicable to all kinds of conceptions, 190-203

Onomatopœia, can be used for things which emit no sound, 204
Onomatopœias, but few necessary, 18
— their function, *id.*
— used by wild children, 20
— abound in savage languages, 20
— reflex, 27
— the widely various forms they assume, 112-114
— are ideal reflections, 114
— for thunder, 115
— modified or rejected when they have fulfilled their function, 128
— suggested roots, 129
— not few in number, 131
— dictionaries of, 132
— the only intelligible roots, 133
— most animals' names are, 140
— and birds, 141 *note*
— are not sterile, 152
— their variety, 153
— are the sound-cells in which speech can germinate, 155
— found in numerals, 162
— their dignity, 166
— their use in poetry, 168

PALAMEDES, 136
Paronomasia, 265
— in the Bible, 266, 272
Perception, its nature, 64
Perrault, quoted, 112
Personification, 214
Phædrus, quoted, 111
Philoxenus, story of, 91
Phonetic types, a mystic term, 123
— — not conceivable, 154
Pictet, quoted, 26, 28
Pigeon English, 126
Plutarch, referred to, 19
Pott, 115, 117
Proclus, 255
Psammetichus, his experiment, 13-21
— probably true, 14
— conclusions from it, *id.*

INDEX.

REA

REALISATION of the Ego, 62
— Relations, of things, are subjective, 208
— imaginary, 215, 216
Representation, 65
Revelations, plurality of, 2
Richter, J. P., 227
Roots, inexplicable theory of, 23, 58 and *note*
— express all parts of speech at once, 59, 197
— a mere 'root' offers no etymology, 95–97
— what was their origin, 107
— correspond to intuitions, 119
— have no independent existence, 120
— the root *ma*, 156
— the root *pa*, 158
— *ta, da, ba*, 159
— other roots, 160–64
— verbal or predicative roots not the earliest, 196
— primary and secondary, 198
— their many-sidedness, 251
— due to the economy of language, 253
Rossignol, 188

SANCTIUS, quoted, 100
Science, martyrs of, 7 *note*
Sensation, nature of, 60
Senses, variety of, 206
— one sensorium, 207 and *note*
— interchange of, 208–210
— analogy between, 211
Simonides, 136
Soul, 220
— analogies for, 221
Sound, the best medium of expression, 79
— elements of vocal, 86
— must have had an original connection with sense, 121–122, 286
— symbolic power of, 186
— its universality, 205
— and light, 209
Sparrow, 145

WOR

Speech, its origin comprehensible, 69. *See* Language
Squirrel, 176
Substance, 207
Sugar, 184
Sumner, Archbishop, 2

TALMA, story of, 76
Tertullian, quoted, 57
Theology, its injurious opposition to science, 7
Thought, steps of its development, 62–70
Thunder, etymology of, 177–182
Tryzus, story of, 74

UMLAUT, 170 *note*
Understanding, 6

VATHEK, referred to, 116
Verbs, 197
Voice, 83
— its mechanical production, 84
— its influence, 83 *note*
Voss, quoted, 75

WEDGWOOD, Hensleigh, his Dictionary of English Etymology, 132
Words, derived from misapplied resemblances, 32–33
— when now invented, are generally onomatopoetic, 37
— correspond to 'representations,' 120
— developed from natural sounds, 121, 127
— not mere crude echoes, 132
— blurred by time, 133
— derived from sensational roots, 133
— surfrappés, 138
— dislike of needless words, 217
— mystic importance attached to, in the Bible, 265–272, 279
— symbolic power of, 280
— fatal force of, 284

Words reflect character, 284 *note*
— steps in their history, 287
— not copies or images of things, 288
— derivation of, 288
— teach us nothing about the non-Ego, 289–291

Words teach us nothing about the Ego, 291–292
— are signs of our conceptions, 293
— their inadequacy at the best, 294
— their importance, 296–298
Writing, 135, 192–196

www.ingramcontent.com/pod-product-compliance
Lightning Source LLC
Chambersburg PA
CBHW030734230426
43667CB00007B/716